WITH THE NINTH LIGHT HORSE
IN THE GREAT WAR

LIEUT.-COLONEL A. MIELL
Commanding 9th Light Horse on formation
Killed in action, Walkers' Ridge, Anzac, 7th August, 1915

LIEUT.-COLONEL CAREW REYNELL
Appointed to command Regiment, 8th August, 1915
Killed in action, Hill 60, Anzac, 28th August, 1915

WITH THE NINTH LIGHT HORSE IN THE GREAT WAR

BY

MAJOR T. H. DARLEY, O.B.E.

WITH A FOREWORD BY
LIEUT.-GEN. SIR HARRY CHAUVEL, G.C.M.G., K.C.B., ETC.
COMMANDER OF THE DESERT MOUNTED CORPS,
EGYPTIAN EXPEDITIONARY FORCE

The Naval & Military Press Ltd

Published by
The Naval & Military Press Ltd
5 Riverside, Brambleside, Bellbrook
Industrial Estate, Uckfield, East Sussex,
TN22 1QQ England
Tel: +44 (0) 1825 749494
Fax: +44 (0) 1825 765701
www.naval-military-press.com
www.military-genealogy.com
www.militarymaproom.com

In reprinting in facsimile from the original, any imperfections are inevitably reproduced and the quality may fall short of modern type and cartographic standards.

FOREWORD

I have been greatly honoured by being asked to write an introduction to the History of the 9th Australian Light Horse Regiment, which was included in my Command during the Great War of 1914-1918, from the 16th March, 1916, to the conclusion of the War.

The great traditions which it had already established on Gallipoli were more than sustained in the Egyptian Theatre of the War.

Very early in 1916, the Regiment, under Lieut.-Colonel W. H. Scott, C.M.G., D.S.O., provided the greater bulk of the Force which took part in the Jif-Jaffa Raid. This raid was of importance as it was the first demonstration of a swift and successful blow by Lighthorsemen across many miles of waterless desert.

The Regiment has also the unique distinction of being the proud possessor of the only Regimental Flag captured from the enemy during the whole campaign.

From the Battle of Romani to the Capture of Damascus, the Regiment always bore its share of the fighting, hardships, and sacrifices, whether the piece was set in the Desert of Sinai, the cold and wet of the Judean Hills in mid-winter, the scorching heat of the Jordan Valley, or the fertile plains of Syria.

No words of mine can do adequate justice to the skill, courage, and determination of the officers and men of the 9th Australian Light Horse Regiment, and it is always with pride that I look back on my long association with them in the stirring days of the E.E.F. Campaign.

        HARRY CHAUVEL,
         Late Commanding,
          The Desert Mounted Corps.

Army Headquarters,
 Melbourne, December 4, 1923.

THE STABLES AT POST 7, SERAPEUM,
Sinai Desert

LIEUT.-COLONEL J. M. ARNOTT, C.M.G.
Commanding 9th Light Horse, Serapeum
Transferred to command 3rd Light Horse Brigade Training Depot

CONTENTS

	PAGE
Chap. I—The Formation of the Regiment	1
II—The Voyage to Egypt	4
III—To Gallipoli	8
IV—Walker's Ridge—Anzac	10
V—Hill 60	19
VI—Rhododendron Spur	21
VII—The Evacuation	27
VIII—The Move to the Desert	31
IX—Serapeum: The Jif-Jaffa Operations	33
X—Serapeum, Suez Canal Zone	39
XI—Romani	43
XII—Desert Operations	53
XIII—El Arish-Maghdaba Operations	60
XIV—Rafa	64
XV—Conditions in the Sinai Desert	70
XVI—Preparing for the Invasion of Palestine	74
XVII—The First Gaza Battle	78
XVIII—Preparations for the Second Gaza	81
XIX—The Second Gaza Battle	84
XX—Minor Operations	89
XXI—The Beersheba-Jerusalem Operations	98
XXII—Dismounted Duty in the Judean Hills	110
XXIII—Belah Camp	116
XXIV—Jaffa	121
XXV—The Es-Salt Operations	124
XXVI—The Auja Bridgehead	133
XXVII—The Return to the Valley	139
XXVIII—Ludd	143
XXIX—The Dash Through. Jenin	147
XXX—The Dash Through. Sasa	153
XXXI—The Fall of Damascus	158
XXXII—Kaukab	163
XXXIII—Homs and Tripoli. The Armistice	167
XXXIV—The Egyptian Rising	173
XXXV—The Return to Australia	177
XXXVI—Conclusion	181
Appendices	183

ILLUSTRATIONS

Lieut.-Colonel A. Meill		*Frontispiece*
Lieut.-Colonel Carew Reynell		*Frontispiece*
The Stables at Post 7, Serapeum		facing page vi
Lieut.-Colonel J. M. Arnott, C.M.G.		,, vii
The Wadi Mukhshieb, Sinai Desert		,, 16
The Country looking towards Maghdaba		,, 17
Turkish Prisoners captured at Maghdaba		,, 32
Part of our Camp at Hod Masaid (El-Arish)		,, 33
Turkish Officer Prisoners captured at Rafa		,, 48
Construction of Trenches at El-Gamli		,, 49
The Regimental Barber		,, 64
Water Cisterns near Khan Yunis		,, 65
Our Leaders		,, 80
Making Roads to Wadi Ghuzze, Gaza		,, 81
Watering Horses at the Wadi Ghuzza, Shellal		,, 96
Gaza before the Attack		,, 97
Padre Finigan, McFarlane, and Burkinshaw		,, 112
Major T. J. Daly, D.S.O.		,, 113
The Author and "Bill" at Marakeb		,, 128
The Jewel of the East—Damascus		,, 129
The Barada Gorge, Damascus		,, 144
Third Light Horse Brigade Camp at Tripoli		,, 145
"C" Squadron, 9th Light Horse, Tripoli		,, 160
Officers 9th Light Horse, Tripoli		,, 161
Embarking at Tripoli for Egypt		,, 176
Our Camp at Zag-a-Zig, Egypt		,, 177
The Quay at Kantara, Suez Canal		,, 192
"The Originals"		,, 193

CHAPTER I

THE FORMATION OF THE REGIMENT

When England declared war, it was at once realized that the Dominions were committed to an active participation in her grave decision. On every hand men clamoured to be allowed to enlist for active service, and foremost amongst the applicants were veterans who had served in South Africa, in addition to younger Light Horsemen eager to emulate that worthy example. All eyes were on the cockpit of Europe, and as the conflict gathered force it was loudly proclaimed that there could be little use for the Light Horse in the theatre of operations.

Egypt, Sinai, Palestine, and Mesopotamia were not thought of, and the effective work to be accomplished by our mounted men in these regions was not foreseen by the keenest prophets. Nevertheless, history, rich in gallant deeds and strong endurance, was about to be written by Australian riders, and in that record the doings of the 9th Light Horse Regiment found a not unworthy place.

On the 5th of October, 1914, orders were issued for the formation of the 3rd Light Horse Brigade, Colonel F. G. Hughes being appointed to the command. The Brigade was to consist of the 8th, 9th, and 10th Light Horse Regiments. Victoria was drawn upon for the whole of the 8th Regiment and one squadron of the 9th, South Australia contributing the balance of that Regiment. The 10th Regiment was raised in Western Australia.

Prior to this order it had been decided to form the 7th Light Horse Regiment of the 2nd Brigade, with one squadron from South Australia, and on this order being countermanded, "B" Squadron of the 7th Light Horse became "A" Squadron of the 9th. This formed a foundation for the Regiment, the balance being specially recruited.

Lieutenant-Colonel A. Miell, Commanding Officer of the 24th Light Horse Regiment, Citizen Forces, an energetic and capable officer of long standing, who had served in the South African War, was appointed to command the Regiment.

The formation of the Regiment was rapidly carried out, the men being enrolled after a searching medical examination at the camp lines, Morphettville. Immediately after being sworn in the recruits were posted to their various troops, and quickly settled down to the new life. Large supplies of clothing and equipment were speedily forwarded by the chief ordnance officer at Keswick, and were as speedily issued to the men by the Quartermaster's staff. The camp was well organized and the men well cared for, rations being both plentiful and of the very best quality.

Strict training was carried out by officers and men, who soon began to show signs of perfect physical fitness for the hard tasks they would be called upon to face at an early date. The horses supplied to the Regiment were a splendid lot, and reflected the greatest credit on the officers on whom the responsibility for their selection and purchase rested.

As soon as the horses had been allotted to the various troops, each member was put through a thorough riding test, much amusement being caused by some, who, although anxious to serve with a mounted unit, had evidently never ridden a horse in their lives. As a result of this test a number of men had to be transferred to dismounted units, much to their disappointment. The remaining members immediately commenced troop and squadron training.

Shortly after the formation of the Regiment, Mrs. Richard Bennett presented a very handsome standard to the Regiment. This standard was a magnificent piece of work, bearing the regimental crest, a lion rampant on a white Australia, the whole being on a scarlet field with a diagonal gold cross. The motto of the Regiment, "Pro Gloria et Honore," was worked in white on the scarlet field. This flag was greatly prized, and was proudly carried by the Regiment on the parade through the streets of the city.

Major J. M. Antill, C.B., who had been appointed Brigade Major to the Brigade, arrived from Melbourne about the middle of November to inspect the Regiment on behalf of the Brigadier. After spending two days, during which he subjected the Regiment to a thorough overhaul, he returned to Headquarters.

A few days later orders were received to shift the camp to Ascot Park, and at the end of November the Regiment was moved to Broadmeadows Camp, near Melbourne, where it joined up with the rest of the Brigade (except 10th Light Horse). The Regiment entrained for this move at Mile End, and after a tiring train journey, arrived at Broadmeadows at 11 p.m. After detraining the horses, the Regiment moved to the camp site. Rain was falling heavily, and as the night had to be spent in the open, the impression formed that night of Victoria was far from complimentary to the sister State.

As soon as day broke all ranks were astir and set about erecting the camp, so that by midday things were fairly settled and the men able to enjoy a much-needed meal and rest. As soon as the lines had been laid out, the Victorian Squadron, under the command of Major T. J. Daly, joined up and made the Regiment complete. The equipping of this squadron was quickly carried out, and the Regiment settled down to serious training.

The whole of the Brigade, with the exception of the 10th Light Horse, now being concentrated at Broadmeadows, training was car-

FORMATION OF REGIMENT

ried out under the personal supervision of the Brigade Commander, special attention being paid to musketry and bayonet fighting. Captain G. F. G. Weick, A. and I. Staff, arrived on appointment as Adjutant. This officer had recently undergone a course of training at the School of Musketry, Hythe, England, and his instruction was of the greatest value to the Regiment.

At Christmas and New Year, a number of all ranks were allowed leave for the purpose of paying a final visit to their relations, but a large number had to stay in camp to attend to the requirements of the horses. Christmas Day turned out very wet, rain falling heavily for some days, the camp being converted into a veritable mud pond, with the result that those who were so fortunate as to remain had anything but a pleasant time.

After the Christmas and New Year holidays, the Brigade, which had by this time been well equipped, was practised in surprise turns out. On the alarm being given, the Brigade would turn out immediately in full service marching order for inspection by the Brigade Major. These turns out were practised at all hours of the day and night.

Early in the New Year the Brigade marched out and bivouacked at Wildwood for two days. During its return to camp, small tactical schemes and march discipline were practised. These two days proved of great value to all ranks, the instruction being carried out in the best possible manner.

Major Carew Reynell, from South Australia, one of the best Light Horse officers in the Commonwealth, was posted to the Regiment as second in command, and threw himself heart and soul into the training of the Regiment. His splendid example and untiring energy did much to bring the Regiment to a high state of efficiency. Day or night, he was ever at his post and ready for any task, however arduous.

In view of the probable early departure of the Brigade for overseas, arrangements were made for a march through Melbourne. On the appointed day, the whole of the Brigade, including transport, paraded in service marching order and marched to the Haymarket, where horses were watered and fed and the men had their mid-day meal. After a general clean up, the troops moved off in column of route and marched through the city, the Governor-General, Sir H. Munro-Ferguson, taking the salute at Parliament House. The Brigade then proceeded to Heidelberg, where it bivouacked for the night. At 7 o'clock the following morning the Brigade moved off on its return to Broadmeadows, carrying out a Brigade scheme during the journey.

Information now came to hand that the Brigade would embark at an early date. All ranks, therefore, worked with redoubled energy to complete the final arrangements, with the result that within a few days all were ready and anxious to be on the move.

CHAPTER II

THE VOYAGE TO EGYPT

On the 11th of February, 1915, camp was struck at daybreak, and the Regiment marched to the docks, where it embarked for overseas, the following officers embarking with the Regiment:

Headquarters: Lieut.-Colonel A. Miell, C.O.; Major C. Reynell, second in command; Captain G. F. G. Weick, adjutant; Major T. J. Daly, Q.M.; Lieut. A. J. Hutchinson, machine gun section; Captain H. Worthington, veterinary officer; and Captain L. O. Betts, medical officer.

"A" Squadron: Major E. Cook, V.D., in command; Lieut. C. Bleechmore, second in command; Lieut. K. McKenzie; 2nd Lieut. G. A. Depledge; and 2nd Lieut. A. E. Dean.

"B" Squadron: Major H. M. Parsons, in command; Lieut. P. Callery; Hon. Captain F. Code; 2nd Lieut. E. T. Pascoe; and 2nd Lieut. E. W. White.

"C" Squadron: Captain W. H. Scott, in command; Lieut. S. McWilliam; 2nd Lieut. A. J. Jaffray; 2nd Lieut. C. R. Stanford; and 2nd Lieut. W. S. Pender.

Captain-Chaplain D. F. McGrath, S.J., also embarked with the Regiment as R.C. Chaplain.

The embarkation was carried out expeditiously and the men were soon settled in their new quarters on board. The "Karoo," H.M. Transport "A" 10, was exceptionally suitable for transport, having a single troop deck capable of accommodating 400 men above the water line, and well ventilated. Men were formed into messes of 20, each mess having two orderlies, who kept the deck and appointments in perfect order throughout the voyage.

The greatest care was taken as to the comfort of the horses, which had been stowed away between decks. Each horse was given 20 minutes' exercise daily, weather permitting, and was afterwards carefully groomed. As soon as the warmer climate was reached, a number of horses were brought on deck. These horses were picked out by the veterinary officer at his daily inspection, and were kept on deck for various periods. Too much praise cannot be given to Major C. Reynell and Captain Worthington for the constant care bestowed on the horses. Both these officers could be found on the horse deck at almost any hour of the day or night. They were well repaid by the fact that on the "Karoo" only two horses died during the voyage out of a total of 402.

Between stable hours each day, classes of instruction were held for officers and N.C.O.'s. Officers received much useful instruction in tactics, map reading, use of the prismatic compass, reports and messages, at the hands of Captain Weick; whilst the men were exercised in musketry, semaphore signalling, and firing with miniature rifles at targets rigged at 20 yards distance. The officers and senior N.C.O.'s were also instructed in the use of the revolver, and were instructed in the use of the sword by R.Q.M.S. Darley.

On arrival at Colombo, the officers and warrant officers were allowed ashore, but the troops were not allowed to land. As large numbers of bumboat men came alongside to sell the various products of the country, the men gained a fair idea of the type of native at this busy port. The beautiful harbour was admired by all on board.

On the following day the "Karoo" put to sea, escorted by the French cruiser, "Montcalm," which remained within view until we had passed Aden. Before parting company, the crew of the "Montcalm" treated us to a display of their gunnery. As the results of the shooting could not be clearly seen, we could form little opinion of its effectiveness. A cheering message was signalled by our French comrades as we parted company.

The "Karoo" arrived off Port Suez on the morning of the 13th of March, and preparations were immediately made for the passage through the canal. A very powerful searchlight was brought on board and rigged in the bows. All ships passing through the canal must carry this light in accordance with the canal regulations. Machine guns were also rigged aloft, as Turkish patrols were known to be moving on the eastern side of the canal. The passage through the canal proved very interesting to all ranks, as at various points camps were seen, garrisoned by Indian troops, who signalled various messages by flag, and Indian cavalry patrols were seen operating in the desert.

We arrived at Port Said and anchored at daybreak on the 14th March, 1915. The port was full of shipping of various nationalities, including a number of captured German steamers, whilst a few units of His Majesty's Navy kept watch and guard over all. Crowds of boats were speedily on the scene, manned by grinning natives, whose antics caused great amusement for the troops on board. The natives' cry of "Gib it bucksheash" soon became familiar to all, and it is safe to say that the bucksheash merchants reaped a good harvest.

As no liquor had been put on board, some of the men were just dying for a drink, and in spite of the warnings as to the filthy habits of the natives, were determined to obtain one. One smart youth, after carefully avoiding the ship's police, got in touch with a native who guaranteed to supply the necessary article. On being asked for whiskey he offered to supply it at the extremely low price of 10/- per bottle. In response to the appeal to "Put de money in de basket," he passed over the side a pound note, and could hardly contain himself as two bottles, nicely labelled, were fished out from under the stern of the boat, and passed up. After a hasty glance round, he pulled them over the side, and, tucking them under his coat, dived below, inviting his mates to join him in the carouse. Drawing the cork of one bottle he passed it lovingly to his mouth and took a great "swig," but the expression on his face when he realized that he had paid a pound for two bottles of sea water baffles description. Needless to say, when he rushed on deck to obtain the life of the drink merchant, the boat was not to be found.

The voyage thus far had been most enjoyable to all. Various concerts had been held and some good talent discovered. Who amongst us all will ever forget dear old Father McGrath singing of his beloved Tipperary, the place of his birth. At 4 p.m. the voyage was resumed, rough weather being met with during the run to Alexandria, which was reached on the morning of the 15th March, 1915.

Immediately on arrival the Regiment disembarked, and in spite of the pleasant time spent on board, none were sorry to get their feet once more on good old mother earth. As the horses were brought ashore they were taken to the railway siding and entrained. One of them, delighted at once more being in the open, broke loose and jumped into the dock. He had the time of his life, swimming from side to side for about an hour, and seemed very disappointed when finally pulled out. On arrival at Cairo the troops were detrained at Kasr-el-nil siding. Baggage was loaded on tramcars and conveyed to Mena camp, whilst the men marched, leading their horses, the camp being reached at 2 a.m. on the 16th.

The day was spent in laying out the lines and settling down ready for the hard training which was still to be undergone. Horses being unfit for riding were exercised daily for one week, after which they were exercised with saddles on, but unridden, for a second week. At the commencement of the third week they were ridden quietly until sound, after which troop and squadron drill was carried out. During the period of exercising horses, all ranks were trained in dismounted work and range practices, the junior officers and all N.C.O.'s receiving special instruction in map reading, field sketching, etc.

Every man in the Regiment was put through a thorough test to ascertain the standard of efficiency of the Regiment, and those who passed were allowed leave from afternoon parades. This was a decided incentive to the remainder, with the result that in a very short time a high standard of efficiency was gained. A route march into the desert (dismounted) was carried out, the Regiment moving out a distance of about nine miles, and returning the following day, carrying out a small tactical scheme during the trip. Mena camp had been well arranged near the Pyramids, many well-stocked shops being included, also several cinema shows.

After a few weeks spent at this camp, orders were received to move to the racecourse, Heliopolis. The move was quickly carried out and training resumed. Prior to this move, the Infantry Brigades had marched out from Mena camp for an unknown destination, making the Light Horse units feel very sore at being left behind. After each hard day's work the troops were allowed leave to visit the town or to proceed to Cairo. These trips were always enjoyable, the city being full of life and with numerous places of amusement. Much amusement was obtained from the natives themselves, especially the shoeblacks with their quaint sayings and the newsboys whose cry of "Egyptian Mail, to-morrow, to-night," was mystifying until understood.

On the 26th April great excitement was caused by the arrival of news that the Infantry had successfully landed at Anzac. A few days later the Light Horse Regiments were paraded and asked if they were willing to leave their horses and proceed to Gallipoli as Infantry. On the question being put, the whole Brigade immediately volunteered. On the 9th May the machine gun sections of the Brigade proceeded to Gallipoli, and the remainder of the Brigade were placed under orders to follow at an early date.

During the few remaining days the men were instructed in the construction of trenches and wire entanglements. As no Infantry equipment was in possession, the men were issued with ruck sacks, and orders were issued that only such articles as were actually needed were to be taken, all other articles to be placed in the kit bags, which were to be stored at the kit base. Thirty men of the Regiment, together with the farriers, were to remain behind to look after the horses under the veterinary officer. Saddlery and spurs were packed in sacks, labelled and placed for safe custody in one of the mess huts, which was boarded up and placed under a guard.

On the morning of the 14th May, 1915, final orders were issued and everything prepared for an early move on the following day.

CHAPTER III

TO GALLIPOLI

At daybreak on the 15th May, 1915, all heavy baggage was dispatched to Helmieh siding and loaded. At 11 p.m. the Regiment paraded and proceeded to the railway, where horses were immediately entrained. The entrainment being completed, the journey to Alexandria was commenced at 1.30 a.m. on the 16th, the strength of the Regiment entrained being 25 officers and 454 other ranks. The first reinforcements, less two men sick, and 50 per cent. of the second reinforcements, being taken to fill vacancies caused by the men left behind with the horses and sick.

Each man took with him to Alexandria his black kit bag containing his personal belongings, and on arrival these were handed over to the care of the Australian kit store, one clerk and three storemen being left in charge. As soon as the horses were detrained, they were placed on board H.M. Transport "Minominee" (X2), a huge vessel, which also carried various other units of the Brigade. By 6 p.m. all troops were on board and anxious to set sail, but it was not until 5 p.m. on the following day that we moved from the quay. The number of troops on board made things far from comfortable, but as this was to be a voyage of short duration, with plenty of excitement in view at its end, all ranks were in the best of spirits.

At 3 p.m. on the 19th May, the transport arrived off Cape Hellas and anchored about three miles from the shore. Here the troops on board were treated to their first thrill of actual warfare by hearing the roar of the guns and by the sight of the huge shells falling on the slopes of Achi Baba. Our aeroplanes were also seen spotting for the gunners, whilst enemy anti-aircraft guns were sending shrapnel shells around them, fortunately without doing any damage. At 5 p.m. the transport sailed for the island of Lemnos without having landed any of the troops, arriving there at 10 p.m.

When day broke on the 20th all ranks were early astir and on deck, admiring the magnificent units of His Majesty's Navy, which were lying at anchor. One battleship was the admiration of all on board, and although anchored at close quarters to our boat, no one discovered that it was not the real thing, but only a dummy rigged up to deceive the enemy, which it appeared quite capable of doing.

At 10 a.m. on the following day, "A" and "B" Squadrons transhipped to the destroyer "Scourge," whilst the remainder of the Regiment went on board the "Scorpion," the boat which, up to that time, had been in more actions than any other unit of the Navy. As soon as the transhipping had been completed, the destroyers put to sea, en route for Anzac, where they arrived at 4.30 p.m., having travelled at a good speed for the whole of the journey. This trip, and the kindly hospitality of the men of the Navy, will long live in the memory of those who shared it. The chief gunner of our boat must have nearly run the boat out of stores, especially beer, by his generosity.

On nearing land, it was noticed that the guns were busy, their loud report mingling with the sharp crackle of the rifles. One large shell fell a few yards astern of the "Scorpion," and a man, who evidently did not realize its serious import, was heard to remark, "By cripes, did you see that fish?" I expect he was thinking of Murray Cod at the time. After a short delay, barges were drawn alongside by tiny naval pinnaces under the command of midshipmen, and the troops were quickly transhipped, the barges being immediately pulled ashore. The capable manner in which these midshipmen (mere boys) manœuvred their unwieldy craft was the admiration of all concerned.

As the barges neared the jetty, the men landed under shrapnel fire, fortunately without casualty, and moved off to the shelter of the hillside, where they bivouacked for the night. It is hard to say what were the feelings of the men that first night spent on Gallipoli, the soil of which had been drenched by the blood of their brothers-in-arms, but it is certain that every man was fully prepared to play his part in the future with true Australian spirit and bravery.

CHAPTER IV

WALKER'S RIDGE—ANZAC

On the 22nd May, 1915, the Regiment moved to Walker's Ridge and took over a portion of the trenches from the Auckland Mounted Rifles. These trenches were extremely narrow, it being quite impossible for men to pass each other except by one man stooping down whilst the other stepped over. The widening of the trenches was therefore immediately started, and a week later was completed. Enemy snipers were very energetic, causing many casualties. Special men were therefore set to work, with periscopic rifles, to quieten them down. A certain officer succeeded in shooting one, and reported his success, but his elation was short-lived as it was discovered that this particular Turk had already been dead for over a week before he succeeded in hitting him.

On the 24th May, in accordance with a request from the enemy, an armistice was granted from 7.30 a.m. to 4.30 p.m., to allow for the burial of the dead. Promptly at 7.30 a.m. all firing ceased, and parties from both sides went out into "No man's land" to perform their sad duty. A boundary line was fixed, the enemy dead found on our side of the line being carried to it and handed over, whilst the enemy did the same on their side. About 3,000 bodies were given decent burial on that day, about 75 per cent. of them being Turks.

Promptly at 4.30 p.m. all parties moved to their own lines, and intermittent rifle fire commenced. Each night the troops stood to arms from 7.30 to 9, and from 3.30 a.m. until daybreak. As soon as it got dark, the enemy appeared to get a trifle nervous, and would blaze away thousands of rounds without apparent reason. As this appeared to be a good way of making them waste their ammunition, it was decided to help them in the good work. To further this scheme dummies were made from sacks filled with straw, dressed in jackets and helmets, and mounted on poles. In the waning light these were shown over the top of the trenches each night, when they would immediately draw a heavy fire from the enemy, who no doubt reported in their next communique that another attack had been abandoned owing to their heavy fire.

On the 28th May, a party of three officers and 60 other ranks were assembled in No. 3 and No. 4 Saps to raid "Turks'" trench, 75 yards away, with the object of capturing prisoners to enable us to identify the units opposite. As the required bombs did not arrive, the raid was abandoned. Had the raid been carried out, it would have been the first one during the war carried out for that expressed purpose. The officers detailed for this task were Lieuts. McWilliam, Miles, and McKenzie.

At 3.17 a.m. on the 29th May, the Turks opened a very heavy rifle fire, under cover of which their bomb throwers advanced. They succeeded in throwing two bombs into our trenches, each killing one man. Rapid fire was opened on the advancing Turks, eight of their bomb throwers being shot down, after which the remainder retired. After re-organizing, the enemy made a most determined attack, but suffering heavy casualties, were again forced to retire. At 6.50 a.m. heavy hostile shelling was directed on our position from the direction of "W" Hill (Kushak-Anafarta), causing severe casualties.

On the 30th May, the enemy made a strong attack against No. 3 outpost, which was held by the New Zealanders. Part of the Regiment was employed in "searching" the ground over which the enemy had to pass with rifle fire. This considerably assisted the New Zealanders in beating off the attack, but we were unfortunate enough to lose a most capable officer during the operation, Lieut. McWilliam being killed whilst directing the fire. In the early hours of June 1st enemy units were noticed to be collecting in the trench opposite Quinn's Post. A heavy fire was therefore brought to bear, with the result that they were dispersed.

The following day the machine gun section which had proceeded to Gallipoli in advance of the Regiment, rejoined. At 10 p.m. on the 3rd June a bombing raid was made on the enemy trenches by Privates J. Souter, N. R. Hayward, J. Pennyquick, and L. Wainwright. The Turks responded with rifle and bomb, causing our party to withdraw. A little later, however, Privates Souter and Pennyquick again advanced, bombing the enemy with effect. On the 4th June 16 volunteers from the Regiment carried out a similar operation with good results.

During the next few days things were fairly quiet on both sides, but no opportunity was missed of letting the enemy see that he could take no liberties. Each evening one of the destroyers would quietly move in close to the shore and carry out a systematic shelling of the enemy trenches, their shooting being perfect. After the allotted number of rounds had been fired, she would calmly move away to sea and disappear in the gloom.

On the morning of the 12th June, the members of the Regiment were subjected to a severe bombardment. The fire, which was exceptionally heavy, opened on the next gully where the Mountain Battery were sheltering their horses. These were quickly driven out and moved to the gully in which we were quartered for shelter. The shells followed, and we came in for a very hot time, many men being hit. The Battery lost 10 ponies and 12 mules killed, besides a number wounded. One shell landed over the quartermaster's store, killing Pte. Alec. Hawson, and severely wounding Pte. R. T. Stewart and Sergt. Frank Maddiford. R.Q.M.S. Darley, who had just moved from where Hawson and Stewart were standing to speak to Major E. Cook (who was also wounded by this shell) had a remarkable escape. Standing in the middle of the burst, with shrapnel pellets flying in all directions, he remained untouched, although the fuse of the shell (3 inches in diameter) passed through his helmet.

Major Cook was attended by the Regimental Medical Officer, Major Follett, and evacuated to hospital. From Anzac he was transferred to the Stationary Hospital at Mudras, and later to the "Blue Sisters'" Hospital at Malta. His wound soon healed, but he unfortunately contracted pneumonia and died, the Regiment losing a valuable officer. The news of his death which was so unexpected, cast a deep gloom over the Regiment, as he was respected and loved by all ranks.

At daybreak on the 27th June, the enemy opened a violent bombardment of our portion of Walker's Ridge. Large portions of the trenches were blown in and a number of casualties inflicted, whilst the 8th Light Horse on our right suffered severely, Colonel White, Major Gregory, and Captain Crowle being included in the list.

For several mornings past it had been noticed that the enemy were in the habit of bringing reliefs down a certain communication trench just before sunrise. This trench, at that time of the day, was extremely difficult to see except by the aid of glasses, but on a distant rise was a small tree which was visible at the first appearance of dawn. Experiments were therefore carried out, and it was found that by setting the sights on the rifles at 225 yards, and sighting at the distant tree, the bullets would drop into the trench. Just before dawn on the 28th June a party of 12 men from "C" Squadron were placed in position where they could plainly see the tree. In order to distribute the fire, the four men on the right and left had their wind gauges screwed over to the right and left respectively. Watch was kept with field glasses for the enemy reliefs to enter the trench, and as soon as this occurred, rapid fire was ordered. A few days later an enemy prisoner who spoke English was brought in. This man took the Colonel along our trenches, and pointed out a portion of their line as being the place where they had had 10 men killed, including their Colonel on the morning of our experiment.

On the 30th June at 12.5 a.m., the enemy guns placed a heavy and well-directed fire on our position, followed a few minutes later by a heavy rifle and machine gun fire, which lasted for about 20 minutes. At 12.30 a.m. heavy firing was heard on our right flank, but the firing on our position died down, and things remained quiet for some time. At 3.40 a.m. observers reported that the enemy were advancing in the direction of numbers 1, 2, and 3 saps in force. The Regiment quickly manned the trenches and opened heavy rifle and machine gun fire on the advancing Turks. Sap 1 was heavily attacked, and a number of the enemy succeeded in entering it, but these were promptly bombed out by Sergeant H. Sullivan of "A" Squadron. About 50 Turks assaulted Turk's Point, but after a stubborn fight were forced to retire.

At 4.30 a.m. the enemy again advanced, but the heavy fire from No. 1 sap prevented them from getting within 20 yards of our position. As the 8th Light Horse on our right were being heavily attacked, the fire of 30 men of "C" Squadron was directed across the front of their trenches with such decided effect that the enemy were again forced to withdraw to shelter. The fire discipline of the Regiment during these attacks was of the highest order, few shots being wasted. There was a total absence of noise and confusion, so that commands were clearly understood and promptly obeyed. Our casualties were one killed and eight wounded. The enemy suffered severely, 54 dead Turks being drawn in over the top for burial, and seven prisoners taken. Many enemy dead were seen too far out to be recovered, but these were collected the following night. The "Anzac Book" in describing this affair, states that Enver Pasha had ordered that our trenches were to be taken at all costs. It also states that the attack was beaten off by the 7th and 8th Light Horse Regiments. This should read "the 8th and 9th Light Horse Regiments," as the 7th were never located on Walker's Ridge.

On the 2nd July, 1915, the Regiment was relieved by the Auckland Mounted Rifles, and proceeded to Rest Gully. The routine of duty was that each Regiment would do two weeks in the trenches and two out. The Regiments at rest had to perform various duties, chief amongst which was the providing of digging parties for improving the trenches and making roads. These parties paraded at sunset, working for about five hours, after which they returned to their lines. During the day various duties were carried out, and a few of the reinforcements received special instruction in musketry. Shell fire on the rest trenches was very troublesome, it being usually the case that more casualties were incurred when at rest than when in the trenches. Whilst occupying the rest trenches, the Regiment had to send one squadron to Walker's Ridge each night as a reserve.

On the 16th July, 1915, the Regiment returned to Walker's Ridge and took over the trenches from the New Zealanders. As extra saps had been constructed, the depleted state of the Regiment through casualties and sickness, made it necessary to place every man in the front line, none being available for support. Special attention was paid to snipers, who had again become a nuisance, periscopic rifles being provided for this purpose. A sharp watch was kept on the enemy to avoid a surprise, as he was known to have received large reinforcements. This was a favourite time for their attacks, as Constitution Day and the termination of Ramadan (the great Mahomedan Festival) were close at hand. The Turks being devout Mahomedans, believed that an attack on the infidel, immediately following Ramadan, would be successful as a reward for their piety. In every case when attacking, they raised a continual cry of "Allah," "Allah" as they charged.

The Regiment after a strenuous time in the trenches was relieved by the 8th Light Horse, and moved to a new rest site at the foot of Walker's Ridge, remaining in rest until the 4th August, when it returned to the trenches on Russel's Top (the name which had been given to our position on Walker's Ridge). Rumours of all descriptions had been afloat for some time, and preparations were made for a big attack on the enemy's position. Colonel Miell made a wager with Major Reynell, in which he bet his issue of rum for three months that we would be in Constantinople before Christmas.

For some nights past huge transports had been seen close to shore, disembarking thousands of troops from England. This work was carried out in perfect silence, without the showing of a single light, the troops being hidden away in the various gullies before daylight, and the transports sent back to their various ports. On the night of the 5th August, a party of 153 reinforcements arrived for the Regiment under the command of Captain Coad. This party moved to the trenches immediately after landing.

Orders were now received that an attack on a large scale would be made against the enemy's position, our objective being a hill known as "Baby 700." The attack of the Brigade was designed to pin down a large number of the enemy to that position, whilst heavy attacks were being directed on various other points. The attack of the 3rd Light Horse Brigade was to be made in successive lines, the 8th Light Horse in two lines of about 150 each being in the lead, and followed by two lines of the 10th Light Horse, whilst the 9th remained in reserve, and gave supporting fire to the movement.

Major C. Reynell was detailed to assist in getting the attacking troops into position, and Major W. H. Scott was attached as guide to the Royal Welsh Fusiliers who were to attack from Monash Gully, the enemy position known as the "Chess Board," in front of Pope's Hill. The 6th August was spent in making the final preparations. Strict orders were issued that no officer or man was to carry any papers or maps, and that all personal belongings and spare clothing were to be packed in the rucksacks and stored under a guard. Each man was to carry 24 hours' rations, and as much water as possible. Each officer and man had a square patch of white calico sewn on the back of his coat, so that they could be distinguished from the enemy, and a few men carried small red and yellow flags for marking the limits of the advance.

Huge supplies of ammunition and bombs were brought up by the Indian Mule Corps detachments, and stowed away at convenient points. Water in sealed petrol tins was also brought up and stored under a guard as a reserve. Orders were read and carefully explained, so that each man would know exactly what was expected of him. After the orders were thoroughly understood, the copies were carefully destroyed.

A demonstration was made against the enemy position with the idea of making him show his strength at this point. This was immediately followed by a perfect hurricane of fire from his position and left no doubts as to his strength and vigilance. It was clearly seen that they had not been idle, but had considerably strengthened their position and constructed a number of new trenches.

At the end of our secret sap was a small tunnel in which each night at dusk a lamp was placed in such a position that its light could be seen from the sea only. This was an aiming mark for the guns of the fleet who often shelled the enemy trenches during the hours of darkness, with good results.

On the afternoon of the 6th August the artillery fire which had been carried on during the last few days, increased in violence, and it was evident that the battle had begun in earnest. Most of our gun fire appeared to be directed against the enemy trenches situated at Lone Pine. After an intense bombardment of this position, the Australian Infantry were seen to charge with the bayonet. It was a magnificent sight, and nothing could stand against its violence. With loud cheers they rushed across the intervening space and into the enemy position, which was of exceptional strength. Reports came to hand that the attack had succeeded and that the Infantry were well established. This news caused great satisfaction to all and greatly increased the confidence in our success for the morrow.

At 4.30 a.m. on the 7th August the Navy opened a violent bombardment of the enemy trenches immediately to our front, whilst the first line of the 8th Light Horse made final preparation for their charge. A few minutes later the firing ceased and the first line of the 8th Light Horse rushed to the attack, led in most gallant fashion by Colonel White of that regiment. They were instantly met by a murderous fire from rifle and machine gun. The attackers had to cross a piece of ground known as "The Neck," lying between Monash Gully on the right and a deep ravine running down to the sea on the left, the distance to the enemy trenches varying from 25 to 50 yards. Our Howitzers on the beach tried to beat down the enemy's fire, and a heavy fire was opened by the Regiment to support the attack.

White and his gallant men were almost immediately shot down, and the second line went over. This was followed at intervals of two minutes by the two lines of the 10th Light Horse Regiment. It has been claimed that several men of the 8th Light Horse actually entered the enemy trenches, but this could not be verified. The enemy had three lines of trenches placed one above the other, and nothing could live in the terrible fire which swept across the intervening ground. It is doubtful whether any man, either before or since, has known such a dense volume of fire. Many of the men were shot down before they could get over the parapet, and our trenches were soon choked with dead and wounded. On the situation being put to the Brigade Commander, the attack was abandoned.

The 8th and 10th Light Horse Regiments were nearly annihilated, the 8th alone having 12 officers killed out of a total of 19, and practically every man who lived to return was wounded. The total casualties of the 8th Regiment amounted to 240 and of the 10th, 136. Although the 9th Regiment did not take part in the great charge, it did not escape altogether but suffered a number of casualties, chief amongst which was its gallant leader, Lieut.-Col. Miell, who was shot dead whilst directing the fire of the Regiment. This gallant officer and gentleman had often stated that his ambition was to lead his splendid Regiment in a charge against the enemy, but fate decreed otherwise, and he met a soldier's death at the head of the Regiment. Sergeant-Major Harvey, a fine old soldier, wearer of the Distinguished Conduct Medal, won in South Africa, was also amongst the killed, and Captain Coad and Lieut. McClaughry amongst the wounded.

On the following day Major Carew Reynell was appointed to command the Regiment. The big attack was still in full swing and every effort was made to pin the enemy down to his position, and help the attack at other points. That the effect of the terrible though glorious failure of the preceding night made its mark on all members of the Brigade cannot be denied, but their splendid spirit never wavered, and with set teeth they went to their task of beating down the fire of the enemy. Away on the left the New Zealanders could be seen making desperate efforts to capture the position from the direction of Rhododendron Spur, assisted by the Australian Infantry and Machine Gun sections.

Heavy fighting took place during the next two days, but things on our immediate front quietened down and the work of reconstructing the battered trenches was carried out. On the 8th August the first promotions to commissioned rank were made, R.Q.M.S. Darley and Sergeants Butler and McDonald being promoted Lieutenants.

About 5.30 a.m. on the 10th August the enemy opened a violent bombardment with high explosive shells, but without doing much damage. During the bombardment Lieut. Darley, S.Q.M. Sergt. Judell, and Corporal Smedley were sitting together in the trench known as the "Broadway" when a large shell, presumably from the "Goben" landed at their feet. With a deafening roar it exploded, hurling Smedley over the parapet into Todd Lane, a distance of about 30 yards, whilst Lieut. Darley was blown round a bend in the trench and along an alley-way for a distance of about 10 yards. Poor little Judell was killed outright, and Corporal Smedley badly wounded. Lieut. Darley, although rendered unconscious, was unhurt.

Smedley was immediately taken under the care of Captain Follett, the Regimental Medical Officer, who dressed his wounds and sent

THE WADI MUKHSHIEB, SINAI DESERT

THE COUNTRY LOOKING TOWARDS MAGHDABA

him to the dressing station on the beach. From there he was transferred to a mine sweeper for conveyance to the hospital ship or to Mudros, but from the time he left the shores of Anzac, this splendid member of the Regiment has never been heard of. A court of enquiry was held to endeavour to clear up the mystery, but the only conclusion that could be arrived at was that he had died and been buried at sea, and that the documents notifying this casualty had been lost in transit.

On the 11th August the general action which had now lasted four days died down, and both sides started to consolidate their positions. Our casualties during the four days amounted to one officer and seven other ranks killed, and two officers and 26 other ranks wounded. The Regiment remained in the trenches for the next 14 days, each day being much the same as the other. Bomb and rifle fire was maintained, all available men being set to work digging new saps and large underground shelters. Several members were also employed in digging tunnels towards the enemy lines for the purpose of laying mines.

All rations and water had to be carried up from the beach daily and as the rise was one of about 400 feet in about three-quarters of a mile, the task of carrying the heavy loads was far from pleasant. The extremely hot weather and the polluted air of the trenches, added to the constant nerve strain was telling its tale on all ranks, and large numbers were evacuated to hospital. The drinking water had to be brought from Malta and landed in kerosene tins from barges. It often happened that the cans were leaky, and on two three occasions the barges were sunk by shell fire. At these times there would be a decided shortage. For some time the allowance was one quarter of a gallon per man per diem, and as this had to suffice for all purposes it was very difficult to make it last out.

When weather was bad and rough seas prevented the landing of supplies rations were cut down, but on the whole they were sufficient and of good quality. For one period of eight weeks bully beef and biscuit was the constant diet, with the result that everyone got to detest the sight of a tin of bully. Bacon, cheese, jam, and rice were also issued when available, and were greatly appreciated. Cooking was a problem, as each man had to prepare his own food in the trenches, using his mess tin for the purpose. One man in his effort to cook rice, filled his billy to the brim with rice, then added water, and put it on to boil. A short time afterwards the rice started to swell and came over the top in waves much to his astonishment, as he had been under the impression that it would boil down instead of up.

On the 25th August a rumour ran round the lines that we were being sent across to one of the islands for a spell. Several of the Infantry Battalions had been over and spent an enjoyable time at Imbros, or Lemnos. A spell was badly needed by all ranks as practically the whole Regiment was in an indifferent state of health owing to the trying conditions under which they had lived for the past three months. Great satisfaction was therefore felt when orders were issued for an early move, and all ranks set to work with a will to make the final arrangements.

CHAPTER V

HILL 60

On the 26th August, 1915, at 3 p.m., the Regiment moved to the beach where they halted and had tea. An hour afterwards they were ordered to fall in, and much to their astonishment were marched through a long communication trench to No. 2 Outpost where they halted for 10 minutes. At this point a guide reported to Lieut.-Col. Reynell, and the Regiment immediately moved off in the direction of the Damijelik Hills. This move was completed by 10 p.m., and the Regiment bivouacked in Karija Dere, which is about four miles north of the position we had evacuated.

The Regiment was now placed under the orders of Major-General Cox, commanding the 29th Indian Division. Early astir on the following day, the Regiment took over a portion of the trenches, and made preparations for an attack which was to be carried out that night. A portion of the enemy trench at this point had to be taken at all cost, and the Regiment had been ordered to undertake the task. After dark the Regiment was assembled and given definite instructions as to their particular duty, the instructions being carefully explained to all concerned.

When paraded the Regiment numbered six officers and 175 other ranks, the whole being under the direct command of Lieut.-Col. C. Reynell. Of this force, one officer and 50 other ranks were detailed to assist the N.Z.M. Rifles in a portion of the attack, and a party of the same number were detailed to assist in holding a position on the right, whilst Major H. M. Parsons with 50 other ranks bombed the Turks out of a trench on the left. Lieut.-Col. Reynell with the remainder were to attempt to capture another portion of the same trench.

At a given signal the whole force rushed into the open to carry out their desperate venture, but were met by a terrible fire from machine gun, rifle, and bomb. Cheering loudly, the gallant party rushed across the open and into the heart of the enemy, where hand-to-hand fighting was soon general. Our losses had, however, been extremely heavy, and the force was gradually driven back to its own lines, leaving the greater part of its number dead on the field, the following officers being amongst the slain: Lieut.-Col. Carew Reynell, Captain Jaffrey, and Captain Callery.

This was a sad blow to the Regiment, especially the loss of their gallant Colonel, an officer and gentleman of the best type, a splendid soldier and born leader. It is safe to say that he was idolized by the members of the Regiment, who would have followed him anywhere. Lieut. J. M. McDonald escaped, and assisted by Pte. G. C. Howell, brought two wounded men to safety under a most galling fire.

Desperate efforts were made to recover the bodies of our dead comrades, and during the following night several were brought in, including those of Colonel Reynell and Captain Jaffrey.

At 1 a.m. on the 29th August, Lieut. J. M. McDonald, with a party of 31 other ranks, bombed their way along a portion of the enemy trench on the left of the position. The 10th Light Horse Regiment then attacked in the centre and captured about 100 yards of trench. Lieut. McDonald's party joined in the final attack, using their bombs with good effect. Shortly afterwards the enemy made a desperate counter-attack which was repulsed with heavy loss. Very heavy bombing was carried on for the remainder of the night, and in several cases our men were wounded by the premature explosion of their own bombs.

Many brave but unrecorded deeds were performed during these attacks, and in the period of hanging on to the position with our small force. The Regiment's casualties during the two days were 15 killed, 18 missing (believed killed), and 45 wounded, making a total of 78, or, roughly, half the force. At 8 a.m. all except 25 men were relieved by the 5th Australian Infantry Brigade, who took over charge of the trenches.

We buried poor Reynell and Jaffrey under the trees on the far side of our little gully, and had just concluded the service when the enemy, who had evidently seen us from their observation post on Hill 971, opened a very heavy shell fire on our position. The parade was quickly dismissed and the men took cover under the hillside. For half an hour the shells fell thick and fast in our lines without inflicting any casualties. The cooks had their piles of camp kettles stacked round the fires in the middle of the gully and these were scattered in all directions by the falling shells. The loss of their dinner did not appear to annoy the men, who treated the matter as a huge joke.

A few days later British Battalions of the 53rd Division arrived and took over the trenches. One officer and 32 other ranks of the Regiment were detailed to instruct them in their new duties, as they were new to the work of trench warfare. At night this number was doubled and whilst being relieved from this duty on the following morning, Lieut. W. Cameron was killed by a shell. Efforts were made to recover the remainder of the bodies of those killed in the attack, and those recovered were given decent burial.

CHAPTER VI

RHODODENDRON SPUR.

The 4th Light Horse Brigade had by this time arrived at Anzac and its units split up to reinforce the other Light Horse Brigades who were all suffering from very depleted ranks. The 11th Light Horse, under Lieut.-Col. W. Grant, had been split up, and their Headquarters and "C" Squadron had been sent to join up with the 9th Light Horse. They had taken over a portion of the position held on Rhododendron Spur, about two miles south of Hill 60, where they were busily employed in strengthening the trenches.

Major W. H. Scott, who had been appointed temporarily to command the Regiment on the death of Colonel Reynell was evacuated to hospital and the Regiment prepared to move to join up with their new headquarters. At 7.30 p.m. on the 7th September, the remains of the Regiment (less the party in the trenches) under the command of Lieut. J. C. Chanter who at that time was the senior officer left with the Regiment, paraded and moved to Rhododendron Spur and reported for duty to Colonel Grant.

It was found that Colonel Grant had taken over the trenches from Colonel Young, of the Auckland Infantry, and had been reinforced by 175 officers and men from the Suffolk Regiment. The outer line of trenches had a frontage of 420 yards, exclusive of a trench which had still to be dug. This new trench increased the frontage to 520 yards, which was a big line for a force of roughly 300 men to defend. The six machine guns of the Brigade were put into position on the apex on the slope of Chunik Bair, and Lieut. B. B. Ragless with 21 men was detailed to hold a position on Table Top, a detached post on the right rear of Rhododendron Spur.

All supplies and stores had to be brought up from No. 2 Outpost on the beach by the Indian Mule Corps. Two parties of 30 each were detailed for digging each night, and parties were sent out nightly into the gully to reconnoitre and to collect arms left there during the heavy fighting of August. Almost immediately after the Regiment entered the trenches, Corporal McDonald was killed by a sniper's bullet, and on the following day one man was killed and three wounded on the position called "The Apex."

Enemy snipers were very active, and men were immediately set to work to beat them down, which they soon succeeded in doing. A mountain gun was brought up to the position and shelled the enemy trench in front of the Apex. After firing about 12 rounds and doing considerable damage, it was withdrawn. On the 8th September, Lieut. McDonald with the men who had been left at Hill 60 joined up and marched to the trenches. The work of improving the defences and cleaning the ground was continued. Shelters for the men were dug and in a very short space of time everything was in perfect order.

A few days later Major General A. J. Godley, commanding the Australian and New Zealand Army Corps, inspected the trenches, and expressed himself as being very pleased with the progress made in this portion of the line.

On the following day the enemy opened a violent bombardment on our position from the direction of "W" Hill. About 50 shells fell in the lines, but owing to the fact that the men were ordered to remain under cover, no casualties occurred, 25 men of the Norfolk Regiment arrived on being attached to the Regiment for instruction in trench duties. These men had just arrived from England, where they had received little training. They were, however, keen as mustard and eager to learn the points of the game, and the idea of attaching them to the Australians for instruction was a good one, as most of our men had been in the trenches for some months and knew the many artful little tricks of Johnny Turk, and how to outwit them.

Our men also derived much amusement from the association. The strange dialect of the newcomers and their inability to cook and look after themselves were a source of wonder to our men, who were becoming quite old campaigners by this time. Much leg-pulling was indulged in during the swapping of lies, our men being experts at relating their daring adventures on the Kangaroo and Prickly Pear farms of wild Australia. The plumes in our helmets were always admired by the men of these units and one and all were told that they were kangaroo feathers.

As it was getting late in the year and a severe winter was expected, warm woollen underclothing was issued to all ranks. Work was also started on the construction of weather-proof shelters. These were constructed under cover of the hillsides and were to be roofed with corrugated iron, but owing to the scarcity of material, the work progressed slowly. Long terraces of shelters were cut in the sides of the hills and temporarily covered with waterproof sheets. As these also gave shelter from shell fire they were the means of saving many casualties.

The enemy were very generous about this time and appeared to have unlimited ammunition and shells. They also had a number of large bombs, almost the size of a soccer football. These were mounted on a stick and were christened broomstick bombs. Several of these deadly missiles landed in our lines, causing serious casualties. On the 14th September the enemy opened a heavy shell fire from the direction of Abdel Rakman. One shell accounted for one killed and three wounded, but the remainder failed in their purpose. On this day Sergeant Richards, who was returning to headquarters from the beach was killed by a shot from Sniper's ridge at long range.

On the 17th September 25 reinforcements arrived from Egypt and the detachment of the Norfolk Regiment returned to their own unit. The 7th Infantry Brigade, under the command of Colonel Burston, took over the Apex and the trenches on the left, relieving the New Zealand Brigade. At 4.30 p.m. the Turks opened a heavy fire along his whole line, and a determined attack was expected to follow. Every gun we could bring to bear on the position opened up in reply, a few of the warships joining in, with the result that the enemy fire died down and the attack, if intended, was abandoned.

At 10 p.m. on the following night Sergeant Wilson went alone into the ravine in front of Fisher's Sap to watch for an enemy patrol which was known to move down the ravine each night. After waiting an hour he heard the patrol approaching along the bed of the ravine. A few minutes later, hearing a noise close at hand, he rose from the ground and saw two Turks, one of whom immediately fired, wounding him in the leg. As the two Turks rushed forward he shot one who fell across the rifle of his comrade, rendering him temporarily helpless and he was quickly bayoneted by the Sergeant. Hearing the noise the remainder of the enemy patrol hurried to the assistance of their comrades, and as they approached Sergeant Wilson threw two bombs amongst them. Four were seen to fall, and Sergeant Wilson made his way back to the sap. Owing to his wound he was unable to climb the steep slope and whistled for assistance. On hearing the whistle, which had been pre-arranged, Privates Belcher and Tomkins went out and helped him back to the trench.

On the 30th September General Birdwood inspected the trenches on our position, and expressed satisfaction at all he saw. For the past five days the enemy had expended a large number of shells on our position, especially that portion of it occupied by Regimental Headquarters, causing numerous casualties, and 21 men were evacuated to hospital.

During the month of October the work of building the winter shelters was pushed forward. The enemy were probably occupied in the same work, as they paid us far less attention. Their guns became active frequently against our 6 inch guns stationed on the beach. This caused a certain amount of interest amongst the men in our trenches who could see the guns plainly, also the strike of the enemy shells. One shell would fall quite close to the guns, whilst the next would fall many yards away. The true sporting spirit soon came to the front, and many bets were made as to where the next shell would land.

About this time an old paddle steamer had been driven ashore by bad weather near No. 2 outpost, and became a total wreck. The troops promptly set to work to salvage anything serviceable and it was soon fit for nothing but firewood. The question of breaking it up was a problem, but the enemy solved it by opening a heavy fire on the wreck. After an enormous expenditure of shells they succeeded in supplying us with unlimited firewood. Each time the firing ceased there would be a rush of diggers to carry away the pieces of timber which had been dislodged, but these men were sometimes caught napping by the unexpected reopening of fire. In such cases they would scurry away like rats into any hole or corner until the bombardment ceased.

No doubt this smashing up of an old wreck was reported by the enemy as a great naval victory: enemy battleship sunk by Turkish gun fire, etc., but the poor old tub was almost in pieces before they fired a round at it, and the expenditure of even one shell by them was unwarranted.

A large consignment of new pattern bombs having arrived, several officers and non-commissioned officers attended at Brigade Headquarters to witness a demonstration of their use and power. On the 1st November General Sir W. R. Birdwood again inspected the position and works. Instructions were also received that the Regiment would hand over the position and proceed to occupy the bivouac of the 8th Light Horse on Canterbury Slope. Very heavy firing took place on our right during the evening, and all troops immediately stood to arms. As nothing came our way, the men were allowed to fall out.

Colonel Young and officers of the Auckland Mounted Rifles inspected the position on the morning of the 10th November prior to taking over in the afternoon. On being relieved by the New Zealanders the Regiment proceeded to the new area and took over a portion of the trenches held by the 10th Light Horse. An order had arrived that all men who had been on the Peninsula since the landing of the Regiment would be sent to one of the islands for a spell. As there were not sufficient of these to make up the required number all those with 90 days' continuous service at Anzac were included.

This party was quickly got together, and at 4.30 p.m. on the 10th November the party paraded at Brigade Headquarters, where it joined up with the parties from the other units of the Brigade. After the party had been addressed by the Brigadier as to their conduct during the period of leave, the party marched to the beach and embarked on lighters. As soon as the party were embarked the lighters were towed to sea and the men transhipped to the S.S. "Osmanieh" for conveyance to Lemnos.

On the 11th November, 1915, the new Regimental area was heavily shelled during the morning, causing slight casualties. A small draft, consisting of nine reinforcements, seven men from hospital and three of the drivers who had been left behind in Egypt, arrived and were sent to the trenches. A lecture on the use of gas was given to the officers at the Headquarters of the Otago Battalion

(N.Z.) at Chalak Dere. Gas respirators were issued to all ranks and a gas alarm parade was held in the evening.

On the 19th Generals Russell and Johnson visited the trenches and inspected the position. A Turkish deserter appeared in front of our lines and was brought in by the sentries. He appeared to be nearly famished, and half dead with cold but was soon revived by means of a good hot meal and drink, after which he was taken to Brigade Headquarters. This man gave much useful information which was duly forwarded to General Headquarters. Various statistics rendered to Brigade about this time showed that over 500 officers and men were absent from the Regiment through various causes, such as wounds and sickness.

On the 27th November, after a bitterly cold day, snow commenced to fall, the ground being quickly covered. At 11 a.m. the next day Private W. A. Barker was shot through the head whilst observing and died before he could be taken from the trenches. All tracks up the hill had become impassable for mule transport, and fatigue parties were ordered to carry up the supplies and water. A Brigade supply dump was therefore formed near Headquarters and put under a guard. Orders were issued to the effect that no supplies would be issued except to an officer, and then only on a written order. As the weather was bitterly cold some of the men decided that an issue of rum was the thing needed to keep out the cold. Just after dark a party under the command of an officer (?) arrived at the dump and presented the N.C.O. in charge with a written order for two cases of rum (four gallons). As everything appeared to be in order, the N.C.O. promptly handed over the two cases, which the officer ordered his men to carry to the lines. The party marched away with the treasure, followed by the officer after he had signed the receipt. Next morning, on enquiries being made, the note proved to be a forgery and no trace of the supposed officer or men could be found, although a number of men appeared to be suffering from severe headache.

This period was the coldest and most trying time the Regiment met with during the whole course of the war. Apart from the snow lying thick in every part of the position, icy winds swept in from the sea, defying all attempts at escape from the piercing blasts. It was a slight touch of the old Crimean conditions, but luckily it did not last long. On the 29th, Pte. C. W. Collins was killed whilst observing from Kidd Sap. It became evident that the enemy were using the snow on our parapet as a background, and it was quickly cleared away. Snow ceased to fall, but the north wind was terrific and freezing.

On the 30th a great change took place in the weather conditions. The sun came out and by mid-day it was quite warm, with the result that a big thaw set in, and the gullies leading to the plain became raging torrents. The possibility of such a happening appeared to have been overlooked, with the result that a number of men occupying low-lying trenches in the vicinity of Salt Lake were drowned before they could reach higher ground. Thousands of men were also evacuated to hospital suffering from frost bite.

On the 2nd December Capt. P. J. Bailey was ordered to proceed to the Island of Imbros to represent the New Zealand and Australian Divisions at a conference in connection with the forming of a rest camp at that place. Leaving at 3 p.m. he embarked on a mine sweeper and proceeded to the island, where he prepared plans for the camp, which were forwarded to Headquarters. Having completed the work he returned to the Regiment. Lieut. N. Malcolm, who had been absent from the Regiment for some months, in hospital, arrived from England, and Lieuts. S. H. Ayliffe and Palmer reported for duty from Egypt.

On the 12th, the commanding officer and adjutants of the various Regiments assembled at Brigade Headquarters to discuss matters in connection with the proposal to evacuate the Peninsula. Field Marshal Lord Kitchener, Secretary of State for War, had visited the position, and after full inspection had decided that the troops must leave. The isolated position of the force, depending on the daily arrival of supply ships for its support, and the difficulty of discharging the cargoes from the open seas, had a lot to do with this decision. Experience had already proved that in rough weather supplies could not be landed, and at such times supplies, and especially water, had been scarce. It was expected that during the long winter months much rough weather would be met with, and as attempts to make breakwaters by sinking large ships near the shore had failed, periods of extreme shortage would be met.

All sick and wounded who had remained for treatment with the 3rd Light Horse Field Ambulance were ordered to proceed to Lemnos, and 40 members of the Brigade were evacuated under the charge of Lieut.-Col. Todd, 10th Light Horse, as the result of this order. The remainder of the Regiment took over new fire trenches, joining up with the 8th Light Horse, who took over part of the line held by the 10th.

CHAPTER VII

THE EVACUATION.

On the 14th December, 1915, orders were received that the Regiment would be held in readiness to march out at an hour's notice, and that two officers and 50 other ranks were to be detailed to remain to hold the line. Capts. B. B. Ragless and J. H. Shearer were the officers selected for this important duty and the men were taken from the various troops. An iron cross, with suitable inscription, having arrived from Egypt, it was taken to Hill 60 and erected over the grave of Lieut.-Col. Carew Reynell, by Pte. Bockleberg. Fortunately for us, the enemy had been quiet for some time and it was noticed that they were working hard on strengthening their position. This left us free to carry on the preparations for the important changes which were about to take place, the Turks evidently being quite in the dark as to our intentions.

In order that no movement on their part should interfere with our plans, scouts were sent out frequently, these usually returning with the report that all was quiet in front. On the 17th December, fresh instructions were received as to the final parties to be left when the Brigade marched out. The units were to be split into three parties, "A" party being commanded by Major S. W. Barlow, "B" by Major W. P. Farr, and "C" by Major H. M. Parsons, whilst Lieut.-Col. L. C. Maygar, V.C., took charge of the party left to hold the position. In the evening a very large fire was noticed in the direction of the beach, and it was later found that a large quantity of stores was being disposed of to prevent them falling into the hands of the enemy.

The following day all officers were called to Brigade Headquarters to receive final instructions. The first party were ordered to march out that night, and in accordance with this instruction seven officers and 150 other ranks marched to the beach at 10 p.m. All remaining officers and men were put into the trenches, the officers taking shifts of six hours each. All troops stood to arms from 5 to 7.30 each morning, and from 7.30 to 9 each evening. On the 19th all ammunition and bombs were disposed of. Small fires were kept burning in the lines, and men kept moving about to deceive the enemy.

In the trenches rifles were fixed with cans attached to the trigger by means of a string. Leaky water bottles were hung over the tins which already contained various quantities of water, in such a way that the water would drip into the cans. When the weight of water in the tin became sufficient it would release the trigger and fire the round with which the rifle was loaded. These water bottles were filled by the party left behind just before they left the trenches with the result that long after the last man had left the Peninsula our rifles could be distinctly heard firing at intervals.

At 12 noon, whilst these preparations were in progress, the enemy exploded a mine under the Apex, doing considerable damage. This was followed by a continual shelling of our position with 4 inch high explosive shells, but probably owing to the few men left in the trenches no casualties were inflicted. At 4 p.m. a second party consisting of five officers and 39 other ranks of the Regiment marched to "Saddle Post," and at 5 p.m. moved to the beach, where they were embarked on lighters. On moving out to sea they were transhipped to H.M.S. "Mars," given a hot meal and made comfortable for the night.

On the following morning the party paraded on the deck of the battleship to receive further instructions. These were to the effect that on arrival at Mudros the troops would tranship to the lighters "Sea Prince" and "Crosswaite" for conveyance to the troopship "Beltana." During the run to Mudros the troops received the kindliest treatment from the officers and men of the Navy.

At 12 noon on the 21st December the party were all safely on board the "Beltana" which was alongside the huge liner "Megantic." At 4 p.m. the "Beltana" sailed for Egypt, Lord Kensington acting as officer commanding the troops on board. After the trying times experienced at Anzac, the change to life on board ship, with regular, well-cooked meals and a decent place to sleep was greatly appreciated, and everyone quickly settled down to make the most of their good fortune. Still, amidst the signs of evident enjoyment, many were sad at heart at the thoughts of the brave comrades who had been left behind for ever on the rough coastline of Gallipoli.

As all good times come to an end much too soon, so did this pleasant trip, the "Beltana" moving into Alexandria Harbour at 7.30 a.m. on Christmas Day, 1915. At 4 p.m. the transport moved to the wharf and the troops proceeded to disembark. They were promptly greeted by their old friends "the wallads," who were evidently expecting a great harvest of backsheash. Cries of "Hello! Australia; Australia very good man; Give it piastre; finish Turkey; Plenty good time, very soon coming," etc., being heard on every side.

The troops immediately entrained and left for Cairo which was reached at 1.25 a.m. on the 26th. From Helmieh siding the troops marched to Racecourse Camp, Heliopolis, where part of the Brigade was already assembled.

The party who had been sent to Lemnos in November for a period of rest were ordered to return to Egypt, and on the 23rd December the camp at Sarpi, Mudros, was struck, and the gear

THE EVACUATION

returned to ordnance. At 11 a.m. on the same date the whole of the Light Horse details at this camp marched to the wharf and were embarked on the transport, "Caledonia," a fine ship of some 12,000 tons. The following totals of officers and other ranks were embarked:

	Officers.	Other ranks.	Total.
Anzac Headquarters	3	6	9
1st Light Horse Brigade	12	365	377
3rd Light Horse Brigade	18	408	426
2nd Light Horse Field Ambulance	2	41	43
1st Divisional Train	11	104	115
1st Divisional Engineers	18	421	439
4th Light Horse Regiment	19	272	291
1st Divisional Artillery	6	300	306
1st Divisional Staff	2	2	4
3rd Light Horse Field Ambulance	4	74	78
Totals	95	1,993	2,088

The "Caledonia" sailed at 10 a.m. on the 24th, that wonderful ship the "Aquitania" being passed at the mouth of the harbour. The following officers were appointed as ship's staff:

Ship's Commanding Officer: Lieut.-Col.W. Grant, 9th L.H.
Ship's Adjutant: Major Maxwell, 2nd L.H.
Ship's Quartermaster: Lieut. T. H. Darley, 9th L.H.
Ship's Sergeant-Major: W.Officer Wasson, 2nd L.H.

Orders were immediately issued that all ranks would wear life belts during the day, and sleep with them during the night as submarines were reported in the vicinity. The Artillery details furnished two crews to man the naval gun mounted on the stern, and three machine guns were mounted for further protection.

The troops settled down quickly to their new quarters and were looking forward to enjoying their Christmas on board. In this they were not disappointed, as the ship's staff made good provision for their comfort, and special rations were issued. In the evening a concert was held, and all spent an enjoyable day. A slight outbreak of measles took place during the voyage, three cases being sent to hospital on arrival at Alexandria. Immediately on arrival at the wharf on the morning of the 27th the troops disembarked and entrained for Heliopolis, where they joined up with the remainder of the Brigade. Major J. W. Parsons, with the remainder of the men who had remained at Anzac, also arrived, having travelled in the same convoy.

On arrival it was found that a number of the members of the Regiment had been taken to form a composite Regiment for service on the western frontier to meet an expected attack from the Sennusi tribes. These men rejoined the Regiment early in January,

1916. All reinforcements in Egypt also joined up with their parent units and the strength of the Regiment mounted to a total of 1,215. Immediate steps were taken to gather together the horses and saddlery which had been left in Egypt and to take a thorough check of all stores and equipment in possession. Stores which had been lost or abandoned at Anzac were made the subject of a board of enquiry, and steps were taken to completely re-equip and re-clothe the Regiment.

The camp on the racecourse was soon put in good order and the Brigade settled down to solid work in mounted training and musketry. The men were delighted at being once more back with their horses after the strenuous time spent as infantry during the long and trying months of the Anzac operations. Each day all available men would parade mounted for Regimental or Brigade drill, whilst those men who could not be mounted received musketry training. The hard work of each day was compensated for by the fact that there was an abundance of amusement, and all men not on duty were granted leave from 6.30 p.m. till midnight.

Each Sunday the Brigade held a massed church parade, followed by a march past. A brigade band had been organized and enlivened the proceedings with their well-known tune, "We are, we are, the 3rd Light Horse Brigade," played to the tune of "Marching through Georgia," a tune no member will ever forget, as we got it for breakfast, dinner, and tea.

A Brigade sports meeting was organized and was well attended, the events being well contested. Several events were won by members of the Regiment, the most important being the Troop Championship, which was won by Lieut. McDonald's troop.

Mrs. Reynell, widow of the late Lieut.-Col. C. Reynell, who had arrived in Egypt prior to the return of the Regiment, had organized and furnished tea rooms in one of the large buildings near the camp. Everything possible was done by her for the comfort of the troops, and her great work was deeply appreciated.

Early in February rumours of an early move into the desert were heard and steps were taken to finalize the equipping of the Regiment, as much still remained to be done in this direction. Orders were received to the effect that the 11th Light Horse Regiment were to re-form, and the officers and men belonging to that unit but who were attached to the Regiment, moved out to No. 2 Oasis camp. Capts. T. A. Brinkworth and B. B. Ragless, of the 11th Light Horse, were transferred to the Regiment, Captain Brinkworth taking command of "B" Squadron.

Major W. H. Scott was appointed to temporarily command the Regiment with Major T. J. Daly as second-in-command. The men selected to remain at the training Regiment, also the horses which were considered to be unfit for the desert campaign, were put together and everything prepared for an early move.

CHAPTER VIII

THE MOVE TO THE DESERT.

On the 27th February, 1916, an advance party under the command of Lieut. T. H. Darley entrained for Serapeum to lay out a site for the Brigade camp close to the Suez Canal, the remainder of the Brigade following on the 28th and 29th. As soon as the Regiment had settled down in its new quarters, training was resumed, and patrols sent out daily into the desert, east of the Canal.

On the 10th March the Brigade moved across the Canal and took over the front line from the 1st Australian Division. The line at that time consisted of a series of strong-posts of which the Regiment took over posts 52 to 62 inclusive from the 5th and 6th Australian Infantry Battalions. These posts extended from Gebel Habeita to Katyb-el-Habashi, and forward observation posts were established three miles in front of that line. The work of completing the trenches, which had just been started, was continued. This entailed a great amount of labour owing to the loose nature of the sand, and it was found necessary to use hurdles covered with a double layer of grass matting. Sand bags had also to be used doubled, as otherwise the sand would silt through.

To get the hurdles into position it was first necessary to dig a trench about four times the required width, then place the hurdles in position on back and front, with stays at the bottom to hold them the required distance apart. Tie posts were sunk some distance out on each side of the trench and the tops of the hurdles stayed back to these by wire. The outside of the hurdles were then banked up, and the fire bench, parapet, and traverses built of sandbags. Every time the wind rose the trenches were quickly filled by the flying sand, and it became necessary to clear out the trenches daily, like bailing a boat in a rough sea. Needless to say, under these conditions the men led a very active life and were in the pink of condition. Artillery positions were constructed in rear of the line.

During the time the Regiment held these posts the horses and transport were camped at Rail-Head, about five miles east of the Canal. A light railway with small motor engines and open trucks had been run out from the Canal for the conveyance of stores and supplies, to within a few miles of the front line. These light railways did splendid work in bringing out water until the pipe lines were completed. Lieut. T. H. Darley was left in charge of the horses and stores, and was assisted by Lieuts. Palmer and Robertson, with one man to each four horses.

On the 29th March Lieut.-Col. J. M. Arnott arrived at Serapeum to take over command of the Regiment. Colonel Arnott, a Light Horse officer of the old school, had left Australia in command of the 7th Light Horse, and had been in temporary command of the 13th Light Horse. On the 4th April the whole of "A" Sub-section of the Canal zone was re-organized. The 10th Light Horse who were on our right flank moved to Rail Head camp, whilst the 8th Light Horse, on our left, were moved to "B" Sub-sector, covering Ferry Post, Ismailia.

In accordance with the new dispositions, the Regiment left half squadrons at posts 7 and 58, and the remainder of the Regiment went into camp at Road Head. The Suffolk and Hampshire Battalions of the 54th (British) Division took over the trench system whilst the Light Horse units were employed for patrol duties and outlying observation posts. A Battalion of the 4th Australian Division held part of the line for a short period, after which it moved back, in support.

The Regiment having concentrated and formed a camp at Road Head, orders were issued to move the horses, transport, and baggage to that place. Up to this time the water supply, being dependent on the railway, had been small, viz., five gallons per horse, and one per man per diem, but on completion of the pipe line a good supply was received. Large tanks, consisting of holes in the sand lined with tarpaulins, were constructed for the storage of a reserve. By this means about 35,000 gallons was kept in reserve at Regimental Headquarters.

Work was commenced on the construction of stables, also on mess sheds for officers and men. All single tents were exchanged for double (lined) tents and erected over holes about three feet deep dug in the sand. The stables and mess sheds were substantial wooden structures, covered with grass matting and proved very serviceable. As the hot weather was close at hand they proved a blessing to man and horse, and were well worth the hard labour expended in their construction. Working parties were also sent out daily to erect wire entanglements and to repair trenches.

Brigadier-General J. M. Antill, commanding the Brigade, inspected the camp and expressed his satisfaction at the progress made, also at the general appearance of men and horses. Hard training was continued, the Regiment parading early each morning to carry out various exercises, and patrols were sent out each day at 3 a.m.

TURKISH PRISONERS CAPTURED AT MAGHDABA

PART OF OUR CAMP AT HOD MASAID (EL-ARISH)

CHAPTER IX

SERAPEUM: THE JIF-JAFFA OPERATIONS

Early in April reports were received that the Turks had thrown out a line of outposts opposite our sector, from the western foot of the Maghara Hills, south-east to Nekhl, with a post at Bir-el-Jif-Jaffa where they were stated to have erected a boring plant and built large cisterns. Jif-Jaffa lies about 52 miles due east of Serapeum on an old caravan route.

Reports also showed that the enemy had established posts at Bir-Barthel-Hegaiib about three miles north of Jif-Jaffa, at Rodh-Salem (north of Jif-Jaffa) and at Bir-el-hama, each post having a strength of about 50 rifles. As the construction of this tank system was a direct menace to our position at Serapeum, Headquarters decided that efforts should be made to wreck them and the plant. Orders were accordingly passed to Headquarters, 3rd Light Horse Brigade, to detail a force to carry out this duty, and a composite force was made up as follows:

Headquarters: Officer to command, Major W. H. Scott, 9th L.H.; Staff attached, Capt. Macauley, G.S.O., 2nd Aus. Div., Capt. H. E. Werne, 8th L.H., Capt. Ayris, 3rd L.H. Brigade.

Light Horse Squadron: Officer commanding, Major K. A. McKenzie, 9th L.H.; Second in command, Capt. B. B. Ragless, 9th L.H.; Troop leaders, Lieut. A. H. Nelson, 9th L.H., Lieut. W. S. Pender, 9th L.H., Lieut. J. M. McDonald, 9th L.H., Lieut. F. J. Linacre, 9th L.H.

Machine Gun Officer: Lieut. L. W. Jacques, 9th L.H.

The non-commissioned officers and men were selected from the 8th and 9th Light Horse Regiments, the composition of the whole force being as follows:

Unit.	Officers.	Other Ranks.	Horses.	Camels.	Remarks.
Light Horse Squadron ..	8	122	138	—	
Engineers	1	8	10	4	
Royal Flying Corps	2	2	2	4	Ground signal apparatus
Wireless Section, R.E. ..	1	8	1	15	Included three Soudanese
3rd L.H. Field Ambulance	1	8	13	6	Two sand carts and five camel cacolets

Unit.	Officers.	Other Ranks.	Horses.	Camels.	Remarks.
Camel Transport Corps .	1	2	3	—	Officers & warrant officers
Camel Transport Corps .	—	29	—	—	Light Horsemen attached as drivers
Camel Transport Corps .	—	95	—	195	Native drivers
Australian Army Service Corps	—	1	1	—	Warrant officer
Bikaneer Camel Corps (Indian)	1	24	—	37	Fighting troops
Guides	—	2	2	—	
Interpreter	—	1	1	—	(French and Arabic)
Officers attached	3	—	4	—	
Grand Total	18	302	175	261	

The camels of the Camel Transport Corps were distributed as follows: For water 88, rations 15, forage 78, ammunition 4, the remainder travelling unloaded to be used in lightening loads where necessary. The Light Horsemen acting as drivers were allowed to ride, but the native drivers walked and led their camels. The Bikanir Camel Corps carried their own supplies on the 12 spare camels shown with that unit. The quantity of drinking water which had to be carried was 2,640 gallons, each camel 30 gallons. This water was carried in flat copper tanks measuring about 24 x 18 x 10 inches, one being hung on each side of the saddle. These tanks (called fanatis) had a hole, fitted with a screw plug, at the top for filling, and a tap at the bottom rear end.

The Light Horse Squadron was made up of the lightest men and the fittest horses, as on account of this being the first operations undertaken by the Light Horse in the desert of the Sinai Peninsula it was highly essential that it should be carried to an entirely successful conclusion, therefore only the most suitable men and horses for the operation were taken. The distance to be travelled was long and trying, whilst the time at our disposal was short. Owing to the heavy sand, orders were issued that nothing would be taken that could possibly be done without, so that the horses would travel as light as possible.

A short time before this the 8th Light Horse had sent a party to reconnoitre and verify reports received to the effect that there were large rock-hewn cisterns containing water in the vicinity of Gebel-um-Mukshieb and Moiya Harab, which lie about 40 miles south-east of Serapeum. An abundant water supply was located and it was therefore decided that the force should march *via* these cisterns.

On the night of the 10th April, 1916, the camel convoy escorted by the Bikanir Camel Corps, moved out and proceeded down the

SERAPEUM: THE JIF-JAFFA OPERATIONS

Wadi Mukshieb, halting near El-Ashubi. The fighting force left Road Head at 2 p.m. on the 11th April and proceeded along the wadi. The force halted from 5.30 to 7.30 p.m., then resumed the march and came up with the convoy at 10.30 p.m.

At 7.30 a.m. on the following morning the whole force continued the march. On reaching a point two miles west of the junction of the wadis, north of Gebel-um-Mukshieb, one troop was detached and sent round to the north and east of the cisterns, as Bedouins had reported that enemy parties had been seen in that locality a few days previously. This troop shortly afterwards reported "all clear," and the column proceeded on its journey, reaching the first cistern, which lies half a mile west of where the wadi turns south to Moiya-Harab, at 11.30 a.m., when it halted.

The travelling down this wadi was very good for some distance, the sand being quite firm, but the last mile was rough and stony. The convoy arrived at 1.20 p.m. in good order, and the camels were off-loaded. During the march down the wadi our aeroplane had dropped a message stating that all was clear except for a few Bedouin camps near Moiya-Harab.

After the mid-day meal three troops were sent out to reconnoitre and report on the water supplies in the area, and altogether nine cisterns were found, hewn in the solid rock. Some were found to be practically empty, but the others were estimated to contain about 140,000 gallons. Having completed the reconnaissance, the troops rejoined at 5.30 p.m., and preparations were made for the final dash forward. It was decided to leave the ambulance, sand carts, and a portion of the Camel Transport Corps at this point under an escort of one officer and 16 other ranks from the mounted squadron, and four Light Horse camel drivers. They were also ordered to guard the wells.

At 7 p.m. the remainder of the column moved off north-east to point 1340, which was reached at 4.30 a.m. on the 13th, and the column bivouacked for the remainder of the night. During this march the Light Horse travelled for 40 minutes of each hour, then halted and dismounted in order to allow the camel portion of the force to keep touch.

At 5.30 a.m. the column moved forward, leaving the Bikanir Camel Corps, Wireless Section, and the remainder of the transport under the charge of Capt. B. B. Ragless, and marched to hill 1082, halting south-west of the hill and out of view of Jif-Jaffa, at 7.30 a.m. The section of the Royal Flying Corps erected their ground wireless plant at the foot of the hill and awaited the aeroplane report which was eventually dropped at 8 a.m., stating that all was clear.

From information previously received it was known that each time our planes appeared over their position the enemy scattered into the hills, therefore the C.O. decided to launch the attack whilst the enemy had lost cohesion. A reconnaissance of the position was made with the aid of field glasses, and orders were issued to Lieut. McDonald to take his troop round the west and north of the hill, and occupy a point about one mile N.W. of the enemy camp.

On the order to move being given the troops moved to their allotted tasks, Lieut. Pender's troop moved to the north-east and passed south of the enemy camp, whilst Lieut. Linacre with his troop, less eight men, was to make a frontal attack. Four men and a machine gun section were kept in reserve, and four men were told off as escort to the engineers, stores, and ammunition.

It was now seen that Lieut. McDonald's troop, owing to the rough nature of the country they had to traverse, would be a little late in arriving at their position. Lieut. Linacre and his troop were therefore sent over the ridge slightly to the north of the enemy's post, the remaining men and reserves moving direct on the post. An enemy observation party were seen to withdraw, whilst a number attempted to occupy position in the hills, but these were headed off by Lieut. Pender's troop. They therefore took up a prepared position near their camp and a brisk fire fight ensued. Although considerably outnumbered and surrounded, they put up a good defence, but after sustaining numerous casualties, surrendered, as their position was hopeless.

Six of the enemy were found to have been killed, and five wounded, too being too seriously wounded to move. One Austrian engineer officer and 34 Turks were captured. The personnel of the enemy post belonged to the second company, 4th Battalion, 79th Regiment, 27th Division, 8th Army Corps, 4th Turkish Army.

According to the statement made by the captured Austrian officer, the post was occupied by a total of 41; it would, therefore, appear that the whole of the enemy force had been accounted for, but two mounted men were seen to gallop away in a north-easterly direction. Evidently these men were just on the point of visiting the post when the attack started.

Our casualties amounted to one man (Cpl. Monaghan, 8th L.H.) and one horse killed. The work of destroying the enemy's tanks and plant was immediately commenced, as it was possible that other enemy forces were in the vicinity, and might hasten to the support of the post on hearing the firing. Two very well-built German artesian boring plants were destroyed, the rods and tools belonging to the drills being thrown down the bores, which were three in number, and about 8 inches in diameter, the deepest being 276 feet. These were subsequently blown in with guncotton, 25 feet from the surface. Large quantities of camp equipment and stores were destroyed, and a number of letters and papers seized.

At 11 a.m. a start was made on the return journey, and the force marched to Point 1340, collecting the Royal Flying Corps Section on the way. On reaching this point, the horses were watered from the fanatis brought up on the camels, and after a short rest the party proceeded to the cisterns, which were reached at 11.30 p.m. The weather throughout the day had been most unpleasant, owing to a very strong Kamseen (hot wind), which blew clouds of sand in our faces so that it was almost impossible to see more than 20 yards. This wind also had the effect of rendering the light portable wireless instruments useless, and communication could not be established.

During the absence of the fighting force, a large number of bedouins made a determined attack on the party which had been left to guard the wells, but after half an hour's fighting they had retired taking their casualties with them.

At sunrise on the 14th, communication by wireless was gained with the 3rd Light Horse Brigade Headquarters, a full report of the operations being despatched. After breakfast the whole party moved homewards, halting at 1 p.m. for the mid-day meal, and to allow the camel convoy to close up. During the halt, congratulatory messages were received from the Brigade and Sector commanders. Whilst these were being read to the men, one of the members of the outpost was seen to be galloping towards the camp at a great pace, and almost as soon as he came in sight it could be seen that the wadi was coming down in flood.

One troop had laid out its lines in the wadi bed, but before the water reached them they succeeded in moving the whole of their belongings to the safety of the bank. The water came down with a rush, the stream being 30 yards wide and from 6 to 10 inches in depth. The water appeared to have the consistency of white paint, and was moving almost as fast as a horse could gallop. Within five minutes the wadi had become a raging torrent, waves breaking from two to three feet high.

This unexpected happening divided the column, one portion being on either side of the wadi, but the march was continued along the wadi banks, the whole force reaching Road Head camp at midnight, having covered the 160 miles in less than three and a half days, thus proving that the Light Horse could be efficiently used in desert warfare.

It will be noticed from the composition of the force that 29 Light Horsemen were employed as camel drivers. This innovation proved of the greatest value, as they also acted as an escort for the convoy, and during the night of the 12th-13th set the pace for the Egyptian camel drivers, who were apt to loiter whenever possible. The prisoners were brought back on the camels whose loads had been consumed.

At 2 p.m. on the 15th March, 1916, the Commander in Chief, General Sir Archibald Murray, wired the following honours and awards:

> Major W. H. Scott, 9th Light Horse, Distinguished Service Order.

Cpl. P. Teesdale Smith, 9th Light Horse, Distinguished Conduct Medal.

Sgt. H. McInnes, 8th Light Horse, Distinguished Conduct Medal.

The following congratulatory messages were also received:

The General Officer commanding wishes to place on record the following telegrams received in connection with Major W. H. Scott's Jif Jaffa party:

From the Commander in Chief, Egyptian Expeditionary Force. Addressed to Major W. H. Scott, 9th Light Horse, O.C. Reconnaissance No. 2:

"I am directed by the Commander in Chief to say that he congratulates you on your success yesterday, and that he has great pleasure in conferring on you the Distinguished Service Order for your good services on April 13th."

Assistant Military Secretary, G.H.Q.

From the Corps Commander to Major W. H. Scott:

"Heartiest congratulations to you and all your command on your ably conducted, gallant feat of arms."

From Major-General Sir H. V. Cox, K.C.M.G., C.B., C.I.E., commanding 4th Division, to 3rd Light Horse Brigade:

"Congratulate Major W. H. Scott, officers, and all other ranks, 9th Light Horse, on brilliant success in raid. Execution reflects great credit on all concerned."

From Major-General H. C. Chauvel, C.B., C.M.G., commanding Anzac Mounted Division, to Brigadier-General J. M. Antill, C.B., commanding 3rd Light Horse Brigade:

"Hearty congratulations to self, Scott, all concerned. Brilliant success."

(Signed) Chauvel.

The Corps Commander, Lieut.-General Sir A. J. Godley, K.C.B., K.C.M.G., in addressing Major Scott's Jif-Jaffa party on the 18th April, said: "Officers, N.C.O.'s, and men of Major Scott's Jif-Jaffa party, I am very pleased to be here to have the opportunity on behalf of all Australians and New Zealanders of the 2nd Anzac Corps of expressing our admiration for the gallant feat of arms which you have performed. We are, one and all, very proud of you. You have carried out an enterprise which can certainly be ranked as being equal to any that has been accomplished during the war and will no doubt be carried out in the future.

"It is unfortunate that more honours on an occasion like this cannot be distributed, but by His Majesty the King graciously consenting to confer the Distinguished Service Order on your commander, he not only honours him, but every one of the command. I again repeat my admiration for the work you have done, and congratulate you."

CHAPTER X

SERAPEUM, SUEZ CANAL ZONE

During the month of May, life at Road Head became rather monotonous. The troops stood to arms at 3.45 a.m. daily, turning out in service marching order and doing an hour's mounted training. On receipt of the "All clear" report from the patrols, the parade was dismissed and the men turned in to stables. Hores were groomed and fed and the men paraded at the mess huts for breakfast.

The building of stables was pushed forward as rapidly as the supply of material would allow, and all single bell tents were exchanged for double, or lined tents, in view of the approaching hot weather. Various duties were carried out daily. Stable parades were held from 11 a.m. to 12.30 p.m. and from 4 to 5 in the evening, the horses being well groomed at each stable parade to keep them in condition. They were occasionally taken to the Canal and given a swim, which appeared to do them a deal of good.

A canteen had been erected near the Canal, and the commanding officer established a Regimental canteen in the lines. This proved a boon to all ranks, as it saved long rides over the desert every time anything was wanted. On several occasions two hogsheads of beer were brought out and distributed to the men at the expense of the commanding officer, Colonel J. M. Arnott, and occasional concerts were held.

On the 30th May, Major-General Sir H. V. Cox, K.C.M.G., K.C.B., C.I.E., caused the following general order to be published:

"In handing over command of this sub-sector of the Canal defences, the G.O.C. places on record the good work done by all ranks of the 3rd Light Horse Brigade in the front line. The cheerful spirit of the men, and the way in which their trying duties are performed, reflects great credit on them and their officers. Their camps and sanitary arrangements are the best I have seen in this country."

On the 1st June, the City of London Yeomanry took over posts 7 and 58, together with the corresponding patrols, thus relieving the Regiment of a big share of its duties.

On the 10th June, a composite force, under the command of Lieut.-Colonel T. Todd, D.S.O., 10th Light Horse, consisting of the 10th L.H. Regiment less one squadron, the 9th L.H. less Headquarters, a detachment of Engineers, a section of the 3rd L.H. Field Ambulance, and over one thousand camels with native drivers, moved out along the Wadi Mukhshieb for the purpose of pumping out the cisterns reported on during the Jif-Jaffa operations, also to drain other large pools which had formed when the wadi came down in flood, and thus deny the water to the enemy.

Major C. C. Dangar, 13th Hussars, Brigade Major, 3rd Light Horse Brigade, and Major W. H. Scott, D.S.O., 9th Light Horse, accompanied the column as staff officers.

The nearest pool to our line lay to the north-west of El-Ashubi, and about 20 miles from our defences. It was estimated that this pool contained five million gallons, and would have made an ideal jumping off place for an enemy attack. The column halted for the night in the Wadi Mukhshieb, about 25 miles east of Rail Head. On the morning of the 11th June, it moved to the cisterns in the vicinity of Gebel-Um-Mukhshieb, arriving there at 10.15 a.m., the work of pumping being at once started by "B" Squadron, 9th Light Horse, who worked 20 pumps. This squadron was afterwards assisted by the 10th Light Horse, the tanks being emptied by 3.30 p.m. on the following day.

At 4 p.m. on the 12th, "B" Squadron, 9th Light Horse, proceeded south to Moiya Harab, taking with them 12 pumps to assist the Middlesex Yeomanry in pumping out the cisterns at that place. This work was completed by 7 p.m., and the column moved back to a chain of large pools in the vicinity of El-Rigum, arriving there at 8 p.m.

When the wadi came down in flood on the 14th April, it brought with it a large quantity of clay matter, which, when the Wadi ceased to flow, deposited itself on the sand, forming an impervious strata. It was therefore decided to cut deep channels through this strata as close as possible to the edge of the water. Digging started about midnight on the 12th-13th, and by noon on the 13th over one million gallons of water had disappeared into the sand, leaving very little serviceable water. The column then moved to the large lake northwest of El-Ashubi and treated this in the same manner. By exploding two large mines in the centre of the lake, the level of the water was reduced between two and three feet, leaving only a shallow pool, which from subsequent reports was found to have completely drained away.

The column, having completed its task, returned to camp, arriving at Road Head at 5 p.m. on the 14th June. During these operations the whole of the country towards Bir-El-Giddi was reconnoitred for roads and water. No trace of the enemy was seen, but we learnt from natives that they visited Moiya Harab the morning after we had left that place. The total amount of water drained away was about eight million gallons.

On the 15th June, Colonel J. M. Arnott was seconded from the Regiment to command the Australian Training Regiment at Tel-el-Kebir, and Major W. H. Scott, D.S.O., assumed command of the Regiment. Routine outpost and patrol duties were carried on during the month of July. Daily lectures were given to officers and N.C.O.'s, mostly on subjects taken from Field Service Regulations. They were also practised in writing reports and in semaphore signalling.

During one of the lectures given by Major K. A. McKenzie, some of those present found it very difficult to keep awake, partly due to the intense heat, but chiefly to the dryness of the subject. At last the Colonel gave up all attempts to keep awake and dropped off into a sound sleep, from which he was rudely awakened by hearing Capt. Chanter ask the lecturer to sound Reveille. The Colonel jumped up with a start and vigorously protested that he had heard every word, but on being asked to repeat the last sentence he caused much amusement by mentioning a few of the opening remarks.

Unanimous verdict: "Guilty."

During this month three officers' patrols were sent out to reconnoitre the Wadi Mukhshieb, El Tassi, and Et Tassa. These patrols were out for over 24 hours at a time, the horses having no water during that time, although the weather was extremely hot. Contrary to expectations, they appeared to be none the worse for their experience.

On the 26th, orders were received to the effect that the 3rd Light Horse Brigade would move to Bally Bunion, and one squadron of the 12th Light Horse arrived to take over the outpost line. The Regiment marched out on the morning of the 27th, 21 officers and 472 other ranks being mounted, and the remainder proceeding by rail with the heavy baggage, under the command of Capt. J. C. Chanter. The wheeled transport proceeded by road under the command of Lieut. T. H. Darley.

The Regiment moved across the desert *via* Ferry Post, and camped for the night about one mile north-east of the Ordnance Depot, Ismailia. The transport, after a very trying march through loose sandy tracks, arrived at 5 p.m. On the following morning the march was resumed *via* El Ferdan and Ballah to Bally Bunion, which was reached at 1 p.m.

Steps were immediately taken to erect a standing camp. Splendid lines were laid out, tents erected, and by nightfall things were looking shipshape and comfortable. Orders were received to the effect that the Machine Gun Sections of each Regiment would be detached to form a Machine Gun Squadron under the command of Major Nicholas, 10th Light Horse. As one Machine Gun Squadron was in future to form part of each Brigade, this squadron was to be known in future as the 3rd Light Horse Brigade, Machine Gun Squadron, and proved one of the best of its kind.

The new organization was found to be of the greatest advantage to all concerned, as it ensured a uniform system of training, and gave the Brigade Commander direct control of the 12 guns of the squadron.

Reports came to hand that a strong body of Turks had been seen in the vicinity of Oghratina, and everything pointed in the direction of a second attempt being made by them to attack the Canal defences. Orders were therefore issued to all units to be ready to move at short notice for an attack on the enemy's left flank, only such men and horses as were fit to undertake three days' sustained effort to be taken. As could only be expected, every man immediately claimed that both he and his horse were fit to carry on for three weeks if necessary, and in most cases they proved it during the ensuing operations.

With the possibility of sustained operations commencing at any moment, steps were immediately taken to complete all necessary arrangements, and officers' patrols were sent out to reconnoitre the country to the north-east for roads and water.

Looking back over a period of three years' service with the Egyptian Expeditionary Force, it can safely be said that the five months spent at Serapeum were undoubtedly the most strenuous in the history of the unit, with the exception of Gallipoli. Periods of greater stress were met with, but for much shorter periods. The scarcity of water, lack of fuel, intense heat, and kamseens made life far from agreeable.

CHAPTER XI

ROMANI

For some months past it had been known that the enemy were collecting a large force in the vicinity of Bir-el-Abd, whilst smaller parties were scattered amongst the hods energetically developing the water supply. A daring raid had been carried out on the Yeomanry Camp at Qatia and heavy casualties inflicted.

At that time, the British line in this sector ran from Mahamdiya on the Mediterranean, South, covering Romani to Katib Gannit, thence in a series of strong posts to protect the light railway from Kantara to Romani, with headquarters at Kantara.

In the early days of August, reconnoitring patrols were sent out daily in the direction of Hod-el-Arras, Hod Jehierat and Hod Abu-Samara, with special instructions as to searching for water.

At dawn on the 4th August the enemy delivered a heavy frontal attack in a determined effort to seize the railhead at Romani. The attack was so sudden and fierce that for a time they made good progress, and the Light Horse holding the point at which the thrust was directed were forced back by sheer weight of numbers. Their splendid discipline and determination, however, held them together and the enemy were gradually forced to withdraw. Heavy fighting continued throughout the day, but towards evening they withdrew to reorganize.

On the morning of the 4th August, orders were issued to the effect that the Brigade would march out at 8.30 a.m. and would travel as light as possible. No news had reached us of the commencement of the enemy attack, and although an early move had been expected, this short notice took everyone by surprise, and caused the greatest excitement.

For eight months the Regiment had been practically in standing camps, looking forward to the time when the enemy would come within striking distance, and the long-looked-for moment had apparently arrived. Everywhere was bustle and excitement, and the instruction to travel light was certainly carried out, as many did not even take a jacket or spare shirt, expecting that a few hours would see them back in the camp which they had gone to so much trouble to make comfortable. They were, however, destined to receive a rude shock, as it was many weeks before they saw a standing camp again.

Only one hour's notice was given, and in that time supplies of rations, forage, and ammunition had to be drawn and issued, and arrangements made as to the stores which were to be left behind. Still, at the stated time the Regiment was on parade, fully equipped and ready to move, with a strength (on parade) of 21 officers, 415 other ranks, and 459 horses. All wheeled transport was left behind, also 115 men and 87 horses under the command of Lieut. A. H. Nelson.

The first orders stated that the Brigade would march *via* Hod el-Arras to Romani, but after proceeding about two miles the direction of the march was changed to Hill 70 which had been held by the New Zealanders. Hill 70 is on the main Kantara-Qatia caravan route, 10 miles north of Bally Bunion, and about seven miles east of the Suez Canal. The Brigade reached Hill 70 at 11.30 a.m. and halted until 5 p.m. Immediately on arrival, the Brigadier left by motor to report to the G.O.C. of the sector, and on his return the Brigade moved to Dueidar, arriving at 10 p.m. and bivouacking for the night.

This point was found to be held by the New Zealanders and Scottish Horse, who found the outposts. During the march, frequent gun flashes had been noticed away on our left and information came to hand of the desperate attack made on the line. Desperate fighting was stated to have taken place on a long hill, covering the camp, afterwards named "Mount Royston" after that splendid old soldier, Brigadier-General Royston, who, a few days later, was appointed to command the 3rd Light Horse Brigade.

At 4 a.m. on the following morning the Regiment moved out from Dueidar as advance guard to the Brigade, followed by the 10th Light Horse, the intention being to attack Hod el-Enna in conjunction with the 5th Light Horse Regiment. On arrival at Bir-el Nuss we gained touch with the headquarters and one squadron of the New Zealand Mounted Rifles, who informed us that the enemy attack on Romani had been broken up, and that a number of prisoners and guns had been taken. As was only to be expected, this information caused general rejoicing, and seemed a good omen for the future. A good well having been found in this Hod, the horses were watered and fed, the men also taking the opportunity to make a good meal.

At 9 a.m. the advance was continued in the direction of Hod El-Enna, but on receipt of information to the effect that the enemy had vacated that place, the direction of march was altered to Bir Nagid and Hod Hamissah. During this move junction was made with the New Zealanders on our left. At about noon, the advance patrols came in touch with a portion of the enemy rearguard, about one mile west of Bir Nagid, who opened fire, but a few minutes later surrendered to our men.

On moving towards Bir Nagid, the sand plainly showed that large numbers of men and camels had passed towards the east. We accordingly increased our pace as much as the heavy sand would allow and soon came in sight of a string of camels loaded with ammunition. These were promptly shot down, but the drivers escaped. The ammunition (about 40,000 rounds) was captured. The main portion of the enemy rearguard which had taken up a position along a line of sand hills, about two miles N.E. of Bir Nagid, opened a heavy fire on "A" Squadron at 12.40 p.m.

Information was brought in that about one thousand of the enemy were occupying a position covering Hamissah, and orders were immediately issued for the Regiment to deploy for action, "A" Squadron in the centre with two troops of "B" Squadron on each flank, whilst "C" Squadron were to make a wide detour to the south with the object of outflanking and enfilading the enemy's position. "A" and "B" Squadrons advanced to within 700 or 800 yards and dismounted, sending their horses to cover. They then opened a brisk fire and pushed forward as opportunity offered.

At 1 p.m. a message was sent to Brigade Headquarters at Nagid, asking that one squadron be sent in support as the whole Regiment was by this time heavily engaged. In the meantime the enemy, seeing the movement of "C" Squadron, began to withdraw in an easterly direction. The led horses were therefore signalled up, and "A" and "B" Squadrons mounted and pushed forward to the foot of the ridge, where they dismounted and went in with the bayonet. A sharp fight took place, and Lieut. Ayliffe's troop captured two officers and 63 men, unwounded, also many sets of arms, and a quantity of stores and equipment. Various other troops captured prisoners in this melee, and when a count was taken the total was found to be 308, of which the Brigade scouts captured 27.

The enemy continued to retire towards a strong position, held by machine guns, covering Hamissah, and at 1.30 p.m. "A" Squadron of the 10th Light Horse arrived under the command of Major Olden. The Inverness Battery, Royal Horse Artillery, had by this time got into position, and quickly put a section into action. This was the first time they had been in action, and their target was a camel convoy carrying machine guns and ammunition at a distance of about 3,000 yards. In spite of the fact that range-taking instruments could not be used, the gunners got on to their target with the first shot, and made splendid practice, their shrapnel being timed to perfection. This somewhat annoyed the enemy, who immediately opened fire on the battery, sending over salvoes of six inch howitzer shells, and the guns were forced to withdraw.

At 2.30 p.m. the remainder of the 10th Light Horse came up and worked round the right flank in conjunction with the Brigade Scouts and "C" Squadron of the Regiment, a number of prisoners and machine guns being captured during the movement.

It was noticed that the enemy machine guns were under the command of German officers and non-commissioned officers, and in one instance, when a party of Turks put up the white flag, a German N.C.O. was seen to shoot the surrendering Turks. At another time when the Brigade Scouts and a troop of the 10th Light Horse under Lieut. J. Lyall were collecting prisoners, a German N.C.O. opened fire with his machine gun on a party of the enemy who were in the act of surrendering. This German no doubt stopped, for the time being, the surrender of about 100 Turks.

During the whole of the engagement the enemy guns made good shooting, our small casualty list being chiefly due to the fact that they were firing high explosive shells which buried themselves in the sand before bursting, with the result that the force of the explosion was almost neutralized by the sand. Cases were frequent where shells fell within six or eight feet of men without any worse effect than the inconvenience of being covered in a shower of sand.

As the Regiment continued to advance, the enemy gunners shortened their range, with the result that when it halted the shells fell amongst their own troops, one shell reaching their ammunition convoy with disastrous results. At the end of the day's fighting it was found that the bag of the Brigade amounted to a total of 10 officers and 415 other enemy ranks, whilst seven machine guns and large quantities of stores had been captured. Although the prisoners appeared to be in good condition they were evidently beginning to feel the strain of having marched on foot through the deserts of the Sinai Peninsula. During the latter part of the great march they had been badly fed and were short of water. In fact the only food the writer saw in the possession of this batch of prisoners was dates collected from the neighbouring Hods.

During this engagement Lieut. A. D. Palmer had two machine guns supporting the Regiment and did excellent work, but late in the day he received wounds which unfortunately ended fatally.

At 6.30 p.m. orders were received to fall back on Bir Nagid where the Brigade would bivouac for the night, the 8th Light Horse finding the outpost duties. After dark the Brigade left Nagid and moved about two miles in a north-westerly direction where it halted and placed an outpost furnished by the Regiment. At 4 a.m. on the 6th, the Regiment left for Hod El-Enna to water the horses, but as the guide failed to find the track through the high sand dunes the Regiment returned to Nagid where it halted, horses and men enjoying a well-earned meal.

At 3 p.m. the Brigade moved to Hod Abu Daren, where it camped for the night. The enemy had continued to fall back after the engagement at Hamissah and contact was not gained during the day, but during the march the Brigade was shelled from the northeast with heavy shells, evidently fired at long range, whilst enemy planes dropped light bombs on the convoy.

At dawn on the 7th, the 8th Light Horse moved off, supported by the Regiment, and shortly after daybreak, about one mile east of Hod Es-Sagia, gained touch with the enemy, who brought a very heavy fire to bear. The 9th Regiment moved up in close support and dismounting, sent the horses back to the Hod, one squadron at a time to water. This move was evidently seen by the enemy, who kept up a heavy shrapnel fire both on the troops and on the Hod during the watering. At 2 p.m. the Regiment took over the line from the 8th Light Horse, who moved back to water, having suffered a number of casualties during the early part of the day.

The Inverness Battery occupied a ridge to the west of Hod Es-Sagia, close to the ruins of a wonderfully well-preserved ancient temple, of which the tops of the pillars and capitols alone stood above the sand, the remainder having been buried by the drift. The Battery did excellent shooting against the enemy convoys, etc., and made them very careful as to their movements. During the afternoon a force, believed to be New Zealanders, was seen to make an advance about two miles to the north, and to become heavily engaged. After dark the Regiment fell back on Abu Daren and established a line of outposts for the night.

On the 8th the Regiment left Abu Daren with the main body of the Brigade and marched to Hod Dhahab, arriving there at about 2 p.m. At 3 a.m. the following morning the Regiment moved off and joined up with the 8th Light Horse who had been on outpost duty. The 8th then moved off as advance guard with the Regiment in support, and followed by the 10th. The advance guard gained touch with the enemy at 6 a.m. about one mile east of Hod Hassaniya where they held a strong position consisting of two redoubts covering Hod El-Bada. These redoubts were well sited and prepared, with good trenches and field fortifications, and it was evident that they had been prepared during the forward move as strong points to be used in the event of a retirement.

The 8th soon became heavily engaged, and "C" Squadron of the Regiment under the command of Major McKenzie was sent up in support and to protect our right flank; but the greater portion had to be diverted to strengthen the centre of the 8th Light Horse line. "A" Squadron under Major H. M. Parsons was therefore sent up to extend the line to the right and to reinforce where necessary.

It was now discovered that there was a gap of about one and a half miles between the left of our line, and the right of the New Zealanders, and "B" Squadron, under Major T. A. Brinkworth, was sent to fill it. "A" Troop of this squadron was sent to gain touch with the New Zealanders, who were seen to be advancing on Abd, touch being gained near El Birdieh. Large enemy movements were observed in the direction of Bir-el-Abd, and the position in the immediate front was found to be strongly held. Several attempts were made to dislodge this force, but these attempts were all held up by heavy rifle and machine gun fire.

It was reported that away to the south in the vicinity of Hod el-Bayud a column, known as "the mobile column," composed of two squadrons of the 11th Light Horse, the City of London Yeomanry, and two companies of the Imperial Camel Corps, were endeavouring to make a wide flanking movement, and to threaten the enemy's lines of communication. It was essential that they should gain possession of Hod Bayud, which was strongly held by the enemy, and, after heavy fighting, the Hod was captured. They watered their horses and held on during the night, but a determined counter-attack in the early morning of the 10th resulted in the Hod being recaptured by the enemy.

It was understood that the duty assigned to the 3rd Light Horse Brigade consisted of holding the enemy in his present position until the turning movement had been carried out, and during the whole of the day the Inverness Battery did excellent work, especially in the early morning when the enemy attempted to launch a counter-attack. At sundown the enemy made a most determined attack on our position, and four men of "A" Squadron were captured. During this attack the enemy advanced within 200 yards of our position, and as a result of the heavy fire brought to bear on them, a party opposite "C" Squadron put up the white flag.

On seeing these flags, Lieut. G. O. Robertson, after ordering his men to cease fire, stood up and went forward to take their surrender, but as he approached, a heavy cross fire was opened by the enemy on the flank, when he was about 100 yards from the enemy, and he fell badly wounded. On seeing the officer fall, No. 84 Corporal Titan Barrington, of "A" Squadron, a big and powerful man, ran forward with great gallantry and determination, and in spite of the fact that Lieut. Robertson weighed over 13 stone, picked him up and ran with him towards our line.

During the whole of this proceeding the enemy maintained a heavy fire, and a number of Turks rushed out in an effort to capture him, yet in spite of his heavy load, and that he had to cover a distance of nearly 100 yards, he succeeded in reaching our lines in safety. No. 462 L.-Corp. Neyland had in the meantime brought up Lieutenant Robertson's horse, and took the wounded officer to safety under intense fire. This officer, it is regretted to state, succumbed to his injuries shortly after his arrival at Kantara Hospital.

Cpl. Barrington was recommended for the Victoria Cross on the evidence of Lieut. Robertson, Major McLaurin, and Lieut.-Colonel L. C. Maygar, V.C., of the 8th Light Horse, who were eye witnesses, whilst L.-Cpl. Neyland was recommended for the Distinguished Conduct Medal, but no awards were made. It is an astonishing fact that one of the bravest deeds of the war should thus pass unrewarded and the two gallant men were not even mentioned in dispatches for their splendid work.

Of the four men captured, only one, Pte. Rose, survived the terrible treatment meted out by their inhuman captors. He passed through Tripoli, Syria, on his release and met the Regiment, which had just arrived at that place from Homs. He stated that when

TURKISH OFFICER PRISONERS CAPTURED AT RAFA

CONSTRUCTION OF TRENCHES AT EL-GAMLI

captured, he and some of the others were wounded, but were immediately taken before a German officer and interrogated. Sgt. H. Sullivan, who had been captured whilst endeavouring to rescue one of the wounded men, was the first to be questioned. On being asked questions of military importance, such as, "Who is your commanding officer," etc., he replied, "I don't know." The German officer immediately replied that he being a sergeant must know these facts, and Sullivan said, "I don't know, for you."

The German then threatened to shoot him and had a machine gun brought and placed in front of him, but still this gallant soldier, of Coromandel Valley, South Australia, refused to give any information whatever. The German, after adopting a very threatening attitude, asked various questions, but seeing the determination of the sergeant not to answer, he finally gave up the attempt. Sergeant Sullivan was reported some time later to have died of dysentery.

The enemy maintained his efforts, continually counter-attacking, but our line held, and at 7 p.m. the enemy retired to their trenches. The 10th Light Horse, who had been held in reserve during the day, now came forward and took up an outpost line in rear of the battle line. As soon as they were in position the Regiment withdrew to Hod Hassaniya for water and supplies.

On the 10th August "B" Squadron moved out at 1 a.m. to support the outpost line. The remainder of the Regiment moved at 4 a.m. and from time to time reinforced portions of the line. During the morning Lieut. Ayliffe with a party of eight men moved south to Bayud and gained touch with the Mobile Column, who were holding the high ridges west of that place, and were being heavily shelled. A portion of this force had to return to Mageiera, about two miles distant, to water, and after carrying out the instructions received, the party rejoined the Regiment.

At 4 a.m. on the following day "A" Squadron passed through the outpost line with the object of finding out the dispositions and strength of the enemy, and were immediately subjected to a heavy fire. They found the enemy to be still in position in considerable force. At 6 a.m. an enemy plane passed over, dropping several light bombs, which fell close to "C" Squadron horses, but fortunately doing little damage. One of our small planes suddenly appeared from the direction of Romani and was quickly spotted by the enemy pilot, who turned his machine, and passing between our plane and the sun, which evidently prevented our pilot from seeing his enemy, turned again and took up a position close in rear of the British plane.

This was the first occasion on which we had seen one of our planes at close quarters with one of the enemy, and all were anxious to see the enemy plane shot down after a thrilling fight, but we were to be sadly disappointed, for as soon as the enemy plane had righted itself the pilot fired a burst with his machine gun, and our plane commenced to fall, evidently out of control, but when little more than one thousand feet from the ground, it straightened out and made a perfect landing about two miles away. The writer, who was with the reserve, immediately mounted and galloped across to see if any assistance was required. Both pilot and observer were found to be badly wounded, the pilot being shot through the shoulder and having his jaw shattered. He had collapsed and momentarily lost control, but with real bull dog courage had regained control and landed without breaking a stay.

Both officers were in a bad way and were quickly conveyed to the Field Ambulance, the pilot succumbing to his wound shortly after arrival. The machine had been struck by about fifteen bullets which passed clean through the body of the machine, and through the back of the seats occupied by both the pilot and observer.

No attempt was made during the day to force the redoubt, and at 7 p.m. the line was taken over by the 8th Light Horse, the Regiment retiring to Hod Abu-Dhahab to water and bivouac. At 4 a.m. on the 12th, the Regiment left bivouac with orders to march to Hassanein and remain in reserve, but on arrival at that place it was found that the enemy had stolen a march on us by evacuating the redoubts during the night.

Brigadier-General J. R. Royston, C.M.G., D.S.O., had arrived at Hassaniya to take over the Brigade from Brigadier-General J. M. Antill, C.B., C.M.G., who had been withdrawn and sent to France. He at once made enquiries as to the condition of the horses, and ordered the Regiment to move forward with all possible speed, and endeavour to pin the enemy down to a position. At 6 a.m. the Regiment passed through the outpost line and moved over the redoubts, which were seen to be well constructed and in an exceptionally good position, commanding the country for miles around. It was apparent that the enemy had paid heavy toll in return for having held up our advance.

A signalling station was established on the redoubt, and the Regiment pushed on towards Bir-Salmana, endeavouring to intercept the enemy. At Salmana the enemy were found to be in strength and holding a strong position, with well-secured flanks. The Regiment therefore took up a position along a ridge about 2,000 yards to the south-west, being promptly subjected to heavy shrapnel and high explosive shell fire. The orders were that as many men as possible were to be shown on a razor-backed sand dune, with the object of drawing the enemy's attention and fire, thus diverting it from the New Zealand Mounted Rifles, who were on our left, and who had a special mission to perform.

Here again the sand neutralized the effect of the shell bursts. The horses and men were occupying a small area and were split up into small parties with intervals and distances of about 20 yards.

The enemy marksmanship was perfect, not a single shell falling outside the occupied area, but in spite of the fact that 56 shells were counted, not a single casualty occurred to man or horse. This was the more remarkable as neither men nor horses shifted their position during the whole time.

At dusk the Regiment withdrew to Hod Hassaniya, where it bivouacked for the night. This proved to be the finish of the engagement known as the Battle of Romani. The Regiment had been continuously on the move since the 4th August, having very little opportunity for sleep and no time or opportunity to shave or clean up—in fact, it is doubtful whether the majority of the Regiment had a wash during that time. Water was extremely scarce, both men and horses having experienced a thirst such as can only be felt by those who have really known the value of water. The whole period was spent under a tropical sun without shelter of any kind, whilst the white glare of the sand seemed to scorch the skin and blind the eyes.

Although the temperature must frequently have reached 120 in the shade, had there been any shade in which to measure it, the men had only their water bottles (one quart) which were filled once per day from the fanatis brought out by camels from Romani. Horses could only be watered when suitable wells were found, and at most got a small drink once in 24 hours. In most cases the water brought up from these wells was absolutely unfit for human consumption and was almost unfit for animals, with the result that many were afraid to give it to their best friend, their horse, and only allowed sufficient to wash the dust from their throats.

The question of transporting rations and drinking water to the various units of the Brigade presented innumerable difficulties. All the work of the Brigade supply branch had to be done by night, in a country covered with high, irregular sand hills, and without tracks or guide marks of any kind. Lights were forbidden and the difficulty of moving long strings of camels, heavily laden, over such country, and in pitch darkness, can only be understood by those who knew the conditions. To get a distance of, say, three or four miles in a direct line, it would often be necessary to travel from 10 to 12 miles winding about in every direction in order to get round these astonishing sand formations, yet never once did the convoy fail to arrive safely or up to time.

The Brigade convoy was under the command of Lieut. T. H. Darley, Quartermaster of the Regiment. Although drinking water was plentiful when the convoys arrived there was no means of storing the water left over after the water bottles had been filled, with the result that what could not be consumed by the men was given to the horses. All rations had to be transported by camels from railhead, Romani, a distance of about 20 miles.

When one recalls the great praise given to the naval officer who guided the British Army to the battle of Tel-el-Kebir, one wonders if full credit has been given to the Light Horseman as a guide and pathfinder. Not only during these operations, but during the whole campaign in the desert, young officers, N.C.O.'s and men had to find their way over vast tracts of country with nothing more than a very ancient map and a compass to work on.

The conduct of all ranks during this period was exemplary, every man performing his allotted task with fine spirit, and it is safe to say that there was not a shirker in the Regiment.

CHAPTER XII

DESERT OPERATIONS

As the enemy had withdrawn for some miles, the Brigade went into camp at Hod Hassaniya for a short rest. Orders were received that the Regiment would occupy Hod Nabit, and the move was made at 9 a.m. As the Regiment marched out from Hassaniya an enemy plane flew over and bombed the camp, causing slight casualties. On arrival at Nabit the horse lines were laid out under the palms, the men constructing shelters of palm fronds. Steps were immediately taken to bring up stores from the camp at Et Maler, the men and horses left at Bally Bunion when the Regiment marched out on the 4th August, having been moved to that place.

The equipment was overhauled and all losses replaced in readiness for future operations. The arrival of a mail from Australia with a few comforts was greatly appreciated, and all ranks settled down to make the most of the short spell after the strenuous time just passed. During the day men and horses kept to the shelter of the palms, but at night all men, except those on duty with the horses, moved to a sand hill about 200 yards from the lines to sleep, it being considered unhealthy for the men to sleep in the Hod.

On the 23rd August "A" Squadron, under Major H. M. Parsons, moved to Oghratina to relieve one squadron of the 10th Light Horse. At 11 p.m. on the 24th the Regiment, less "A" Squadron, with the balance of the Brigade, and in conjunction with the New Zealand Brigade, moved out to make a reconnaisance of the country to the north of Salmana, with the object of rounding up enemy patrols and Bedouins, who were known to be assisting the enemy.

The 10th Light Horse moved as advance guard, and at 8 a.m. on the 25th arrived on the high ground overlooking Hod Geisi. Patrols were immediately sent out in all directions, and "B" Squadron was sent out towards Ganadil. The only enemy seen was a party of Camelry on the eastern horizon, but these were too far away for pursuit. The country in the vicinity of Bir-el-Geisi consists of a series of wind-blown sand hills rising to a razor edge. The sides of these dunes in the direction of the prevailing wind were a gradual slope; the lee side falling away at the natural angle of the repose of the sand, the angle of slope being about one and a half in two. In many places it was absolutely impossible to take horses over them with the result that the base of the dunes had to be traversed until a break or low place was found. This often necessitated travelling from twice to three times the actual distance on the map, to get to any particular place, besides which the heavy sand made it difficult for the horses.

After having made a thorough reconnaisance of the surrounding country, the Brigade, with the Regiment as advance guard, proceeded *via* Ganadil, to Hod Mushafat, and after watering horses returned to bivouac, arriving at 7.30 p.m. Outpost lines were thrown out each night, and patrols were sent out each day before sunrise.

On the 31st, the Regiment, with a section of the Machine Gun Squadron and a section of the Field Ambulance, with two sand carts moved to Bayud to assist the Mobile Column in making a drive between Hod el-Bayud and el-Aweida. The object of this drive was to endeavour to cut off and capture enemy patrols who were very active, and were constantly interfering with our telephone lines. The Regiment left bivouac at 6 a.m., "C" Squadron being sent to a point 10 miles south of Hod el-Bayud. No enemy being encountered during the march, the squadron returned to Bayud at 1 p.m., and the whole column returned to camp.

On the 2nd September, one squadron was sent out to form an outpost line, Baya-Bayud, connecting with the Imperial Camel Corps on the right and the N.Z.M.R. on the left, patrols being pushed out in front one hour before daybreak, but no enemy were seen. A few days later the Brigade took over the Bada-Abd-Hod-Hishia line, and the Regiment moved to Hod Amara. On alternate nights the Regiment found the outposts and inlying picquet, the 10th Light Horse being detached from the Brigade.

On the 15th, the Regiment, under the command of Major T. J. Daly moved out as an advance guard to the Brigade, and proceeded *via* Bir-el-Abd to Hod Salmana which was the point of rendezvous for a reconnaisance in force of Bir-el-Mazar. Arriving at Salmana at 4 a.m. on the following morning the Brigade took advantage of all possible cover as a protection from aeroplane observation. At 9 a.m. an enemy plane flew over the lines and after dropping a few bombs flew low and opened fire with his machine gun, causing a few casualties. The plane was eventually driven off by rifle fire.

At 5.30 p.m. the Brigade advanced, the Regiment forming the advance guard, and halted at a point 3½ miles east of the Hod where the remainder of the force, consisting of the 2nd Light Horse Brigade, the Ayrshire and Inverness Batteries, and the Hong Kong and Singapore Mountain Battery joined up. This mountain battery was an exceptionally fine unit, and made excellent shooting with their small but serviceable guns, which were carried on pack mules. The guns on being dismounted were distributed over various loads, the gun on one pack, mounting on another, and the wheels on a third, together with the tools. Ammunition for these guns was also carried in leather panniers on mules. In spite of this distribution, it was astonishing to see how quickly the guns could be assembled and brought into action by their highly-trained teams, which consisted mostly of Indians.

The 3rd Light Horse Brigade were to proceed to a point some distance to the south of Bir-el-Mazar, and at a stated time to advance on the enemy position, but if the enemy were found to be in strength, the attack was not to be pressed. Lieut.-Colonel W. H. Scott, D.S.O., having joined up at Salmana, was given the task of guiding the Brigade to its appointed position. The night was pitch dark, and the country to be traversed was filled with every possible kind of obstacle for mounted troops, but in spite of these difficulties, daylight showed that the troops were in the exact position ordered.

The column moved off at 10 p.m., proceeding east, and at 2 a.m. the direction was changed to the south. Winding its way along the foot of the enormous sand dunes, the column constantly changed its direction in order to get back to its proper course. At 4.30 a.m. a point two miles south of Mazar was reached, and at 4.45 a.m. "C" Squadron was fired on by an enemy post which was promptly rushed and captured. The direction was now changed to the north-west, "C" Squadron moving on the right and throwing out flank patrols; "A" Squadron deployed on the left of "C," and "B" on the left of "A," the line being extended by one squadron each of the 8th and 10th Light Horse Regiments. The 2nd Light Horse Brigade who were making a demonstration against Mazar from the west, joined up with our left flank.

A number of the enemy could be seen moving about the main redoubt one mile to the north, and several trenches were seen, well manned, at a range of about 800 yards. Numerous rifle-pits were located at various points, the position appearing to be a difficult proposition owing to the scattered nature of the defences. As soon as our force came in sight, the enemy opened a brisk sniping fire, but with little effect. As the Regiment moved forward to the attack an order arrived from headquarters to withdraw as the position was reported by aeroplane as being strongly held. As the Regiment withdrew the enemy opened fire with field and machine guns, and Lieut. Slattery was killed. This officer had only received his commission three days before, but had served through Gallipoli as a non-commissioned officer, and later as Regimental Sergeant-Major.

During the forward move it was noticed that at frequent intervals small fires were lighted on the sand dunes some distance in front, and it became evident that Bedouins were advising the enemy of our approach. These small fires were followed by a big fire in the centre of the enemy position, as a signal to their scattered posts to be on the alert. At 7 a.m. the Regiment halted at Sabahet-el-Mustabib, the horses being fed and the men having breakfast.

The return journey was commenced at 11 a.m., the route being along the ancient caravan route and telegraph line. As the horses had not been watered for over 24 hours, arrangements had been made to send out a large camel convoy, each camel carrying 30 gallons of water to a point eight miles east of Salmana. The water arrived safely, but the arrangements for its distribution were faulty, and some units went very short. Troughs were erected in such a manner that in some cases the horses could not get near them without being wedged in and disturbing the horses who were drinking at other troughs. The whole of the water supply was put in the troughs before the first unit arrived, with the result that the lucky first arrivals used up about twice their share, and left none for the rear units.

Salmana was reached at 7.30 p.m., and the column bivouacked for the night, leaving at 4 a.m. on the following day for their camp at Amara. The heat during these operations was intense, men and horses suffering severely from thirst.

Shortly after arrival at Amara Lewis guns arrived and were issued to the several Regiments. Teams were selected and trained whilst the remainder of the Regiment carried out the usual routine of outpost and patrols, and the many other duties which fall to the lot of a mounted unit on service. During the whole of the desert campaign the work of carrying the railway line forward had been pushed steadily on. The line which had terminated at Romani had now been carried many miles into the desert, and each day saw an appreciable advance. Thousands of Egyptian labourers commonly known as "The Gippy Labour Corps," were employed in laying the sand track, whilst others, more skilled in the work, were laying the sleepers and rails, and it was astonishing to see the rate at which the line advanced.

As strong winds were prevalent and in a very short time completely covered the lines with loose sand, it was necessary to build a screen of scrub along the northern side of the track. In many places steep embankments had to be built, this being done by the natives bringing baskets of sand and dumping it at the required spot. A double pipe line was also laid alongside the line, to carry drinking water from Egypt, the construction of these lines keeping pace with the railway. Railway stations of a very substantial nature were also built at various places, being constructed of tubular bricks made on the spot by native labour.

A wire road was also constructed from Romani across the desert, this road being eventually carried through to the outskirts of Gaza. The idea was a novel one, the road being constructed of small mesh wire-netting pegged down to the sand, which was first levelled. The road was roughly four yards wide, the widths of wire-netting being joined together, and something like 600 miles of netting was used in its construction. This road enabled the Infantry to march through the desert with a certain amount of ease and comfort, the rate of march being about three miles an hour under ordinary circumstances, but when necessary this rate was considerably increased. The road also enabled light cars, mostly Fords, to travel through the desert.

On the 3rd October the Regiment took over the outpost line, Bada-Abd-Hishia, from the 10th Light Horse, Headquarters, "B" Squadron camping one and a half miles east of Abd, whilst "A" Squadron took the right, and "C" the left of the line, the 5th Mounted Brigade holding the sector on our right. Two officers' patrols were sent out each night to reconnoitre the country towards Salmana, and a party were sent out each day to patrol the country towards Ganadil.

Two days later a composite squadron composed of two troops of "A," one troop, and the Lewis guns from "B," and one troop from "C" under the command of Major McKenzie, with Capt. C. Bleechmore as second in command, proceeded to Ganadil and bivouacked for the night. Their orders were to the effect that they would move from that place in such time as would allow them to reach Bir-el-Kasseiba at daybreak, and reconnoitre the surrounding country for tracks and water. This work was most efficiently carried out, and the squadron returned to camp at sundown.

About this time enemy planes had become very active, their chief object being to obstruct the work of the railway construction party, on whom they would daily cast a shower of bombs, much to the disgust of the Gippy labour corps. These labourers, being non combatants and of the same religion as the enemy did not consider it by any means fair dealing on the part of the Turks, and loud and strong were the Arabic curses hurled at the enemy pilots. At Abd an enemy pilot dropped his morning hate, in the form of a shower of light bombs, amongst a party of about 4,000 Gippy labourers, who promptly scattered in all directions. Parties were sent out mounted to round them up, but it was some hours before they were got back to their work. It was only necessary for one of our men to walk past a party of these men, looking skywards, to see them immediately drop their tools and scatter.

On the 12th October the outpost line was advanced to a line one mile south of Bir-Ganadil to Katib-Ganadil, thence north to Sharket-el-Bardawil. Headquarters were established half a mile west of Bir-Ganadil, whilst "C" Squadron were placed about eight miles east of Salmana. This squadron had to send their horses 12 miles each day to water. Patrols were sent out daily to watch the enemy, one Turk being captured who gave much useful information as to enemy movements, strength, positions, etc.

On the 18th the 8th and 10th Light Horse Regiments took over the outpost line, and the Regiment went into bivouac about three-quarters of a mile north of Hod Willega, supplying three troops on alternate nights for outpost, connecting the right of the 10th Light Horse with the left of the Yeomanry Brigade.

On the 23rd the Regiment, with the rest of the Brigade, marched to Et Maler, south of Romani, arriving there on the 25th about 3.30 p.m. This move ended the first phase of the Desert Campaign. The Regiment had moved out at one hour's notice on the 4th August, expecting to be out for a few days only, and leaving practically all their gear, including their greatcoats, behind. It was therefore a cheering sight to find the details which had been left at Bally Bunion waiting for them with a comfortable camp already pitched, and their spare gear, or rather, what was left of it.

Of all the sights seen in Egypt not one created half as much interest amongst the members of the Brigade as did one large tent in this camp. Before it came into view of those in rear one could judge from the noise ahead that something unusual was astir, and on topping the rise the mystery was explained by the sight of a large marquee almost hidden in piles of cases. Closer inspection settled all doubts, for bottles which unmistakably contained beer could be plainly seen. Needless to say the work of fixing up the horses was quickly carried out, and the Regiment formed up to storm the position, a duty which it carried out in a manner worthy of its reputation.

During the stay at this camp the men were given short spells of leave to visit Port Said, a privilege that was greatly appreciated. A thorough inspection of all saddlery and equipment in possession was made by the Quartermaster, steps being immediately taken to complete deficiencies and repairs.

After a month spent in this camp orders were received for the Brigade to take the field, and on the 23rd November, 1916, it moved out and marched *via* Negiliat to El Khirba, where it camped for the night, continuing the march the following morning *via* Afein and Abd to Salmana. On the 25th the Regiment moved at 10 a.m. to Mustafig which was reached at 3.15 p.m., moving again on the 26th to Kasseiba where "B" Squadron relieved a company of the Imperial Camel Corps, and the balance of the Regiment, together with the Brigade, proceeded to Malha.

On the 1st December the G.O.C. and Staff, with a number of Regimental officers, made a reconnaisance due south to the Maghara Hills about 20 miles from bivouac. No large parties of the enemy were met, but the party was fired on from the foothills.

For the next few days the Brigadier constantly exercised the Brigade in small tactical schemes and field firing, the Regiments turning out in full fighting order, and carrying one day's rations for man and horse. Alarm "turns out" were constantly practised, the smartest time made by the Regiment being seven minutes from the signal to the whole Regiment being formed up ready to move.

On the 14th December the Regiment proceeded to Arnussi to take part in a Divisional Training scheme, returning to bivouac at 6 p.m. Enemy planes bombed the Regiment during the move, but without effect. Christmas billies arrived from Australia, and were much appreciated.

CHAPTER XIII

EL ARISH-MAGHDABA OPERATIONS

At 6 o'clock on the 20th December, 1916, orders were received for the Brigade to proceed to the Divisional rendezvous at Bir Gympie. The Regiment marched at 8 a.m. with a strength of 23 officers, 464 other ranks, and 539 horses, arriving at Gympie at 5 p.m., where horses were watered and supplies drawn. The Brigade rested at this point until 11 p.m., then moved to take part in the general advance on El-Arish. The Regiment passed through Um-Zughla in the direction of Bir-el-Masmi and halted at 6 a.m. in full view of the famous and ancient town of El Arish.

Information came to hand that the 1st Light Horse Brigade had passed round the town and found it had been evacuated. The Regiment was therefore ordered to move to Hod Masaid, situated about two miles west of the town, where it bivouacked for the night. At 6.30 on the following morning the Brigade moved to a point half a mile south-west of the town. It was quite evident that something of very special nature was about to take place as orders were issued to draw extra rations and forage and to place all spare gear in dumps under a guard, the men retaining only such articles as were absolutely necessary.

At 6 p.m. on the same day (22nd December) the Regiment paraded and marched to the rendezvous of the Anzac Mounted Division in the bed of the Wadi El Arish, about two miles south of the town. It was pitch dark and the night was bitterly cold when the troops dismounted to await the arrival of the convoy, which should have met the troop, but had not arrived. Everyone was anxious to get on the move, but hours passed before the convoy eventually arrived, it having travelled some distance along the Rafa road before the mistake was discovered.

Immediately the convoy halted everything was bustle and excitement. Parties were sent from each unit to draw its portion of the supplies which had to be man-handled from the supply section to the unit, where it was split up and reissued to the squadrons. Every available water bottle was filled, as a scarcity of water was expected during the operations about to be carried out. As the appointed time for the move had long passed, everything was rushed, as success depended on the troops being in the desired positions at daybreak.

El Maghdaba is situated on the banks of the Wadi El-Arish, about 23 miles, as the crow flies, from the sea. Except from a

EL ARISH-MAGHDABA OPERATIONS

military point of view, it was a place of no importance, but standing in a natural defensive position it was well garrisoned with a view to holding up our further advance. It could also be used by the enemy as a starting place for a turning movement against our right flank. It was clear to all that no further advance could be made in our direct line until this menace to our communications was removed, and the C. in C. decided that the Anzac Mounted Division would efficiently carry out this duty.

At daybreak, shortly after arrival at El Ria, the Regiment took up a position about 3,000 yards north of Maghdaba. From this point the 1st Light Horse Brigade could be clearly seen closing in to the attack. At 9.45 a.m. the Brigade commenced to move round the enemy's right flank, whilst the New Zealanders occupied some prominent sandhills; the Inverness and Leicester Batteries, Royal Horse Artillery, being between them and the Camel Corps. These batteries immediately opened fire on the redoubts, thus enabling the advancing troops to gain ground. The enemy up to this had laid low, but he prepared to give his usual display of defensive fighting and opened heavy and accurate fire at ranges of from 1,000 to 1,200 yards.

The Regiment now took up a position on the left of the New Zealanders and was supported by the 8th Light Horse. The two Regiments dismounted and advanced in extended order. The country at this particular point was practically level for a distance of 2,000 yards, whilst the enemy trenches were on a slight rise, and so placed that their fire would sweep the whole plain. A few grassy hillocks dotted over the plain afforded slight cover, but these were few and far between. As the Regiments advanced the line was shortened by the 8th Light Horse advancing on a slightly different direction, and two troops were dropped back as support.

When about 1,000 yards from the enemy position snipers and Lewis guns were pushed forward to cover the advance, which was made by alternate rushes, troop by troop, each troop supporting the advance by rapid fire. The heavy and accurately-placed fire of the enemy began to take effect, and a number of casualties occurred, but by 2.30 p.m. the line had been advanced to within 500 yards of the position, and drew the attention of the enemy gunners who opened a brisk fire with shrapnel.

The line was now straightened up and reserve ammunition brought forward for the Lewis guns. At 3.15 p.m. the line again advanced by rushes of 25 yards, whilst the batteries kept up a brisk fire on the redoubts. On arrival at 150 yards from the redoubts, the line laid low for a spell, and at 3.45 p.m. bayonets were fixed ready for the final rush. At a given signal the whole line leapt to their feet, and, rushing forward with wild cheers, carried the outer trenches, many of the enemy being bayoneted before the remainder surrendered.

Our machine guns, which had been in rear supporting the move by overhead fire, now came forward, and together with the Lewis guns and rifles, opened a heavy fire on the enemy position to our right thus enabling the Camel Corps and New Zealanders to advance. In the meantime the 10th Light Horse had moved round the right flank for the purpose of cutting off any attempt at escape.

The 8th and 9th Regiments now advanced against the buildings from which rifle fire was being directed, the 8th Light Horse capturing a battery of light guns during the move. As the prisoners were being rounded up news arrived that the 10th were hard pressed on the far side of the buildings, and Major McKenzie with 50 men were immediately sent to their support. General Royston called for two mounted troops, and as the horses had just arrived, these were despatched under the command of Capt. J. C. Chanter, but this party on arrival found that the enemy force had already surrendered to Major McKenzie's party. Major McKenzie with "C" Squadron did excellent work during the day, and to them fell the honour of taking the first enemy trench.

The Air Service was by no means idle during the day, our pilots skimming the enemy trenches frequently and doing good work with their machine guns. They also dropped a liberal supply of light bombs on enemy strongpoints, doing considerable damage and with good moral effect.

This was the first action in which the Lewis gun teams had used their new guns, their work showing great initiative and tactical judgment, special credit being due to Cpls. McKenna, Harley, and Carter for the manner in which they handled their teams, reconnoitred the position, and brought effective fire to bear with economical use of ammunition. Tprs. F. Gruddas and Fulwood did splendid work in bringing up supplies of ammunition under heavy machine gun fire, whilst the stretcher bearers, Tprs. Crack and Currie, did excellent work amongst the wounded.

The Regiment had little time to collect prisoners, but five officers and 154 other ranks taken in the first trench were handed over to the Division. It had been stated that the enemy had destroyed their water service when all hope of a successful resistance had been abandoned, but this was found to be incorrect, and both horses and men drank to their heart's content from his abundant supply. A party was sent out to collect the wounded and bury the dead, whilst another party from one of the Brigades was sent to clear up the battle ground.

A plentiful supply of wood was found, and as the night was drawing in and was bitterly cold large fires were lighted. It was indeed a strange sight to see our men and the Turks, who one hour before had been fighting a bitter fight, sitting side by side round the fires, sharing their evening meal and cigarettes, apparently on the best of terms.

EL ARISH-MAGHDABA OPERATIONS

At 11 p.m. the Division moved off on the return journey, arriving at Laffan at 3 a.m., where it halted and bivouacked. The huge column of prisoners arrived at 4.30 a.m. and halted. A convoy of 400 camels had been sent out from El Arish, and at daybreak each enemy prisoner received a ration consisting of one tin of bully beef, one pound of biscuits, and one quart of water. For the purpose of distributing these rations the prisoners were paraded in line, and were told off in parties of 20, under their own officers and N.C.O.'s. Each party was then given 20 tins of meat and one tin of biscuits, and were marched off a short distance, where the supplies were distributed amongst the party. It is doubtful whether they had ever received such a generous ration during the whole of their desert campaign.

At daybreak the Division resumed the march to El Arish, and went into bivouac at Hod Masaid, which was reached at 9 a.m. on the 24th. The operations had been a severe test on the endurance of both men and horses, as three night marches had been done during the past four nights, with plenty of hard work during the intervening days.

That the operations were an unqualified success is proved by the fact that the whole garrison of roughly 2,000 had been captured, together with a large quantity of stores, a battery of guns, and many machine guns. The prisoners were a mixed lot, representing many tribes, but were all of fine physique. Several Germans were amongst the bag, and one black officer was seen. After a short rest and meal they were conducted to El Arish and sent to Egypt.

The work of the transport was very trying throughout these operations. When the force moved from the Wadi El Arish on the night of the 22nd, the transport camels allotted to the Brigade were collected and marched to the supply depot on the beach at El Arish by Capt. T. H. Darley and loaded with further supplies. At 10 a.m. on the 23rd this party commenced the long and trying journey to Maghdaba, 80 per cent. of the camels carrying drinking water. By continuous marching Maghdaba was reached at 9.30 p.m., and the supplies were issued to the various units. The convoy immediately started on the return journey, arriving at Laffan at 2 a.m. where it halted. After the prisoners had been rationed the two convoys were moved back to El Arish, arriving at 3 p.m. on the 24th.

CHAPTER XIV

RAFA

Christmas Day of 1916 was spent under the beautiful date palms of Hod Masaid, which runs parallel with the beach of the Mediteranean at a distance of about 200 yards from the water. A good supply of provisions being on hand, the Christmas dinner was marred only by memories of absent friends. In the evening, fuel being plentiful, several fires were lit, and sitting round them the men swapped lies about their past deeds. Many of these yarns would not bear investigation, but were evidently the result of the good cheer dispensed during the day. Naturally the recent fight at Maghdaba was the chief topic, and if the number of prisoners stated to have been captured by different men had been totalled, it would have considerably outnumbered the whole Turkish army.

On the following day Lieut.-Colonel Sir Philip Chetwode, accompanied by Major-General Sir H. Chauvel, attended a full parade of the Brigade, and warmly congratulated all ranks on the splendid work done by them during the Maghdaba operations. He also dropped a hint that there were prospects of more work of a similar nature at an early date.

The Regiment remained at Masaid until the 1st January, 1917, when, owing to the difficulty of transport, orders were issued, and the Brigade moved down to Railhead, at Kilo 139. The weather conditions became very bad, day after day being cold and wet. As the troops had no tents shelters were made of blankets and palm fronds, but these only afforded partial protection.

A few days later, the line having been carried as far as Masaid, the Brigade moved back to the shelter of the Hod, much to the satisfaction of all concerned. Camel convoys passed through from Kilo 139 daily on their way to El Arish, carrying stores of all descriptions, and it became evident that a new move was pending.

Information now came through to the effect that the enemy, driven from his position at El Arish, had retired to a line marking the boundary between Egypt and Palestine, running from the sea to the Gulf of Akabar. His chief position on this line consisted of a series of redoubts at Rafa, and it was evident that he was prepared at this point to offer a stout resistance to our further advance, whilst stronger lines of resistance were being prepared in the rear.

The fall of Maghdaba, which had been considered an exceptionally strong position, and the capture of its entire garrison, had been

THE REGIMENTAL BARBER

WATER CISTERNS NEAR KHAN YUNIS

a great blow to the enemy, and made him a bit doubtful as to his ability to hold the Rafa position against a sudden onslaught by our mounted force. He also considered that having been once caught napping such a surprise could not possibly occur again in view of the dispositions made to guard against it. The position of the redoubts had been well chosen, having a splendid field of fire on all sides, and they were manned by, roughly, 3,000 men, supported by a number of well-placed guns.

Considering the exposed nature of the approaches, an attack on this position presented many problems; still the G.O.C. decided that it must be taken without delay. The force available for this enterprise consisted of the Anzac Mounted Division (less the 2nd Light Horse Brigade), the 5th Mounted Brigade (Yeomanry), and the Imperial Camel Corps, with three batteries of Royal Horse Artillery, and one Mountain Battery, a total of roughly 3,500 rifles and 16 guns.

Taking all things into consideration, the General Officer Commanding, Sir Philip Chetwode, was taking considerable risk in marching 30 odd miles from his base to attack so strong a position with so small a force, added to which was the possibility that the enemy would be able to rush forward reinforcements from Shellal as soon as information of the attack reached there.

The element of surprise was not overlooked, and if successful in this direction the effect on the nerves of the enemy, which had already been sorely tried, would count for much. It can safely be said that not a man of our force had the slightest doubt but that Rafa, with its whole garrison, would be taken whenever the General gave the order to attack. A sure sign that the enemy were a bit nervy was the constant visit of their planes to make sure that we were still in camp.

Shortly after mid-day on the 8th January, 1917, the Regiment, with the rest of the Brigade, under the command of Brigadier-General Royston, moved to the Divisional rendezvous about one mile east of the Wadi El Arish, each man carrying three days' rations for himself and horse. Horses were watered and the whole force moved off in the direction of Rafa at 4 p.m., reaching Sheikh Zowaid at 9.30 p.m. A halt was made at this place until 1 a.m., the men being instructed to get as much rest as possible. The night, however, was the coldest that had been experienced in the desert, and sleep was almost impossible, the men having no cover.

At 1 a.m. sharp the advance on Rafa was commenced, and from then till daylight talking and smoking were forbidden. These orders were implicitly obeyed, everyone recognizing their importance. One troop of "A" Squadron, under Lieut. R. C. Sharp, was pushed out as a right flank guard to the Brigade, whilst one troop under Lieut. E. M. Luxmoore guarded the left flank.

F

About 6 a.m. the column reached a point two miles south-east of the redoubts on El Magruntein, and the left flank guard was fired on by the Turkish outposts, who fired a few Very lights as a signal. This post was immediately rushed and captured. A short halt was now ordered whilst General Royston and staff, together with certain regimental officers reconnoitred the position. As the light improved the strength of the enemy positions could be clearly seen as they stood out prominently on the hillside, the approaches being absolutely void of cover, whilst practically every inch of the ground for a distance of 2,000 yards could be swept by rifle and machine gun fire.

To the east, at about 800 yards from their main position, stood a solitary tree which acted as a reference mark for the remainder of the day. The surrounding country was pleasing to the eye, being firm and grassy, whilst standing crops of barley were plentiful and formed a great contrast to the sandy desert which had been our home for the past year. A few Bedouin encampments scattered about added a finish to the picture.

After a hasty meal the Brigade moved further east, and passed two large stone pillars making the boundary between Sinai and Palestine, and at last we were operating on enemy territory. The thoughts of all ranks as they passed into the oldest historical country in the world can be better imagined than described, whilst the fact that a successful conclusion to the day's operations would clear the enemy from a British Protectorate had undoubtedly a great moral effect on the men.

The Brigade halted at this point and dismounted, remaining in reserve until 11 a.m. New Zealanders could be seen working round the enemy's eastern flank, with the 1st Light Horse Brigade moving to a position on the left. As these troops came under fire, they extended, and the sight was one to thrill the observer, the troops moving into position as calmly as if carrying out a peace manoeuvre. The Inverness Battery R.H.A. had by this time got into position and were placing a well-directed fire on some parties of the enemy who were endeavouring to escape to the east.

The enemy position had been split into four groups for the purpose of the attack; "A" and "B" groups were allotted to the Imperial Camel Corps, "C" to the 3rd Light Horse Brigade, and "D" to the 1st Light Horse Brigade, whilst the New Zealanders were to make an enveloping movement round the eastern flank, to cut off all possibility of escape.

At 11 a.m. the 9th and 10th Light Horse Regiments and the 3rd Machine Gun Squadron were ordered into action. The Regiments advanced mounted in extended order, each leaving one squadron to act as support. At 11.40 a.m. the leading troops came under fire and, dismounting, sent their horses to the cover of a small ridge, continuing the advance on foot. "A" Squadron's Lewis gun was placed on the extreme left of the line and after advancing about 800 yards the Regiment took up a position on a slight rise which afforded slight cover to men, and opened a brisk fire on the enemy trenches to our immediate front.

Our batteries were sweeping the enemy position with shrapnel and high explosive shells, whilst the machine guns were raking their trenches with bursts of rapid fire. The enemy's fire was extremely heavy but a little erratic, evidently due to nerves, but this proved a great blessing for otherwise our casualties must have been very heavy. At 2.30 p.m. the situation remained unchanged on our immediate front, but away on our right the 1st Light Horse Brigade were seen to be advancing, small parties of the enemy being seen to surrender. The Imperial Camel Corps, like ourselves, appeared to be unable to make any headway without incurring heavy casualties, and the Artillery were ordered to concentrate their fire on our objective, whilst the heaviest possible rifle and machine gun fire was poured into the group, with the result that the enemy's fire slackened considerably.

A t 3.20 p.m. a message was received from Brigade Headquarters ordering a general advance to commence at 3.30 p.m. General Royston rode along the line and gave instructions that the advance should be timed by the 10th Light Horse on our right. Lieut. Brown, 3rd Machine Gun Squadron, brought two guns into the line, to give covering fire to the advance.

At 3.45 p.m. the extreme right of the line, 1st Light Horse Brigade were seen to be falling back, and the enemy's fire at once greatly increased. Many of the enemy stood up in the trenches in order to get better aim, thus affording our Lewis gunners a splendid target, which was taken full advantage of. At 4.10 p.m. Lieut.-Colonel D. Fulton, 3rd Light Horse Regiment, asked for covering fire, as his Regiment was hard pressed. A message was also received from Major Robertson, 10th Light Horse, to the effect that two troops of that Regiment were retiring, and asked the Regiment to cover the retirement of the 10th Regiment if necessary.

The Turks were putting up a great fight, and for the moment appeared to have the upper hand. Their aeroplanes were constantly flying overhead dropping light bombs on every available target. They were able to accurately estimate the strength of the attacking force, and the information thus obtained and transmitted to the trenches seemed to give the defenders fresh heart, and they became confident that they could hold out and wait for the large reinforcements which were hurrying to their assistance from Shellal and Khan Yunis.

Our gunners fought splendidly; the Hong Kong and Singapore Batteries bringing their small guns into the advanced line.

About this time men were seen moving about on the sand hills north of the enemy position, and waving discs, painted black and white, which had been issued to all units for the purpose of disclosing their position to our artillery, as shells from one of our batteries were falling close to their front line. A message was therefore sent to the Brigade, drawing attention to this, and the shelling ceased.

The order was now given to fix bayonets, and the Regiment advanced by short rushes, accompanied by the Imperial Camel Corps, but after a short advance orders were received for the whole force to retire, the Regiment to cover the retirement. Before this order could be obeyed the whole situation suddenly changed. The New Zealanders, under General Chaytor, had steadily worked round the enemy's flank without attracting much attention, and having already received information that strong enemy reinforcements were approaching, he immediately closed on the enemy left flank, and attacked with the bayonet.

Seeing this move, General Royston galloped out in front of the Brigade, and ordered them to advance. With loud cheers the men rushed forward with the bayonet and the position was won, white flags making their appearance in large numbers. At the moment when things looked blackest and the men were unwillingly preparing to retire the whole situation changed like a flash, to the great delight of all ranks.

Rafa had been captured with small loss to ourselves, and the whole of its garrison were prisoners in our hands, together with their guns and considerable stores. The splendid fight put up by the enemy was testified by the heaps of dead and wounded in their trenches, which also spoke volumes for the coolness and accuracy of our fire. Capt. J. C. Chanter, of "C" Squadron, with a few members of the I.C.C. pushed on and took a battery of four guns, together with a number of prisoners.

Enemy reinforcements, estimated at 2,000 men, with guns, were actually within sight during the latter part of the engagement. They sent up several flare signals, but receiving no reply evidently decided to take no risks by coming to closer quarters. Had their commander pushed forward with his large force he may have been able seriously to interfere with our plans and save some of the garrison.

On the rally signal being blown the Regiment assembled and moved off to take up an outpost line facing east, covering the ambulance and stretcher bearers in their work of mercy amongst the enemy. At 9 p.m. the Regiment, less "A" Squadron which had been detailed to escort the prisoners, moved off to Shiekh Zowaid, arriving there at 2 a.m. on the 10th. Horses were watered after having been 36 hours without a drink, and the troops bivouacked for the night.

At 7.30 a.m. on the 10th the column commenced the return journey, arriving at Hod Masaid at 1.30 p.m., "A" Squadron with all available wagons being left to clear up the battle area and collect the stores. They also searched the whole area for any wounded who may have been missed in the dark, and buried the dead. One of our aeroplanes flew from El Arish and dropped parcels of medical comforts at Sheikh Zowaid for the small field hospital which had been erected.

On the 12th January Major-General Sir H. G. Chauvel addressed the Brigade and congratulated all ranks on their magnificent effort at Rafa.

At last Egyptian territory was free of all enemy forces, and the war could now be taken into enemy country.

CHAPTER XV

CONDITIONS IN THE SINAI DESERT

Having completed our true desert operations and followed the paths of great leaders of the past, of Thothmes and other ancient leaders, and also the road traversed by Napoleon in his campaign to Egypt, a short chapter on the conditions which prevailed during our sojourn in the Sinai Desert may not be out of place.

In the regions of Serapeum, which lies on the Suez Canal, midway between Lake Timsah and Little Bitter Lake, where we operated during the first period of our desert campaign, a plain runs from the Canal to a distance of about five miles east, and here rises to a ridge of sand hills, in height from 300 to 500 feet. The sand across this plain was fairly coarse and inclined to be gravelly, but as one proceeded further east for a distance of about 25 or 30 miles, over rolling hill and wind-swept sand dunes the sand became much finer until the foot of the Makhasa and Maghara Hills is reached where the ground becomes stony and gravelly.

There is absolutely no water in this area except that retained in the rock-hewn cisterns mentioned in the account of the Jif Jafa operations, or left in open pools formed by the flooding of the Wadi Mukhsheib, which was reported to come down in flood at varying intervals of from one to four years. In large, but scattered areas, the country is covered with tufts of camel grass, thorn, and other rough vegetation. The only trees in this area were a few tamarisks along the banks of the Wadi.

Animal and bird life is practically non-existent, except for an occasional gazelle, and in some places a very pretty little rat. Lizards of various kinds are prevalent, the chameleon being the most popular amongst them. Its power of changing colours ranges between the grey of the sand and a dull green. These little reptiles caused endless entertainment in their method of catching flies by smartly ejecting their tongue and catching their victims at any range up to about 10 inches.

The Scarab beetle, a black and scaly creature, was also a source of entertainment in the manner in which he treated horse dung. He would get a small portion between his hind legs and work it into a small ball, then roll it round and round over other dung, increase its size to about that of an ordinary egg. He would then start on his journey home, walking on his forelegs, head down, and pushing his treasure along with his hind legs. If he came against any obstacle

CONDITIONS IN THE SINAI DESERT

he would quietly climb on top of the ball, view the situation, and getting down again would clear the obstacle with ease. Arrived at the nest, the female beetle lays its eggs in the ball, and it is put aside for them to hatch. At times it was not unusual to see a party of men place several beetles and the result of their labour in the centre of a three foot ring and wager on which would be first out. Needless to say, the odds were very uncertain.

During the months of April and May, Khamsins, meaning 50, referring to the period of 50 days over which heavy windstorms from the south may be expected, were prevalent. These winds blew with terrific force, carrying with them clouds of sand which made it quite impossible to see for any distance.

On moving to Romani the desert changes, in that a strip of country along the coast about 12 miles across at its widest part and narrowing down to three at its narrowest, between Salmana and El Arish, contains every few miles palm groves, known as Hods. These Hods as a rule run from north-west to south-east, and on the south-west side there is usually a large wind-blown sand dune. In these Hods water, slightly brackish, can be found at a depth of a few feet, the surface of the Hods being in most cases little above sea level. These Hods vary very much in size, some being 1,000 yards long, but seldom more than 150 yards wide. During September and October the dates are ripe and make delicious eating when taken straight from the palm, being large and juicy. The horses got into the habit of stripping big bunches, but were always careful to eject the stones.

Up to the time the Regiment left Bally Bunion bell tents were provided at the rate of one to eight men. On moving to Romani for operations tents were left behind and the men had to improvise shelter from any material available. During the Romani action a few waterproof sheets were captured from the enemy, and numerous Bedouin carpets made of goat-hair and wool. The bivouack sheets were made of duck, five feet square, with buttons and button holes along each edge, so that they could be joined together to form shelters, with pointed poles, in sections, used in their erection. At Rafa and Maghdaba many more of these sheets were captured, so that practically each man in the Regiment could form a shelter. Towards the end of 1917 sheets of a similar nature were issued by the Army Ordnance, each man being given one sheet and one pole. On arrival in bivouac, each two men would make a shelter of their two sheets and poles, but as the sheets were square it left both ends of the shelter open, so that they were of little use in wet weather.

At Serapeum a Regimental Canteen was organized, but on leaving for the Romani operations this was wound up. From time to time, as occasion demanded, canteen stores were purchased to supplement the rations, and retailed to the men at cost price. At a later date sections of the A.I.F. Canteen were pushed out with the Brigade, and the British Canteen also came forward. These canteens were exceptionally well run and were always well stocked. In some of the British canteens a good hot meal could be secured at almost any hour, which was a great boon to men travelling apart from the Regiment.

The whole of the regimental transport during the desert campaign was carried out by camels, the number allowed being as a rule 73, each being able to carry a load of not exceeding 300 lbs. for long periods. These camels were not attached to the Regiment, but belonged to the Camel Transport Corps, being sent to the Regiment each day under the charge of natives. All camel drivers were Egyptians, but the officers and N.C.O.'s of the Camel Corps were British. Each camel was watered every third day, and the column would travel for many hours at a rate of slightly over two miles per hour. Under normal conditions they were given a short rest at the end of each four hours.

Rations were brought from the base at Kantara to Railhead where they would be loaded on camels for distribution amongst the advanced depots. The main artery of the railway from Kantara followed the old caravan route through Romani, El Arish, and finally through Gaza to Ludd and Tul Keram, where it joined the Turkish railway. Branch lines were laid to various points, one being to Shellal and Beersheba, and another to Jerusalem. From Tul Keram the line ran through Jenin, El Afuleh, Semakh, on the Sea of Galilee, to Damascus, Beirut, Alleppo, and on to Constantinople.

The portion of the line laid by the Army was 4 ft. $8\frac{1}{2}$ in. gauge, which is the standard gauge for most European countries. The personnel employed in the construction of this railway were British Royal Engineers and Egyptian labourers, also a number of Australians who had had experience in railway construction. At times the work was speeded up, as much as two miles of bed and track being laid in one day. Engines were brought from England, and it was a curious sight to see on their tenders the familiar L. & S.W.R. (London and South Western Railway).

In the early stages the line was not ballasted, except with sand. The Khamsins during their season frequently covered the line in a layer of sand, causing the engines to jump the rails. It also blew the sand from under the rails, causing them to shift and hold up the traffic. As the railway was being built pipes were laid to carry water to the front line.

With the Field Ambulances the methods of carrying the wounded varied, some being carried on cacolets, stretcher-like arrangements on each side of a camel saddle. Some of these were arranged for lying and others for sitting patients, but were very uncomfortable to ride in. Light carts were also used, the wheels being covered with broad iron bands, called sand tyres, to prevent them sinking in the loose sand. Sleighs were also used, running in broad runners and drawn by two horses, each sleigh carrying one patient.

Ruins and ancient relics (mostly in possession of the inhabitants) were often discovered. At El Fisiat, north of Mazar, were the ruins of an old Christian Church and Monastery. Many of the monks' cells were still in existence, and many of the pillars still clearly showed the crosses in relief on them. Old pottery and glass vessels, some in a good state of preservation, were found, and on one occasion when putting down horse lines at Hod Nabit some coins of the Justinian period in a very high state of preservation were discovered. In Bedouin camps some fine beaten copper dishes, evidently of great age, were often seen; also flint-lock pistols, clumsily-made daggers, and scimitars.

On the whole, both horses and men kept in fine condition. The horses, which could not be taken faster than a milk except over very short distances, soon acquired the habit of walking at a fast rate, and when the desert was crossed there was not a single horse in the Regiment which could not walk well above the average pace.

It is safe to say that the desert, with its trackless wastes, perfect quietness, and wonderful nights, especially at full moon, appealed to most men, and there are many who will look back at this period as being one of the most interesting in their lives, and in their quiet moments will sigh for such another experience.

CHAPTER XVI

PREPARING FOR THE INVASION OF PALESTINE

After the battle of Rafa intense training was carried out in musketry, signalling, mounted and dismounted attack, and various tactical schemes, the Regiment remaining at Hod Masaid. One Hotchkiss gun was issued to each Regiment for instructional purposes, and the Lewis guns were withdrawn.

About the beginning of March the formation of the mounted forces was subjected to various changes, and placed under the command of General Sir H. Chauvel, the force being known as "Desert Corps." Our Brigade was taken from the Anzac Mounted Division and together with the 4th Light Horse Brigade and the 5th and 6th Mounted Brigades (Yeomanry) went to form the Imperial Mounted Division.

On the 9th March the Brigade moved to El Burj, and on the 13th moved along the beach to Bir Abu-Hamthala where it bivouacked for the night, moving again next day to Bir Abu-Ashunnar, at which place it remained until the 16th. At 6 a.m. on that date the Regiment, with a strength of 15 officers and 356 other ranks, moved out to make good the line, Abasan-el-Kebir, Khan Yunis. One section of the 3rd Machine Gun Squadron and Light Horse Field Ambulance being attached. "C" Squadron moved along the beach to Tel-el-Marakeb, whilst the remainder of the column moved through Rafa to Khan Yunis, which was known to be held by the enemy.

On reaching the cross-roads, two miles north-east of Rafa, "A" Squadron were detached and moved south-east to make good Abasan-el-Kebir, the move being completed by 9.30 a.m. The remainder of the column moved direct on Khan Yunis, which was reached at 9.15 a.m. and found to be clear of the enemy. On reaching the high ground, one mile east of the village, our patrols came in contact with, and were fired on, by enemy patrols, who after a brief fire fight retired in the direction of Gaza.

Regimental Headquarters was established at Beni Sela, about one mile south-east of Khan Yunis, and strong patrols were sent out to reconnoitre the Wadi Ghuzze, eight miles distant. The main object of these operations was to discover roads and water and at the same time to cover the work of the Engineers who were developing the water supply at Khan Yunis.

The country over which the Regiment had passed during the day was well grassed, large patches being covered with standing crops of barley. It was a great treat to all ranks to be able to move at a faster pace than a walk after the long, weary months spent in the desert campaign.

On the 19th March the Regiment, in conjunction with the 8th Light Horse, endeavoured to round up enemy patrols in the vicinity of Khan Yunis. The 8th, under the command of that fine old soldier, Lieut.-Colonel L. G. Mayger, V.C., moved along the beach to Deir-el-Belah, thence to Tel-el-Shabani, whilst the Regiment accompanied by the Machine Gun Section and Field Ambulance proceeded *via* Rafa and Fukhari to the vicinity of Abu Sitta. On arrival at this place "A" Squadron was detached to cover the country towards Sheik-el-Nakhaur, and the Field Ambulance was left at Abasan, the remainder of the column moving to Goz-el-Taire ridge.

Joining forces with the 8th Regiment at this point, a drive was commenced in the direction of Khan Yunis. This was completed by 11 a.m., but no enemy were seen, and the Regiment moved off to water, leaving the 8th on observation. On the 21st the Brigade moved along the beach to Tel-el-Marakeb.

On the 22nd March the Regiment took up an outpost line stretching from the sea at a point about one mile north-east of Deir-el-Belah to Abasan-el-Kebir. An hour before dawn patrols were pushed out in front of this line by each squadron. One of these patrols, consisting of one N.C.O. and seven men, encountered a troop of Turkish Cavalry on the Gaza Road about one mile north-east of the Wadi Ghuzze. The patrol, which was hopelessly outnumbered, was forced to retire, being pursued by the enemy cavalry, who succeeded in capturing Pte. Gilbert, whose horse was exhausted.

At 5 a.m. on the following day the outpost was withdrawn and the Regiment joined the Brigade in a reconnaisance in force of Gaza. The Regiment took the right flank and the 10th the left, whilst a Regiment of Yeomanry were sent towards Mansura to watch our flank. By 11 a.m. the Regimental Headquarters had been established at El-Sheluf, about two miles south of Gaza.

From this point an advance was made towards Ali Muntar. "A" Squadron occupied a position about one mile south of that place and immediately encountered opposition. About 700 Turkish infantry advanced to attack this squadron, but were driven back by rifle fire, assisted by enfilade fire brought to bear by "C" Squadron on their left. The Artillery in the fort at Ali Muntar now opened fire, and the order was given to withdraw. Under cover of the advance the General Staff and staffs of the infantry Divisions had made a reconnaisance of the defences for use in the forthcoming operations.

It was seen that during the occupation of Rafa the main body of the Turkish Army had devoted all their energy to preparing a strong defensive line from Gaza to Beersheba. Ali Muntar, the famous hill overlooking Gaza, and commanding the country for miles around, had been strongly fortified, and was a network of trenches and gun emplacements. The city itself, which is surrounded by giant cactus hedges, had been thoroughly entrenched, whilst the cactus hedges themselves formed a formidable obstacle to an assaulting force.

Ali Muntar stands out as a natural fortress on the south-east corner of the city and has played many important parts in the history of Gaza. It was on this hill that Samson was stated to have pulled down the pillars of the temple. Thousands of men in past ages had died on its slopes, and it was evident that many more were doomed to the same fate in the near future.

Lying behind Ali Muntar the town of Gaza could be clearly seen, with its narrow streets and flat-roofed houses, whilst clear and distinct the minaret of the mosque towered above all in its centre. A red crescent flag, which is the distinguishing flag of the Turkish Medical Service, flew from its top, no doubt with a view to securing its safety from our gun fire.

Our airmen were very active in obtaining information as to the nature and progress of the defensive works, a splendid and complete series of photographs being obtained by them.

A strongpoint on the Gaza-Beersheba line had been made at Sheik Narran. The amount of work put in by the enemy at this point was astonishing. Line upon line of trenches had been dug in the hard ground, and were protected by three rows of funnel-shaped pits about 10 feet in diameter by eight feet deep, separated at the top by a thin crust of earth about six inches wide. These pits made an advance on the trenches practically impossible, and as all the earth had been cleared away they could only be seen at very close range. They had also dug pits for their horses, which looked like a long line of loose boxes, thus enabling their cavalry to keep close at hand and under cover from our fire.

This tremendous amount of work turned out to be labour in vain, as they vacated the position without a fight and retired, evidently having found that the position could be easily outflanked, and they had no wish to repeat the disasters of Rafa and Maghdaba.

Preparations were now pushed forward for an attack in force on the Gaza position. Five days' rations were to be carried for all ranks, in addition to the iron, or emergency ration. In order to do this 26 saddle horses were trained to carry improvised packs made of canvas in the form of large saddle bags, each side being large enough to take two 25-pound tins of biscuits and two dozen tins of bully. This brought our number of pack horses up to 49 per Regiment, and as the improvised packs caused endless trouble, it was found necessary to leave one extra man with each four pack horses, which meant a big loss to the firing line which was already far below strength, the squadrons, when dismounted, numbering about **60 rifles.**

PREPARING FOR INVASION OF PALESTINE

On the 25th March, 1917, the Regiment with the remainder of the Brigade moved to Deir-el-Belah where it bivouacked and received its final orders for the operations against Gaza which were to commence at dawn.

CHAPTER XVII

THE FIRST GAZA BATTLE

Two Divisions of British Infantry had been brought forward to assist in the big task, viz., the 52nd and 53rd British Divisions, together with their Artillery. Some heavy batteries had also been brought forward and made a welcome addition to our force which now numbered close on 70,000 of all arms.

As far as could be gathered from the available information it was intended to capture Gaza by a frontal attack to be delivered by the Infantry, whilst the mounted troops and Camel Corps swung round to the left and attacked in the rear, thus cutting the enemy communications.

At dawn on the 26th March the whole country was enveloped in a thick fog, the first experienced, which made it impossible to see for any distance, and the recognition of landmarks became impossible. In spite of this, the mounted troops moved off at the allotted time, crossing the Wadi Ghuzze at Sheikh Nebban and moving through Shiekh Abbas to the vicinity of Siahan.

A position was taken up at this point to prevent enemy reinforcements moving up from Hareira, which lies about 10 miles south-east of Gaza, on the Beersheba road. The fog, which might have been turned to our advantage, as the attacking Infantry could, under its cover, have advanced right up to the outskirts of Gaza and Ali Muntar, proved the reverse, as when it lifted the Infantry were found to be far in rear of their positions. An enemy plane could be heard buzzing overhead waiting for the fog to lift. When this happened it flew over the surrounding country, the pilot firing smoke signals over each body of troops, thus giving the range to their gunners.

About 9 a.m. the sun was shining brilliantly, and some distance ahead the Anzac Mounted Division could be seen moving in a north-easterly direction, disappearing a little later behind the Mansura ridge. The Anzacs were to hold the line from Huj to the sea, and the Imperial Camel Corps from our left to the Wadi Ghuzze. Clouds of light dust could be seen in the direction of Beersheba, and it was evident that enemy cavalry were moving to the assistance of their comrades at Gaza.

The Brigade halted on the Mansura ridge, near Tel-el-Ahmar at 10 a.m. and awaited orders. News was received that the Anzacs had succeeded in completely isolating Gaza, and that they had

THE FIRST GAZA BATTLE

captured the commander of the 53rd Turkish Division, together with his staff officers and escort, as he was entering the town to direct operations.

The booming of heavy guns was heard and high explosive shells began to fall on a ridge half a mile south of the Brigade. These were evidently fired from Abu Hareira, and although the fire was kept up for some hours it is doubtful whether they caused a single casualty. As there were a number of wells in the vicinity the opportunity was taken to water the horses after which they were given a small feed, and the men snatched a hasty meal.

At about 3.30 p.m. the Brigade received orders to move rapidly to a position near Australia Hill. As the Brigade up to this time had taken no part in the fight everyone was delighted at the prospect of doing his share. Moving at a fast trot the Brigade reached Anzac Ridge, now the Headquarters of the Anzac Division, and here orders were given to the Brigadier that the 3rd Light Horse Brigade was to intercept and hold off the large enemy reinforcements, consisting of about 4,000 infantry and 2,000 cavalry, which had been reported as advancing from the direction of Huj.

The 10th Light Horse were detached to act as a reserve, and the remainder of the Brigade galloped out and occupied a chain of small hills about two miles east of Gaza, completely blocking the path of the enemy reinforcements which were advancing in various columns at a distance of about two miles. The Regiment took the right of the Brigade line, and gained touch with the Berkshire Yeomanry who were on our right.

This new force of the enemy which had to be dealt with had evidently been marching for some hours as their rate of march was below normal and they appeared tired. As soon as they came within 2,000 yards the Brigade opened fire, and the Notts Battery, which had pushed well forward, opened a heavy shrapnel fire, which appeared to be well on the target. At 5 p.m. the Yeomanry on our right were heavily engaged and our line was pushed well forward and strengthened by some armoured cars and a portion of the 8th Light Horse. As this new move threatend the enemy's flank they were obliged to fall back slightly. As darkness approached our line was shortened and an outpost line taken up.

During these movements the Infantry had delivered their assault against the formidable Ali Muntar, and in spite of heavy casualties had succeeded in taking a number of the outer works, but could not drive the stubborn Turks from the main position. The British Infantry made a splendid show as they advanced by waves in the face of a withering rifle and machine gun fire, their movements being as orderly as if on a peace parade.

Much to the surprise and disgust of all ranks, orders were received to the effect that the whole force would retire during the night to the Wadi Ghuzze. It was the first time our force had received such orders, and everyone wondered at the cause, some doubting the genuineness, but as they were verified shortly afterwards it was realized by all that there must be some good and sufficient reason for them.

The 3rd Light Horse Brigade were to cover the retirement, and remained in position until 2 a.m., at which time the 8th Light Horse were ordered to withdraw. At 3 a.m. the Regiment withdrew, acting as rearguard to the whole force, and moving round to the east and south of the defences made for the Wadi Ghuzze.

The Turks during the night had sent large reinforcements from Sheria, and when in the vicinity of Siahan our flank guards got into touch with them. "C" Squadron, in conjunction with the armoured cars, formed the rear and flank guards, and from this point to the Wadi fought a continuous rearguard action, doing splendid work in checking the enemy's advance, and allowing the whole column to pass in safety over the Wadi.

The enemy now opened a continuous shell fire from the south, and the Regiment altered its formation to columns of sections, moving in echelon, and by continually altering the pace and direction succeeded in completing the retirement with only two casualties, two horses being wounded. The Wadi was crossed at 7 a.m. and the Regiment proceeded to Deir-el-Belah, a distance of four miles, where the horses were watered, the Regiment then moving to Goz-el-Taire, where it bivouacked.

It was now learned that the Infantry had been severely mauled during the attack, their casualties against Ali Muntar alone being, roughly, 3,000. The fact that Gaza had not fallen was not due to any lack of vigour or fighting efficiency on the part of any of the troops, but was considered to be due to the heavy fog which delayed the assault for so many hours.

OUR LEADERS
(Left to right) Lt.-Genl. Sir Philip Chetwode (foreground), Lt.-Genl. Sir H. G. Chauvel, Bgdr.-Genl. J. R. Royston

MAKING ROADS TO WADI GHUZZE, GAZA

CHAPTER XVIII

PREPARATIONS FOR THE SECOND GAZA

The short period between the first and second Gaza battles was one of strenuous work for all ranks. It was no secret that another attempt would be made at an early date, and smarting under the failure of the first attack, all ranks were determined that Gaza would be ours in the near future.

The Brigade was based on Belah where there was an abundance of water, but carried out operations daily in the direction of the Wadi Ghuzze and Tel-el-Jemmi, taking up an outpost line each night along the Goz-el-Taire ridge.

At 9 a.m. on the 29th March, 1917, the Regiment moved to the beach at Marakeb, where both men and horses enjoyed a swim. At 3 p.m. the Regiment moved to Belah where it bivouacked until the 16th April. Two squadrons were sent out daily and working parties were provided for the purpose of constructing large reservoirs near Tel-el-Jemmi. These reservoirs consisted of huge holes in the ground lined with tarpaulins, and were filled with water brought from Khan Yunis.

Large forces of Infantry were moving up from the Canal zone, and a number of guns, far heavier than anything previously used on this front, also arrived. These guns were drawn by caterpillar tractors and immediately moved to their allotted positions. Our Air Force, which had been sadly neglected, also received substantial additions to the number and quality of its machines.

Late one night a strange rumbling noise was heard, and all sorts of conjectures were made as to its cause, but it was not till daybreak that the true facts were known. It was a fact hard to believe, but investigation proved that at last the famous tanks had arrived and had been stowed away under the palms in a small cactus-bordered paddock.

The enemy were known to have enormously strengthened their position. They had brought forward thousands of extra men and had prepared a number of strong positions on the Gaza-Beersheba line, with complete network of trenches from Gaza to Abu Hareira, whilst the famous Ali Muntar had been made a perfect honeycomb of works.

On the 16th April, the Regiment took over the right sector of the Goz-el-Taire outpost line from the 12th Light Horse, and at 6 p.m. moved with the remainder of the Brigade to the Wadi Sheria, where a new outpost line was formed, its right covering the junction of the Beershaba-Khalasa Road, and its left covering Mendur, "C" Squadron gaining touch with the Infantry at Sharta, one mile north-east of El Mendur. Twelve Hotchkiss rifles (automatic) were now issued to all mounted units to replace the Lewis guns, which were withdrawn, they being classed as an Infantry weapon. Extra pack horses to carry these guns and their ammunition also arrived, and the training of these and the guns' teams were pushed forward, a reserve team being trained for each gun.

Enemy Cavalry, mounted on small Arab ponies and armed with lances, had been frequently seen, but all efforts to draw them into close quarters failed, as immediately any body of our troops showed themselves, the enemy withdrew.

A new pattern gas helmet was issued, and all ranks were trained in its use. When instruction had been given in the method of wearing the helmet, each squad were made to run round for some minutes so that they would get used to the method of breathing through the mouthpiece. This exercise always caused great amusement to those who were not wearing the helmet at the time, by the grotesque appearance of those undergoing the exercise, who, it is safe to say, did not join in the amusement. On becoming familiar with the breathing apparatus, each man was marched through a specially constructed chamber filled with poison gas.

The enemy had been very quiet for some time, and appeared to have all his energies centred on digging operations, but on this particular morning, whilst the troops were having breakfast, they were startled by a number of reports of heavy guns in the direction of Gaza. Our Rail Head had been advanced as far as Belah, and as a natural consequence huge supply and ammunition dumps had sprung into being close to the station. A large hospital had also been erected half a mile north-west of this point, and another about 300 yards north of the line.

These were considered to be well out of range of any of the enemy guns, and free from attack except by air craft, which it was the duty of our anti-air craft gunners to keep at a distance. On this morning, however, large high explosive shells began to drop in the supply depot enclosure with steady persistence, whilst an enemy plane could be seen spotting for their gunners. This airman was evidently no respecter of the Red Cross, as a short time later shells began to fall in the hospital area, causing a number of casualties amongst the sick and wounded. The gun used was evidently a long range naval gun, probably taken from the "Goben" or "Breslau."

It was now evident that the railway could not be pushed further forward until Gaza had been taken, but with the expectation of this being accomplished in the near future gangs of workmen were kept at work preparing the ground for the laying of the line as far as the wadi.

PREPARATIONS FOR SECOND GAZA

Although only three weeks had elapsed since the first battle of Gaza, the enemy position had undergone a remarkable change. A complete chain of redoubts had been constructed along the Gaza-Beersheba Road, the most important and formidable being at Resm Atawineh, about seven miles south-east of Gaza, with strong posts guarding its flanks at Sheikh Abbas and Kirbet-Erk. They had evidently no intention of allowing their flanks to be turned during future operations.

How the Regiment made a closer acquaintance with the redoubt at Atawineh will be told in the next chapter.

CHAPTER XIX

THE SECOND GAZA BATTLE

The British Force engaged in the second battle of Gaza numbered between 50,000 and 60,000, the composition of the Force being as follows:
 1. East Force (Lieut.-General Dobell) consisted of the 52nd, 53rd, and 54th Infantry Divisions.
 2. Desert Column (Lieut.-General Chetwode) consisted of the Anzac Mounted Division (Major-General Chauvel), the Imperial Mounted Division (Major-General Hodgson), and the Imperial Camel Corps (Brigadier-General Smyth, V.C.).
 3. Detachments, Royal Air Force, Armoured Cars, and Tank Corps.

The enemy numbers in the zone of operations were estimated at about 25,000, but this figure is probably far below the estimate. This force, in view of the strength and strategical advantages of their positions, made the task confronting our force a formidable one. Still no one, from General to Private, doubted that Gaza was as good as taken.

The scheme of operations appear to have been as follows:
 (a) The seizure of Sheikh Abbas by the Infantry;
 (b) The capture of the redoubt at Atawineh, and the position at Khirbet-Erk, by the mounted troops;
 (c) The capture of Gaza by East Force, whilst Desert Column carried out a holding attack against Abu Hareira.

To the Imperial Mounted Division, consisting of the 3rd and 4th Light Horse Brigades, the 5th and 6th Mounted Brigades (Yeomanry), with the Imperial Camel Corps attached, was allotted the task of capturing the redoubt at Atawineh.

On the 17th April, the Regiment stood to arms at 4 a.m., and patrols were pushed well out to the front. These patrols returned at 6.30 a.m. and reported "All clear." Several crossings, suitable for wheeled traffic, had been constructed over the Wadi Ghuzze, and at 11 a.m. the Regiment moved forward to El Mendur, where horses were off-saddled and watered.

At 2 p.m. the Regiment, less "B" Squadron, moved out to reinforce the working parties of the 8th Light Horse at Aseiferiyeh, which were being disturbed by enemy patrols. At 6.30 p.m. the work was taken over by the 12th Light Horse, 4th Brigade, and the Regiment returned to bivouac at Tel-el-Jemmi. On the 18th the Regiment,

THE SECOND BATTLE OF GAZA 85

with the Brigade, moved out to support the 6th Mounted Brigade on outpost, and halted two miles south-west of El Mendur, returning to bivouac at 10 a.m.

The Brigadier and Commanding Officers proceeded to El Aseiferiyeh at 10 a.m., and made a reconnaissance over the ground in the direction of the Atawineh position. Whilst this reconnaissance was being carried out parties of enemy riflemen were pushed out to keep our officers as far as possible from their position, but the reconnaissance was successfully carried out and the party returned to camp.

A party of reinforcements arrived from the Training Regiment at Moascar at about 8 p.m., being conducted from Belah by Pte. Elsdon. Immediately on arrival these men were provided with rations and ammunition, and posted to their respective troops, ready for the strenuous work at hand. Every man in the Regiment was served with extra ammunition, making the total 250 rounds per man, which was to be carried into action, as it was considered that the replenishing of supplies during the fighting would be practically impossible.

At 9.30 p.m. the Regiment moved off with the rest of the Brigade, *via* the Wadi Sheria, to the vicinity of Aseiferiyeh, at which place they left the horses under the charge of Capt. B. B. Ragless, the intention being to make the attack dismounted from this point. The wheeled transport of the Brigade, containing the reserves of ammunition and water, had been left at the wadi under the command of Capt. T. H. Darley, with orders to move up to the line at 9 a.m. on the following day.

It now became known that the Infantry attack against the position at Sheikh Abbas had been entirely successful, and already rumours were going round to the effect that the enemy were preparing to evacuate the whole line, but this appeared to be stretching imagination to the limit. These rumours, however, put everyone in a good mood, and seemed to promise great success.

At 3 a.m. on the 19th April, 1917, the Regiment, less horse holders and pack leaders, moved forward in attack formation. The 10th Light Horse, on our left, joined up with the 4th Light Horse Brigade, whilst the right of the Regiment gained touch with the 5th Mounted Brigade, the 8th Light Horse being held in reserve. At 4 a.m. the line advanced, and by daybreak was well up on the high ground beneath the first Turkish redoubt, where it was met by a very heavy fire, the advance being held up.

For some unknown reason, the 5th Mounted Brigade had checked its advance about 1,000 yards in our rear, thus leaving the right flank exposed. Away to our left, the Infantry and Imperial Camel Corps were heavily engaged, and one of the tanks could be seen to have been knocked out of action, and to be in flames. It was very difficult at this point to locate the enemy as the sun was behind them, but the slightest movement of our line could be clearly seen from their position. We were fortunate to have a good crop of barley to lie in, but any movement of the stalks immediately drew a heavy shower of lead.

The 4th Light Horse Brigade, moving forward on our left, enabled us to advance, and at 9 a.m. the enemy's first line of trenches was rushed, and about 20 prisoners taken. These men were found occupying a series of shallow pits, but as the pits were facing west, no use could be made of them. As we were on the high ground, and near the redoubt we were to take, the enemy paid us special attention with his field guns, shells of all descriptions falling rapidly from the direction of Sausage Ridge and from the direction of Gaza.

At 9.30 a.m. the line was re-organized, and it was found necessary to swing back the right flank in order to conform to the movement of the Yeomanry Brigade, which was still some distance in rear. During these movements, the Regiment was heavily shelled and sustained many casualties. The swinging back of the right flank left a gap between the 10th Light Horse and the 4th Brigade, and the 8th Light Horse were moved into the line, leaving the Brigade without a reserve.

From this time till noon, a heavy rifle and Hotchkiss gun fire was brought to bear on any targets appearing, but mainly on Atawineh redoubt. At noon it was noticed that the 5th Mounted Brigade were moving up, and orders were issued to the right flank to conform to the movement, which was a preliminary to the attack on the redoubt. Just how this attack was to be carried out, no one seemed to know, as none of the Regiments had more than about 170 men in the firing line to start with, and all had suffered heavy casualties, with the result that by this time things were looking far from bright.

On the order to attack being given, the Regiment responded with its characteristic dash. On topping the rise, it became fully exposed to the enemy, who seized the opportunity to pour in a withering fire from every available weapon. An attempt was made to get to grips with the Turks, but the heavy fire forced the Regiment to fall back to cover after suffering heavy casualties.

At 2 p.m. the remains of the Regiment were re-organized and again moved forward, the men digging small pits for themselves with their bayonets, whilst the enemy continued his unwelcome attentions. As it was seen that we were not likely to effect a break through, and were receiving far too much attention from the enemy, a party of New Zealanders were sent to our support, and fought through the rest of the day with the Brigade, showing splendid courage.

At 2.30 p.m. one squadron of the Bucks Hussars (Yeomanry), under the command of Major Cripps, galloped to within a short distance of our position, dismounted, and reinforced our line. It was an inspiring sight to see this squadron gallop up, under heavy gun fire, and as far as could be seen, no casualties occurred to their

THE SECOND BATTLE OF GAZA

horses. It made us wonder why we had dismounted and marched so far with our heavy loads of ammunition in the early hours of the morning.

At 4.30 p.m. the enemy commenced a counter attack, but being met by a well-directed and sustained rifle fire, were forced back to their line. A short time later they made a second and more determined attack. For some distance they were in dead ground, but as soon as they came into view the rifle and machine gun fire from our line took all the heart out of them, and they were again forced to retire hastily to the shelter of their positions.

The sight of the enemy coming into the open was a most welcome one, as it was seldom that they could be induced to leave their cover, and all ranks felt that it was a great opportunity to get a bit of their own back—which they did. From now until dark a heavy fire was maintained by both sides, and at 7.45 p.m. orders were received for the Brigade to retire. As it was now quite dark, the horses were brought up to within half a mile of the line, and the Brigade moved back to El-Munkelieh, which was reached at 10.30 p.m.

The men had had their water bottles filled the previous afternoon and had to rely on that supply and a few biscuits for their meals during the day. It was an extremely hard day under a scorching sun, and those who got back to Munkelieh were thoroughly done up; still, after attending to their horses and drawing rations, the Regiment was sent on outpost. Throughout the day the fighting had been particularly constant and the fire intense, the enemy artillery causing many casualties. Their planes were also constantly passing overhead, and dropped a number of light bombs.

The casualties of the Regiment consisted of nine other ranks killed, seven officers and 61 other ranks wounded, one officer and six other ranks dying before they could be evacuated to hospital, making a total of 77 casualties. Unfortunately, a few of the wounded died after reaching hospital. The signallers of the Regiment suffered exceptionally heavy casualties, as out of a total of 15, 12 were either killed or wounded.

Throughout the day all communication between the Regiment and the Brigade had to be maintained by telephone, it being impossible to use visual signalling owing to the absence of cover. The manner in which the signallers carried out their arduous and dangerous duties was a splendid example to all.

During the afternoon the commanding officer, Lieut.-Colonel W. H. Scott, D.S.O., was wounded by a fragment of shell, and Major T. J. Daly assumed command.

A few words must be said in appreciation of the splendid work of the Regimental Medical Officer and his staff throughout the day. In spite of the exposed position of their dressing station, each case as it was brought to them received the best of attention and skill, and it was undoubtedly due to their splendid efforts that so many of the wounded recovered. The stretcher bearers, as usual, carried out their duties in the same self-sacrificing manner as was characteristic of them throughout the whole campaign.

To say all ranks were disappointed at the failure of the attack hardly describes the feeling which existed, but that failure was not due to any lack of determination or bravery on the part of the troops engaged. The policy of passively allowing the enemy to build a long line of strong positions, on ground previously taken by our troops, could never be understood, but seemed to be a repetition of the mistakes made at Gallipoli.

The British casualties sustained during this second attempt to oust the Turks from the Gaza line were estimated at 15,000, but the failure led to important changes being made in the personnel of the General Headquarters Staff. It remained to be seen how the change would work out, but from the moment the troops saw the new Commander-in-Chief they felt confident that success would crown their future efforts, nor was their confidence misplaced.

CHAPTER XX

MINOR OPERATIONS

Shortly after daybreak on the morning following the attack on Atawineh, large forces of the enemy were seen on the move, and word was received from Brigade Headquarters that it was believed the enemy would attack. Work on the trenches was pushed forward as rapidly as possible, but the expected attack did not take place. At 10 a.m. the 10th Light Horse, who had been in reserve, relieved the Regiment, which went to rest until 6 p.m., at which hour it moved off to reinforce the 8th Light Horse. The Regiment was split up into several parties, and all hands were put to digging until midnight.

At 2 a.m. on the 21st, the Regiment stood to arms and continued digging operations. A few shots were exchanged between our scouts and enemy patrols, but the main body of the enemy seemed to be content to remain behind their positions. At 10 a.m. the Regiment took over the right of the outpost line, extending it as far as the small wadi south-east of Munkelieh, where touch was gained with the 5th Mounted Brigade. The work of constructing a trench system was continued throughout the day, and at 6 p.m. the line was taken over by the 6th Mounted Brigade. The Regiment, with the remainder of the Brigade, then marched to Mendur, where it bivouacked.

On the 22nd the Regiment sent large working parties to Tel-el-Jemmi for trench digging. These parties returned at 6 p.m., and shortly afterwards the Brigade moved to Abasan-el-Kebir. On the 24th the Regiment proceeded to the beach at Belah, where men and horses enjoyed a good swim, returning to Abasan at 6 p.m., where it remained until the 26th, on which date the Brigade moved to Marakeb.

On the 28th April, 1917, the Regiment, together with one section of the Machine Gun Squadron and a detachment of the Field Troop, Engineers, proceeded *via* Abasan to El Shauth, where it was attached to the 6th Mounted Brigade for duty. Its particular duty was to take over the protection of the El Gamli crossing from the Warwickshire Yeomanry. Regimental Headquarters were established at Khudri, and "A" and "B" Squadrons commenced digging redoubts on the high ground south-east, and overlooking the Wadi Shanag, which is a branch of the Wadi Ghuzze, whilst "C" Squadron took up an outpost line on the eastern side of the Wadi Ghuzze, covering the crossing. Patrols, consisting of one sergeant and eight other ranks, were sent out to Goz Mabruk and Kh-el-Far, touch being gained with the 22nd Mounted Brigade at El Fara.

Our patrol at El Fara exchanged shots with an enemy patrol, killing one, and bringing in his horse and papers. During the remainder of the month digging operations were continued, as an enemy attack was expected on the 1st May. Patrols were constantly sent out, and frequently encountered parties of enemy Cavalry, sometimes 200 strong. The enemy constructed a strong post on the high ground overlooking the Khalasa-Gaza Road, and occupied it with a force of about 400 men.

On the 30th the mobile rations (special operation supplies) were handed over to the 5th Mounted Brigade, thus enabling the Regiment to mount 26 horses which had been used for carrying the improvised packs, and on the 4th May the Regiment rejoined the Brigade at Khan Yunis. During the time the Regiment was attached to the 5th Mounted Brigade it had no wheel transport, all rations and forage having to be brought out on pack horses from Weli-Sheikh-Nuran, a distance of about five miles.

Late on the 6th May the Regiment moved, with the rest of the Brigade, to carry out an attack on the enemy position at El Buggar. Reaching Esani at 11 p.m., the force halted until midnight, when it moved forward, the Regiment forming the advance guard. At 1 a.m. the Brigade deployed, two squadrons of the 8th Light Horse on the right, with one squadron in support, and "A" and "B" Squadrons of the Regiment forming the left of the Brigade, with "C" Squadron in reserve.

The advance was continued, El Buggar being reached just as day was breaking. A heavy fog made observation difficult, but numerous enemy patrols were seen and engaged. In face of our forces' determined advance, these parties withdrew, the El Buggar position being occupied practically without opposition. At 8 a.m. the Brigade commenced to withdraw, the Regiment acting as rear guard, El Gamli being reached at 11 a.m., and the horses watered and fed. At 12.30 p.m. the Brigade moved to Abasan-el-Kebir and bivouacked.

During the next few weeks the Regiment was employed in improving the defences along the banks of the Wadi Ghuzze, whilst Hotchkiss rifle teams, signallers and other specialists received particular training. Owing to the constant movement of troops and transport in all directions the whole of the surrounding country was soon covered with a layer of dust as fine as flour, and as strong winds were prevalent eyes and throats began to suffer from its effects. Parties were therefore set to work to clear tracks, marking these by mounds of earth placed every five yards on either side, and all troops were warned to move *via* these tracks.

Sore throats and septic sores were extremely prevalent, about 120 men being evacuated to hospital. To shelter the men from the fierce heat large square pits were dug and roofed with timber and

MINOR OPERATIONS

grass matting, each pit being large enough to accommodate eight men. These shelters proved very comfortable and were much appreciated.

The presence of large black scorpions and tarantula spiders proved a source of annoyance, and it was seldom a man moved his blankets without finding one or the other under them. The sporting fraternity soon took advantage of this, and, placing a good big scorpion and a tarantula in an oblong biscuit tin would wager on the fight to the death of these bitter enemies. The fight is most cases ended in the death of both, but the one who lived the longest was considered to be the winner.

Owing to a breakdown in the water service the Brigade moved back to the beach south of Marakeb on the 20th. Two days later, at 4.30 p.m. the Brigade moved to Abasan, and at 7 p.m. proceeded to Goz Mabruk where the Wadi Ghuzze was crossed, the 8th Light Horse acting as advance guard. The object of the operations was to protect a party of engineers, reinforced by a party of one officer and 26 other ranks from each Regiment, who were proceeding to destroy the enemy railway between Beersheba and Asluj. The Brigade took up a position in the locality of Yahia, five miles west of Beersheba, touch being gained with several enemy patrols who fell back on our approach. At 4 p.m. the Brigade withdrew, the Regiment covering the withdrawal.

The operations were entirely successful, the demolition party having succeeded in destroying a large portion of the line, including several spans of a very long bridge over the Wadis. The party returned to Abasan, and Lieut.-Colonel W. H. Scott, D.S.O., also arrived on return from hospital.

On the 28th May the Regiment, with the remainder of the Brigade, left bivouac at 8.30 a.m. and proceeded to Shellal, where it bivouacked on the western side of the Wadi Ghuzze. At 5 p.m. an enemy plane dropped bombs in the vicinity of the camp, but was driven off by anti-aircraft and machine-gun fire. Lieut.-Colonel Scott, who had only just returned from hospital, was again wounded by a falling bullet from one of the machine guns and was again evacuated to hospital, Major T. J. Daly assuming command of the Regiment.

The wheeled transport which had been left behind when the Regiment first commenced desert operations had been brought forward to Belah, and a portion of it, viz., four G.S. and two limbered wagons and the water cart were sent out to join up with the Regiment at Shellal.

At 3 p.m. on the 31st May the Regiment with one section of the Machine Gun Squadron and two sections of the Field Ambulance crossed the Wadi Ghuzze a little north of Shellal. Colonel J. M. Arnott, a former commanding officer of the Regiment and at this time Commandant of the Light Horse Training Depot, Moascar, accompanied the column.

The object of the operations was to make an effort to capture enemy patrols which had been seen daily in the vicinity of El Magam and Kh-Erk. On clearing the Infantry outpost line on the east banks of the Wadi, "A" Squadron was thrown out as an advance guard, with "C" Squadron, less one troop, as right flank guard. When in the vicinity of El Negili the 8th Light Horse could be seen advancing on Kh-Erk from the north. The Regiment therefore altered its direction to the right and pushed on to join up with the 8th. As the advance guard reached the Wadi Sheria the enemy artillery opened fire on the crossing with high explosive shell, but "A" Squadron succeeded in crossing without casualties. "B" Squadron took up a position in the Wadi, whilst "C" Squadron were sent south to protect the right flank.

No enemy were captured, although large numbers were seen in the distance. The two Regiments were therefore ordered to return, and reached bivouac at 9.30 a.m.

On the 7th June the Brigade moved forward to carry out a reconnaissance in force. On arrival at Karm, Lieut. Linacre and 40 other ranks were detached, whilst the Brigade moved forward. At Karm was an unoccupied farm, surrounded by large cactus hedges, which enemy patrols were known to visit frequently, and Lieut. Linacre was ordered to occupy this position for the night. During the time the Brigade was driving out towards the enemy this party prepared defensive positions inside the cactus hedges so that their presence would be completely hidden. An explosion was also caused near the farm to arouse the curiosity of the enemy, in the hope that they would send forward troops on the following morning to ascertain its cause.

As the Brigade withdrew they took back with them the horses of Lieut. Linacre's party, which by this time had been well hidden, and the long night vigil commenced. Early the following morning enemy patrols were seen in the distance, but unfortunately none of these approached the farm, and the ruse failed. The same trap was, however, laid a few days later by the 4th Light Horse Brigade, and was entirely successful, as a complete troop of enemy cavalry made straight for the farm. The hidden troop reserved its fire until the enemy were within 100 yards of the farm, when they opened with every rifle, the enemy being practically annihilated.

"B" Squadron was sent out the following morning to bring in the dismounted men, and pushed forward to the high ground east of Karm, but no enemy were encountered. Patrols were sent out daily and small brushes with the enemy were frequent.

On the 17th June the Regiment suffered a sad loss, No. 3131, Pte. H. G. Smith, of "C" Squadron, being drowned whilst gallantly attempting to rescue three French infantrymen who had got into difficulties whilst bathing in the sea at Marakeb. Letters of appreciation of the gallant conduct of Pte. Smith were received from the

MINOR OPERATIONS

Commandant of the detachment Francais in Palestine, and from Capt. T. A. Tarrance, R.A.M.C., attached to the 5th Mounted Brigade.

Throughout the remainder of the month continuous protective duties were carried out, and as far as possible training of various kinds was practised. During the month the force underwent slight reorganization, a Yeomanry Division being formed. The 6th Mounted Brigade, which up to this time had constituted part of the Imperial Mounted Division, was transferred to the new Division. Lieut.-Colonel W. H. Scott rejoined the Regiment from hospital and Major Daly resumed the duties of second in command. On the same day the Regiment proceeded to the camp at Abasan, being relieved by the 6th Light Horse Regiment, Anzac Mounted Division. The Australian Mounted Division now became the Divisional Support, the Anzacs holding the outpost line, with the Yeomanry Division in reserve at Marakeb.

On the 19th July the Brigade moved in support of the Anzac Mounted Division which had been attacked by two regiments of Turkish cavalry. The enemy cavalry had been driven off, but their artillery continued a heavy fire, whilst a couple of Taubes dropped bombs. On reaching Essani the Brigade bivouacked for the night. At 4.30 on the following morning the Regiment moved across the Wadi as advance guard to the Brigade, and pushed forward towards Beersheba, "B" Squadron and one troop of "A" forming the vanguard, whilst the remainder of the Regiment formed the main guard.

In the vicinity of Abuyahia enemy patrols were encountered, but these withdrew on the vigorous advance of our patrols. A position was occupied about one mile east of El Hatira, and two troops of "A" Squadron were sent out to a point about two miles to the northwest to make good the cross-roads near Towal-el-Habira, gaining touch with the Anzac Division.

The enemy now commenced to show fight, but were driven off, and at 11 a.m. orders were received to retire. This was carried out by withdrawing the advanced posts through the supports. The enemy followed these parties, but were checked by the fire of the original supports, which then retired in turn from the right, the last troop to withdraw being Lieut. M. O. Farmer's troop of "B" Squadron.

Gaining confidence in view of our retirement the enemy rapidly closed on this last troop. Lieut. Farmer allowed them to come within 100 yards, then ordered rapid fire which drove them back in disorder, after suffering many casualties. The withdrawal was then carried out without further incident, Gamli being reached at 3 p.m., where the horses were watered, the Brigade proceeding to bivouac, which was reached at 6.30 p.m.

On the 22nd July the Brigade moved to the beach at Marakeb. For the next few weeks the Regiment underwent a course of intensive training, special attention being paid to musketry. Practice was carried out daily on the 30 yards range and greatly improved the shooting efficiency of the Regiment.

On the 18th August the Brigade moved to Abasan, handing over the old camp to the 6th Light Horse, and taking over new lines from the Dorset Yeomanry. Lieut. Hogan and 17 other ranks proceeded to Kantara to undergo a course of instruction in railway construction.

A few days later the Regiment moved to Shellal where it joined the rest of the Brigade at 4 p.m. At 3 a.m. on the 24th the Brigade moved across the Wadi and occupied the line of hills east of Karm. Lieut. Linacre's troop was sent to Two Tree Farm to gain touch with the Division on our left. "B" Squadron found a Turkish infantryman wandering about, and from information obtained from this man it appeared that he had been driven away from their lines on suspicion of being a cholera (germ) carrier.

At 7.30 p.m. a special patrol was sent out under the command of Capt. B. B. Ragless to reconnoitre the Girheirinlieh area. An enemy patrol was found to be guarding the water at Birifties, and was promptly driven off. The enemy showed little movement during the day, but at 2.30 p.m. two of their planes flew over and dropped bombs on the led horses, but without results. This escape was evidently due to the fact that the horses had been placed in small groups, each group being at a distance of about 150 yards from the next. At 3.30 p.m. the force withdrew to Shellal, at which place it bivouacked for the night, returning to Abasan on the following day.

On the 18th September the Regiment moved to Um Urgan, arriving there at 11.30 a.m. and taking over the lines of the City of London Yeomanry. Patrols were sent out daily across the Wadi and many brisk skirmishes took place with the enemy. On the 23rd Sgt. Suter of "C" Squadron with a patrol of six men when moving in the direction of Hill 720 was charged by a troop of Turkish cavalry. Sgt. Suter, at 50 yards range, shot their leader with his revolver, and the brisk fire of his patrol drove the remainder off in disorder.

In view of coming operations parties of officers of all arms of the service were frequently sent out to observe the lay of the land around the various enemy positions. The Brigade on these occasions was sent out to form a protective screen and hold off the enemy patrols.

On the 6th October the Commander-in-Chief, General Sir Edmund Allenby, visited the area, and the Regiment was ordered out at short notice to carry out a scheme, so that he might judge the efficiency of the Brigade. The Regiment proceeded to El Shauth, where, in conjunction with a section of the 3rd Light Horse Machine Gun Squadron, a combined mounted and dismounted attack on an enemy position was carried out. On the conclusion of these operations, General Allenby expressed himself as being entirely satisfied with the work of the troops.

On the 8th two taubes flew over the lines with the evident intention of bombing. Splendid shooting on the part of our anti-aircraft gunners resulted in one of them being shot down. This plane dropped about one mile east of our lines, and was the first enemy plane we had seen shot down.

During the past few months the lines of communication had been vastly improved. The railway construction party with their Egyptian labourers, working like ants, had made wonderful improvements in the line from the Canal to Belah, and had constructed a branch line to Shellal. This branch left the main line at Rafa, at which place a station had been built on the old battle ground. The pipe line had also been largely extended to meet the growing demands made by the large forces of all arms, and was being brought forward as rapidly as possible.

It was remarkable to note the confidence all ranks seemed to have in their new Commander-in-Chief, and no one doubted but that the next move would be disastrous to the Turks. He was constantly seen at all points of the front line, and if not actually in sight, his presence seemed to be felt.

A large number of new planes had also been received, and a 'drome had been built at Belah. The newer type of machine put our airmen on more equal terms with the enemy pilots, and they not only began to hold their own, but to give the enemy a taste of what they themselves had to put up with in the past.

The Sikh Pioneers (Indian) at Shellal constructed a wonderful trestle bridge over the Wadi Ghuzze, the bed of which at this point was about 50 feet below the banks. A branch line was also laid to Gamli, and a huge reservoir constructed in the Wadi bed. This was soon filled from various springs and provided a sufficient supply for some time to come. When this work was completed a light line was laid from Gamli to Karm, which proved to be of great value during the Gaza-Beersheba operations.

As the Brigade had served for a long period in the front line it was withdrawn for a rest, and proceeded to the beach at Marakeb. Sea bathing, combined with the splendid bracing air of the Mediterranean soon brought all ranks to their normal state of health, whilst the rest and good feeding made a vast improvement in the condition of the horses, with the result that the Brigade was soon fit to undergo the most severe operations.

The sport side of the question was not overlooked, and a good boxing tournament was held, at which Sgts. Suter and Harley greatly distinguished themselves. A good afternoon was also spent in witnessing the sports of the 5th Mounted Brigade, which were splendidly organized. Lieut. Hargraves won the open jumping event at these sports. Some capital concerts were also given by the various concert parties, practically all British units, and no member of the Brigade will forget the fine shows given by the concert party of the H.A.C.

In view of the impending operations we were soon back amongst the dust, scorpions and tarantulas of Abasan-el-Kebir, and working hard at putting the finishing touches to our preparations. The wheeled transport was organized in three echelons, "A" echelon consisting of tools, ammunition, and water; "B" 1, supplies, and "B" 2 baggage. Special load tables were arranged, and every driver given definite instructions, so that whenever orders were received the whole transport could be correctly packed and paraded in the shortest possible time. Surprise turns-out were practised frequently, and, without a single exception, the transport of the Regiment was quickly paraded with every wagon correctly packed as per load table.

Our airmen had also put the past few weeks to good use, and had taken extensive photographs of all the enemy positions. These photographs were quickly joined together and splendid maps printed from them. With the assistance of these photographs the Infantry built exact replicas of the most important enemy positions, complete in every detail, even to the barbed wire entanglements. The Infantry units who were selected to attack these special positions during the big operations were thus enabled to carefully study every aspect of the position, and make their plans accordingly. They also practised attacks on these models, so that all ranks would know exactly what was expected of them when the actual day arrived.

Although the Light Horse units had not been told what their particular task would be, they were given to understand that to a very large extent the result of the action would depend on full use being made of their mobility by their commander, Lieut.-General Chauvel.

On the 27th October, 1917, the Brigade moved out at short notice to support the 8th Mounted Brigade, Yeomanry, who were reported as being heavily engaged near the eastern bank of the Wadi Hanafish. The hills in this locality had for some time been occupied each night by the enemy cavalry, but it was not considered advisable to allow them to retain the position by day. Orders were therefore issued to the effect that our outpost line would occupy that position daily, and this had been done, sometimes without resistance, whilst at others the Turks seemed inclined to dispute possession, with the result that sharp engagements occurred.

On this particular occasion the Yeomanry had occupied the posts for some hours when suddenly a large body of Turkish infantry, supported by cavalry and guns, deployed from the cover of the Wadi and made a determined attack on the position. They succeeded in completely enveloping the position on Hill 720 and annihilating the small party of Yeomanry who were defending it before support could be given.

WATERING HORSES AT THE WADI GHUZZA, SHELLAL

GAZA BEFORE THE ATTACK. *Captured German Photo.*

MINOR OPERATIONS

The Yeomanry on Hill 630 fought bravely, and despite the fact that they were completely surrounded and suffering heavy casualties, held out until reinforcements arrived. It was stated later that the enemy intention had been to seize the light railway which had been pushed out from Gamli. The 9th and 10th Light Horse Regiments which had been rapidly pushed out, occupied the ridge at El Buggar in the face of considerable opposition, and brought an enfilade fire to bear on the Turks who were still holding Hill 720, making their position an unenviable one.

Large bodies of the enemy were observed moving at various points supported by their artillery, and indications pointed to a big enemy offensive. Our batteries having got into a suitable position opened a heavy fire on Hill 720, making the enemy cavalry rush to the shelter of the Wadi, whilst their infantry commenced to fall back.

Late in the evening the infantry of the 74th Division moved forward and dug in on El Buggar ridge, the mounted troops returning to bivouac. It was whispered that the following morning would see the commencement of the great battle, which was to drive the Turks from the Gaza-Beersheba line, but those who knew the strength of the various points in that 14-mile line realized that the task was no light one, and that the next few days would prove very strenuous indeed. Still, no man doubted but that at last we were on the point of a big forward move.

CHAPTER XXI

THE BEERSHEBA-JERUSALEM OPERATIONS.

Ever since the second battle of Gaza on the 19th April, the enemy had worked night and day on strengthening the line from Gaza to the foot of the Judean Hills, beyond Beersheba. This line was by the 27th October considerably strengthened and presented a formidable barrier of strong points and redoubts. The task of breaking such a line, held by a determined enemy, was one to tax the skill of any commander, and the fighting efficiency of his troops to the utmost. There appears to be no doubt that the enemy commander felt confident that he would be able to again bar our further progress.

Our force had also undergone considerable changes since the failure of the 19th April. Large reinforcements had been brought up, the air force had been considerably increased, and all arms had undergone special training to fit them for their great task.

A still greater change was that we had now a Commander-in-Chief, who, being himself a cavalryman, knew to a fraction to what advantage a large, spirited, and resourceful body of cavalry could be put; also one who would not hesitate to take the risks so essential in an adventure of this nature. That under his dispositions the Cavalry would play a great part in the coming operations was evident to all as the time approached, and many were the conjectures as to when and where they would be sent to make the effort.

From observations recorded at the various reconnaissances it appeared to be impossible to outflank the force at Beersheba, owing to the range of hills, which seemed to close right on to the eastern side of the town, and it was evident the enemy thought the position impregnable at this point. General Allenby evidently did not share this opinion, as it was at this point that he thrust the Anzac, Australian, and Yeomanry Mounted Divisions, under the command of General Chauvel. The manner in which they carried out their difficult task reflected the greatest credit on all concerned.

At 3 p.m. on the 28th October, 1917, the Regiment with the remainder of the Brigade, less the 8th Light Horse Regiment, moved from bivouac in column of route to the Divisional starting point, two miles east of Tel-el-Fara, which was reached at 5.30 p.m. The march was then continued to Bir-el-Esani, which was reached at 11.30 p.m., and the troops bivouacked. The march had been a severe one, the tracks being very rough, the transport and pack animals beginning to show signs of the heavy work.

THE BEERSHEBA-JERUSALEM OPERATIONS 99

The Brigade rested at Esani until 5 p.m. on the 29th, when it moved to Khalasa, a distance of about nine miles. It was found that the wells had been blown in by the enemy, but a party of engineers, assisted by members of the Camel Brigade soon effected temporary repairs, and we were able to give our horses a good and much-needed drink. The dust along the line of march was stifling, whilst the soft and dry nature of the track over which this large body of troops and transport passed made the work of the gun teams and transport extremely heavy.

On the 30th October orders were received for the attack which was to be delivered on the following day. The Australian Mounted Division, of which we formed part, were to support the Anzac Division, which was to proceed *via* Asluj along the road running north-east to the Wadi Imshash, thence along the Wadi to the cross-roads, and along the road to Iswainin. From this point the defences on the east and north-east of Beersheba, including Tel-el-Saba, were to be attacked and captured.

In support of this move, the troops of the 20th Corps were to attack the enemy works on the Ras Channam-Hableim Hill, with a view to an advance on Beersheba from the north.

Between 9 and 10 a.m. on the 30th October an hostile plane flew over Khalasa and was promptly engaged by our airmen. A spirited fight took place and was eagerly watched by the large bodies of troops in the vicinity, as on the results of this fight much depended. Hearts almost ceased to beat as the enemy plane appeared to have the advantage, but by skilful use of his machine our pilot succeeded in bringing his adversary to the ground, thus preventing him from returning to his lines with the valuable information he had collected, and our attack from the east on the following day came as a most unwelcome surprise.

At 5.30 p.m. the Regiment moved with the Brigade from Khalasa, arriving at Asluj at 8 p.m. The march was splendidly organized, and the spirit of the men excellent. At midnight the march was continued to Iswaiwin, a distance of about 31 miles. Rains had recently fallen in this area, which kept down the stifling dust, and allowed the troops to arrive at the point of concentration in a much fitter conditions than would otherwise have been the case.

At 9.30 a.m. on the 31st October Lieut. Ayliffe with his troop was despatched to the north-west, and Lieut. Mueller, due north. Their orders were to locate the enemy and report on his dispositions. Within one and a quarter hours Lieut. Ayliffe returned and reported having found the enemy to be holding Ras Ghanna in strength. Lieut. Mueller pushed further north than was anticipated and did not rejoin prior to the Regiment moving. At 2 p.m. the Regiment moved to Iswaiwin to support the New Zealand Mounted Brigade in their attack on Tel-el-Saba.

On moving to Bir-Salem-Abu-Irgeig the Brigade came under heavy shell fire, but reached their position with only slight casualties. By 3 p.m. the battle of Beersheba was developing and the mounted troops on our right were closing in on the enemy positions. The right flank at this time presented a wonderful spectacle, for as far as the eye could see mounted units and horse batteries were galloping into position.

Our Artillery had opened an intensive bombardment of the enemy positions, and the thunder of the guns on our left convinced us that the 60th Division were pushing their attack. At 3.15 p.m. the Regiment moved to the closer support of the N.Z.M.R. Brigade. The country over which the Regiment passed was slightly undulating and broken by small Wadis. The move was made in column of sections at a steady trot, the front being increased and diminished at intervals, and the direction changed frequently, when out of sight of the enemy observation posts. During the move the Regiment was heavily shelled, but reached Tel-el-Saba without casualty just as the position was surrendered to the New Zealand Brigade.

Tel-el-Saba is one of those enormous mounds of earth, stated to have been constructed by the Crusaders for defensive purposes. This had been improved by the enemy with a complete system of trenches and bristled with machine guns; it was also supported by well-placed batteries of field guns.

About 5.30 p.m. an enemy plane flew over, dropping bombs on "C" Squadron and a section of the 3rd Machine Gun Squadron who had taken cover from gun fire behind the hill. The casualties from these bombs were exceptionally heavy, 13 being killed, three officers and 17 other ranks wounded, 32 horses killed, and 26 wounded. Amongst the wounded was Lieut.-Colonel L. C. Maygar, V.C., a fine old soldier, and sad to say he succumbed to his injuries before he reached hospital.

As the horses had not been watered since the previous afternoon the Regiment proceeded to Wadi Saba where they were given a good refreshing drink.

Just before sunset the 4th Light Horse Brigade were seen to make a magnificent charge against the enemy trenches. Although mounted and armed with only a rifle and bayonet, they galloped clean over the enemy position, causing the utmost consternation amongst the Turks, and this charge can almost be said to have decided the day. News was received at 6 p.m. to the effect that the town of Beersheba, considered by the enemy to be impregnable, had been captured.

The Brigade was detailed to furnish the outpost line, and took up a position with the Regiment on the right, and the 10th on the left, the 8th remaining in support. During the night the enemy continued his artillery fire, and much trouble was caused by snipers, several of whom were captured. About an hour after sunrise "A" Squadron were left in the outpost line, and the remainder of the Regiment went into support. A patrol was sent out under L.-Cpl. Gregory, and brought back as prisoners a Turkish medical officer and five men. The medical officer spoke excellent English and informed us that the flank attack by our mounted troops was entirely unexpected and unprepared for by the enemy.

On the afternoon of the 31st October, Capt. B. B. Ragless, with Lieut. J. Kildea's troop of "B" Squadron, left the Regiment in the vicinity of Iswaiwin and moved to Beersheba, where, on arrival, Capt. Ragless assumed the duties of the first British Military Governor of that place.

On the 1st November "C" Squadron escorted a party of 1,300 Turkish prisoners from Beersheba to the Headquarters of the 20th Corps at Taweil-el-Haberi. The day was spent by the remainder of the Regiment in cleaning-up operations in and around Beersheba. The Infantry took over the outpost line, and the Regiment moved to a position about one mile south-east of the town, where it bivouacked.

During the day enemy planes dropped bombs without causing casualties. On the 3rd, two large parties were detailed to assist in repairing the wells, which had been partially destroyed by the enemy prior to their evacuation. Water for both men and animals was extremely scarce, and the work of reconstruction was of the greatest importance. At 5 p.m. "C" Squadron rejoined the Regiment.

On the following afternoon the scarcity of water, which was becoming very pronounced, compelled the Brigade to move back to Karm. The whole distance was traversed through thick clouds of choking dust, it being impossible at times to see the head of the horse one was riding. Owing to the difficulty of keeping touch between units orders were issued that the heads of columns would keep close up to the unit in front. It is said that one commanding officer who had been carefully carrying out these instructions found after marching for about three hours that he had been going round in a large circle, carefully hanging on to the tail of his own regiment. Karm was eventually reached at 10 p.m., both men and horses having a good refreshing drink before bivouacking for the night.

At 5 a.m. on the 5th the Regiment, with the Brigade, moved to Ilimara. "C" Squadron moved forward and took up an observation line through Two Tree Farm and Abu Shawish, covering the railway which had been pushed out to that place. At 7 p.m. the remainder of the Regiment moved up and took up the night outpost line.

It was made clear that the Brigade had been concentrated at this point for the following reasons: 1. To cover the gap between the 20th and 21st Corps; 2. To protect railhead from any possible hostile attacks; 3. To take up the pursuit of the retreating enemy should the Infantry action succeed.

During the whole of that day and night the roar of the guns which were furiously bombarding Gaza could be distinctly heard, the sky during the hours of darkness being a blaze of light from the continuous flashes. It became quite evident that Gaza, with its famous Ali Muntar, was receiving its final knock-out.

The bombardment increased in violence during the morning of the 6th November, as the Regiment moved back to Abu Shawish. From this point a splendid view was obtained of the Infantry attack on the Rushdi system. The Infantry, who had fought so splendidly against tremendous odds in the two previous attacks, moved forward in splendid style under the cover of a heavy Artillery creeping barrage, which moved forward as each position was taken with the bayonet.

At 3 p.m. the Regiment received orders to move, at a good pace, to point 550, where orders were received for the Regiment to occupy the night outpost line. On taking up the line from the Turkish Viaduct at Kh Kanwukah to the Wadi Imelih, the right flank linked up with the Infantry who were by this time well established in the Rushdi System, having captured that position late in the afternoon. It was clear to everyone that things were going well with our forces, on orders being given to proceed to Karm at daybreak on the 7th, in readiness for a rapid move to Sheria, via Imlieh and Abu Irgieg, which the day before had been strong enemy positions. At Abu Irgieg orders were received to push on the Notts Battery and the Field Ambulance to Sheria. This place was reached at noon, and on arrival welcome information was received to the effect that Gaza had been captured.

At 4 p.m. the Regiment, with the remainder of the Brigade, moved forward to the Wadi Sadeh, and in conjunction with the 10th Light Horse, on the right, proceeded to take an enemy position which was thought to be occupied but proved to be deserted. Line after line of enemy trenches were passed which had been carried by the Infantry with cold steel, and there was every indication that the enemy had put up a stubborn resistance. Large numbers of enemy dead and wounded were lying around, and a few of our own men awaited burial.

Information now came through to the effect that the remains of the enemy force which had occupied Gaza were retreating, closely followed by our Infantry in the coastal sector. The Brigade now moved to a point three-quarters of a mile east of Sheria railway station where orders were received to support the Anzac Division in clearing the ridges north of Sheria, which were being held by the enemy rear guards. The Regiment, with the 10th on its right, galloped in extended order over a succession of ridges, meeting with slight opposition, and taking a number of prisoners. After a long gallop the pursuit was broken off near Khirbet Ameidat, the enemy having retired with great rapidity.

At dawn on the 8th the Regiment moved out as advance guard to the Brigade. The Regiment was instructed to occupy the line Wadi

THE BEERSHEBA-JERUSALEM OPERATIONS 103

Durber to Kh-el-Kofrhan, with the 10th on the left, and the 5th Mounted Brigade on the right. At 4.50 a.m. patrols from "A" Squadron captured an enemy outpost of two cavalry and three infantrymen. At 5 a.m. the Regiment crossed the Wadi Ezzaideh, closely followed by the remainder of the Brigade. Dawn was just breaking when the right flank of the Regiment came under a heavy rifle and machine gun fire, but owing to the bad light, some minutes elapsed before the enemy's position could be located.

"A" and "B" Squadrons were quickly in action, "A" occupying a position about 600 yards from the enemy, with "B" in support. The remainder of the Brigade now came up under heavy shrapnel fire and moved to the flank. The two squadrons, together with a section of machine guns, poured a heavy fire on the enemy position with good effect, and they were forced to withdraw, leaving a number of prisoners in our hands. As the squadrons pushed boldly forward the enemy retired in the direction of Huj. At 10 a.m. a short halt was made to allow the 10th Light Horse to move up on our right, and the whole force moved to make a vigorous thrust towards Huj, whilst the Notts Battery harassed the enemy retirement.

The Turks had taken up a very strong position, supported by many guns, and the Yeomanry Brigade were seen to form line, and with drawn swords, make a most gallant charge over the broken ground, in the face of heavy rifle and shell fire.

"A" and "B" Squadrons continued to push on, and the right flank patrol, under L.-Cpl. Bennett, gained Nebi Huj where, after shooting down the escort, they captured two 5.9 howitzers. By mid-day the whole of Huj was in our hands; "A" Squadron with the machine-gun section capturing large quantities of war material and over one thousand rounds of big gun ammunition. Before retiring the enemy had endeavoured to burn his ammunition dumps, but the vigorous action of Major H. M. Parsons with his squadron prevented this.

At 1 p.m. a request was received from Colonels Williams and Cheap, asking for reinforcements to enable them to reorganize after their charge, as the enemy appeared to be contemplating a counter-attack. Two squadrons were sent to their support, whilst "A" Squadron with the Machine Gun Section pushed on to a point one and a half miles north-east of Huj. "B" Squadron was shortly afterwards pushed forward about three-quarters of a mile, and Lieut. Mueller with a patrol shot down the team of a 4-inch gun and forced the escort to retire, leaving a second gun about 400 yards to the right. A team of bullocks was captured and hitched to the captured gun, but all efforts to shift it failed, probably due to the fact that the Turkish bullocks did not understand the language of the wild and woolly Australians or the terms of endearment that were lavished on them.

At 2 p.m. Lieut. Hargrave with his troop pushed forward with great boldness to the high ground west of the junction of the Wadis, and shot down part of the escort of a 15 c.m. gun. By a heavy and well-directed rifle and hotchkiss gun fire he prevented a strong enemy force from removing the gun. Lieut. P. T. Smith, D.C.M., with his troop, and Lieut. McGregor with a troop of the 10th Light Horse came up and charged the remainder of the escort, capturing the gun and 10 prisoners. About the same time Lieut. Little, 3rd M.G. Squadron, pushed his sub-section which was attached to the Regiment well forward to the Wadi and shot down the team and escort of a 12 c.m. gun, which was also captured.

The flat country in the vicinity of Bureir and Sinsin now presented a wonderful sight,, as thousands of disorganized enemy troops could be seen retiring in a north and north-easterly direction. It was unfortunate that these could not be vigorously pursued, but as the horses had been extremely hard worked and had not been watered for 33 hours the task was impossible. Two troops of the Regiment were sent to the 5th Mounted Brigade to assist in the burial of the dead, and rejoined some hours later.

The Regiment was now sent to attack a series of enemy positions in the Wadi Jemmameh, assisted by two squadrons of the 10th Light Horse. The Regiment rode up under heavy shell fire, dismounted and advanced on foot toward the Wadi. As the broken ground of the Wadi was reached the enemy fire grew intense, and it was noted that the high ground on the north side of the Wadi was strongly entrenched and held in force by the enemy. The Wadi bed, which at this point was nearly a mile wide, contained a number of snipers who seriously interfered with the advance.

The Regiment pushed forward with great determination, supported by the 10th Light Horse and the guns of the Notts Battery, and succeeded in clearing the western portion of the enemy position. As the Turks were driven from one position they fell back on other prepared positions to the east and opened a heavy fire on the advancing troops. The 2nd Light Horse (1st Brigade) now moved up on our right, but could only make slow progress. In spite of the galling fire our line pushed forward in extended order over the rough ground of the Wadi, clearing it to within a quarter of a mile of the main trenches. The enemy now appeared in large numbers on the high ground in the vicinity of Khirbet Bahlawan.

The 2nd and 3rd Light Horse Regiments of the 1st Brigade pushed forward their line, and at 4 p.m. a message was received from the Headquarters of the 1st Light Horse Brigade asking for all possible support for the 3rd Regiment, which was about to gallop the ridges in their immediate front. The horses of the 3rd Regiment were brought up along the small Wadis in readiness, and at a given signal the Regiment mounted and rode forward.

THE BEERSHEBA-JERUSALEM OPERATIONS 105

The Turks observing this movement and having a lively recollection of similar tactics at Romani and Beersheba, fled from their positions and retreated in disorder towards the Huj road, pursued by our mounted troops until darkness put an end to the operation. A fair number of prisoners was taken, also a number of guns, transport vehicles, and a large quantity of war material. Shortly before dusk 28 British planes flew over in battle formation, bombing and machine gunning the retreating Turks. "A" and "B" Squadrons, with "C" in support, took up an outpost line, joining up with the Infantry on the left and the 10th Light Horse on the right.

The day had been full of exciting moments. It was quite a new feature to be able to get the wily Turk in the open, as the artful Jacko seldom fought unless he was behind good defensive works which practically hid him from view. In this instance he was driven from pillar to post, and those who succeeded in getting away will never forget their experience. The spirits of our men were excellent, but our horses were showing signs of the continual movement, and were badly in need of water.

At 2 a.m. on the 9th November the horses were sent to water in the Wadi Jemmaneh, and never was a drink more richly deserved. The wells were very deep and the water scarce, with the result that it was not till 6 a.m. that they returned. The Regiment remained in its position until 5 p.m., at which time it moved off as advance guard to the Brigade. The route taken was *via* the northern side of Kh-el-Hummum, Kh-Zeidan, Tel-el-Hesi to Arak-el-Menshiyeh. The country passed over was extremely rough and had it not been reconnoitred by daylight the Regiment would have had the responsible task of finding a road for the Division over unknown country in the dark. The Regiment watered at the Wadi Hesi and arrived at a point two miles from Menshiyeh at 11.30 p.m., where it took up an outpost line astride the railway for the night.

Early the following morning the Brigade was again on the move, the route taken being along the eastern side of the Turkish railway. When passing Arak-el-Menshiyeh the Regiment came under heavy shell fire from the direction of Zeita. The enemy were found to be holding the high ground around Summeil, their left flank resting on the railway. Patrols were pushed out to Ijseir, which was found to be unoccupied. During the whole of the morning the enemy showed great activity and continually changed his dispositions.

At 11 a.m. the enemy made a determined advance against our right flank, causing our patrols to fall back on their supports. Two troops of "C" Squadron were sent to protect the right flank, and the enemy advance was checked. Lieut. Hargraves with a troop of "A" Squadron was despatched to search an area in the vicinity of Menshiyeh, and on his return reported having seen a number of wounded Turks, also large quantities of rifle and gun ammunition.

Five aeroplanes, which had been partially destroyed by fire, were also seen, as were a number of motor lorries and huge quantities of war material near Menshiyeh, which place had been evacuated.

At 4 p.m. orders were received to attack Summeil in conjunction with the 4th Light Horse Brigade, and with the 5th Mounted Brigade in support. The Regiment was sent forward in advance, patrols being sent out to try to locate the 4th Light Horse Brigade. At 6.30 p.m. touch was gained with two squadrons of the 4th Light Horse Regiment, but the remainder of the Brigade could not be located. A conference was therefore held by the commanding officers, who decided that as it was getting dark and as the country to be traversed had not been reconnoitred during daylight, the attack should be postponed. The 8th and 9th Light Horse Regiment therefore threw out an outpost line and the Brigade bivouacked.

At daybreak on the 11th November Lieut. Stevens was sent with a troop of "A" Squadron to reconnoitre Summeil, and later reported it to be clear of the enemy. The Regiment moved to the high ground one mile north-east of the railway station, and on arrival the horses were sent to water. On return they were off-saddled for four hours, this being the longest spell they had been off-saddled since the 4th November. At 4 p.m. a move was made to a point one mile south of Faluje where the Brigade bivouacked.

At 5.30 a.m. on the 12th "A" Squadron moved out and occupied the high ground between Berkusie and Tel-el-Safi, the last-named place being the site of the ancient "Gath." Information had come through to the effect that the enemy had withdrawn from Berkusie, and were occupying Safi in force. At 8 a.m. the remainder of the Regiment concentrated half a mile north-east of Faluje and awaited developments. At 2.30 p.m. an urgent message was received to the effect that the enemy were attacking Berkusie in force, and the Regiment was ordered to reinforce the 5th Mounted Brigade at that place.

"B" Squadron, under Captain B. B. Ragless, was immediately sent into the line north of Berkusie village, "A" Squadron having already occupied that place. One troop of "A" had been sent to Tel-el-Safi and had reported that a large force of the enemy had arrived by rail and had detrained at El-Tine. This body of the enemy had immediately moved in the direction of Berkusie.

About 3 p.m. the enemy concentrated his artillery fire on Berkusie with the evident intention of covering the advance of about 4,000 Turkish infantry, who were moving south on each side of the line. At 3.30 p.m. the enemy force on the western side of the line were seen to take up a position, whilst the force on the eastern side continued to advance.

The enemy now pushed forward with great determination causing our Artillery to withdraw. The 5th Mounted Brigade also withdrew to a position 1,500 yards north-east of Summeil, the Regiment covering the withdrawal. By 4 p.m. the enemy had advanced to within 100 yards of the position held by "B" Squadron, which hung on gamely to allow the machine gunners of the 5th Mounted Brigade time to withdraw their guns.

As soon as the 5th Mounted Brigade had gained its new position the Regiment withdrew and occupied a ridge slightly in advance of the 5th Brigade, where they were joined by two squadrons of the 8th Light Horse. The enemy continued to advance, occupying the village and a ridge in its vicinity. Their determined efforts to continue the advance from this point were frustrated by the heavy rifle and machine gun fire from our position. As darkness fell both sides threw out protective lines and settled down for the night, which passed quietly.

At daybreak the enemy were seen to be holding Berkusie Ridge in force, small enemy parties being observed working their way forward on the low hills north-east of Summeil. At 5 a.m. an observation line was pushed out, supported by the 10th Light Horse. Lieut. Bridger-Lane was sent with a patrol to Zeita, and on return reported the place to be clear. The Notts Battery shelled the enemy positions with excellent effect, the Turkish gunners retaliating by shelling our position during the whole of the day, causing a few casualties. By 1 o'clock the enemy were seen to be retiring in the direction of Junction Station, where the Beersheba-Jerusalem and the Jaffa lines unite.

Away to the north our Infantry and Cavalry could be seen pressing forward to the attack of an enemy rear guard position. At 2.30 p.m. the Regiment was relieved by the 10th Light Horse and proceeded to Ijseir and after replenishing its supplies moved one mile south-east of Tel-el-Turmus.

At 5 a.m. on the 14th the Regiment moved to join the Brigade, and at 8.30 the Brigade commenced the march to Wadi Sukhreir, north of Esdud. The ride was very interesting, and in every direction was found large quantities of enemy stores and munitions which had been abandoned in their flight. This was mute evidence of the demoralized condition of the enemy forces. The natives of the villages passed through seemed to be delighted at the arrival of the British troops, and appeared to have suffered great hardships at the hands of their late protectors (?). Although they had no idea as to how they would be treated by our force they were delighted to think that at last they would get a little fair dealing.

At 1.30 p.m. the Brigade halted to water the horses which had been 56 hours without a drink. They were only allowed a small drink, but during the remainder of the day they were watered five times, and by evening appeared to be quite fit and ready for more hard work. The men took advantage of the good water supply to wash their clothes and have a much-needed bath, the Wadi presenting the appearance of Glenelg by the number of bathers, but minus the prettily-coloured bathing suits, as the costume worn was the same in every case.

During the day our Infantry columns could be seen moving steadily along the main Gaza road, which led north to Junction Station. This point had been stoutly defended by the enemy, but had been captured after a dashing charge made by the Ghurkas, the piles of dead testifying to the energy that they put into the fight. Much material and rolling stock was captured at this point, but a large supply of grain and coal had been burnt before the troops could save it. The railway station had been partially destroyed by fire and explosives the previous night as the main body of the enemy passed through in their retreat.

The 15th and 16th November was spent in resting the horses, whilst the units reorganized and repaired saddlery, etc. At 10 a.m. on the 17th the Regiment moved *via* Beshshit-Katrah, thence to Salmah which was reached at 4.45 p.m. "B" echelon wagons joined up with the Regiment at this point, and brought with them an Australian mail, which was rapidly sorted and delivered.

At daybreak on the 18th November, 1917, the Regiment moved to Mansura, crossing the Jaffa-Jerusalem road at Abu-Shuskeh, thence to El-Kubal, and relieved a regiment of the 7th Mounted Brigade. Enemy shelling and machine gun fire was continued all the morning from the direction of Latron and Amwas which lie at the foot of the Judean Hills, where the road to Jerusalem enters. At 10 a.m. one of our airmen dropped a message to the effect that about 4,000 Turkish infantry with 100 horse transport were passing through Jerusalem from Bethlehem to a point on the Nablus road, six miles north of Jerusalem, and that this force presented a splendid bombing target. The message was forwarded by a galloper to Headquarters at Abu Shusheh.

At 11.15 a.m. orders were received from Brigade for the Regiment to advance and occupy Bir Main. "C" Squadron was immediately sent forward supported by three troops of "B" and "C" Squadron, and ordered to occupy the line Bir Main, Kh-el-Hadithaieh with "B" from the last-named place to Kh-Baraduh. The 8th Light Horse Regiment which had been placed under the orders of the C.O. 9th Regiment took up a position on the right of "B," and "C" Squadron and gained touch with the Yeomanry on their left.

Headquarters and "A" Squadron, with two sections of the M.G. Squadron and "A" echelon transport, moved in support and were subjected to heavy shell fire from concealed guns, the water cart being entirely destroyed and its precious contents lost. By 1.30 p.m. the Regiment had occupied its allotted position, and orders were sent to the O.C. 8th Regiment to push forward to Kh-el-Kusr. The Regiment, less one squadron, now pushed forward to Deir Enb, but owing to the roughness of the ground and strong enemy opposition progress

THE BEERSHEBA-JERUSALEM OPERATIONS

was slow. The Notts Battery, R.H.A., during the whole of the time made excellent shooting and inflicted heavy casualties on the enemy.

At 4 p.m. orders were sent to "A" Squadron to reconnoitre Yald, while "B," supported by the 8th Light Horse Regiment, pushed on to Deir Enb, and "C" Squadron maintained touch with the Yeomanry in their advance on Beit Sirra. Sgt. Masson with a patrol of "A" Squadron reconnoitred Yald and reported it clear of the enemy, but the high ground to the east of the village, strongly held. At 4.30 p.m. orders for the withdrawal were issued, and by 6 p.m. the Regiment, less "C" Squadron, had retired out of range. All efforts to gain touch with "C" Squadron failed, and the Regiment proceeded to Junction Station which was reached at 11.30 p.m. It was found later that the O.C. "C" Squadron on failing to locate the Regiment reported and was attached to the Yeomanry Division.

On the morning of the 19th as "C" Squadron had not rejoined patrols were sent in the direction of Kukab, but failed to find any trace of the missing force. During the morning the Brigadier informed the C.O. that the Regiment would represent the Brigade in the operations against Jerusalem, but owing to the non-arrival of "C" Squadron this order was cancelled and the 10th Regiment detailed.

On the 20th patrols were again sent out but failed to locate "C" Squadron, but early on the 21st information was received to the effect that they were with the Yeomanry Division at Beitunia, eight miles from Jerusalem.

At 10 a.m. the Brigade moved, *via* the Jerusalem-Gaza road to Mejdel, at which place it arrived at 6 p.m., and bivouacked amongst the sycamore trees in the sandhills, two miles north of Askalon. "C" Squadron rejoined the Regiment at this place on the 24th, the Regiment remaining in camp until the 27th, having a general clean up and a much-needed rest.

At 10 p.m. on the 27th orders were received for the Regiment to move to Deiran. At 11.30 p.m. the march was commenced, Wadi Sukhreir being reached at 2.15 a.m., where the column halted for one hour to feed the horses. At 3.15 the march was resumed, the column passing through Yebnah at dawn and arrived at Deiran at 6.30 a.m., where it bivouacked.

CHAPTER XXII

DISMOUNTED DUTY IN THE JUDEAN HILLS.

On the 28th November, 1917, orders were received for the Brigade to reorganize preparatory to carrying out dismounted operations in the hills. Lieut. Ayliffe and 25 other ranks were detailed for relay post duty between General Headquarters and Desert Mounted Corps. This became necessary owing to the winter rains, which had now set in, making the roads impassable to the motor cycle despatch riders.

At 11 p.m. the Regiment moved out as advance guard to the Brigade and proceeded *via* Anabeh to Berfilya, which was reached at 4.30 a.m. on the following day. The Brigade was ordered to gain touch with the 52nd and 54th Divisions, and a patrol under the command of Lieut. Freebairn was sent out. This patrol succeeded in locating the Divisions, and returned at 9 a.m.

At 3.30 p.m. the Brigade moved to El Burj where the Brigade dismounted and handed over the horses to a party under the command of Major T. J. Daly. Capt. B. B. Ragless took charge of the led horses of the Regiment with one man to each four horses, and two officers per squadron. This party left immediately for Deiran, "A" echelon of the Transport remaining with the Regiment; also 33 pack horses and horses for the Commanding Officer and Adjutant.

At 6.45 p.m. the Regiment consisting of 223 dismounted personnel moved up and took over the front line of the 4th Royal Scots and the 4th Scottish Fusileers. Our sector covered a frontage of approximately one thousand yards, and was divided into three posts, "A" Squadron taking the right, "C" the left, with "B" and Headquarters in the centre. The line ran practically east and west across the hills, 1,000 yards north of El Burj. Touch was gained with the 8th Light Horse on the right, but connection could not be made with the 54th Division, who were reported to be holding a position 1,000 yards to the left of "C."

It was found later that they had fallen back some distance, and at midnight one troop of the Gloucester Yeomanry were attached to the Regiment and put into the line about 800 yards to the left of "C." The surrounding country was a mass of hills, the valleys being strewn with huge boulders which made the work of the patrols extremely difficult.

At daybreak on the 30th touch was gained with the 54th Division by a patrol of the Yeomanry. The enemy paid us particular attention throughout the day with artillery and machine gun fire, also throwing a large number of rifle grenades on our position. The enemy were noticed to be moving about from point to point, and were evidently preparing a strong defensive position. At 4 p.m. orders were received to the effect that the 4th Light Horse Brigade would take over a portion of the line, and these troops relieved the 8th Regiment which in turn took over the position occupied by the Regiment.

As soon as these moves were effected "A" Squadron relieved the Gloucester Yeomanry and "B" took up a new position 800 yards to the north-west. The new position was splendidly placed, as in the event of attack both these posts could direct their fire right across the front of the central position occupied by the 8th Regiment.

All these posts were quickly joined up by duplicate telephone lines with Regimental Headquarters and from there to the 54th Division. A section of the Machine Gun Squadron was attached to both "A" and "B" Squadrons. During the night enemy shelling was intense, the telephone wires being repeatedly cut, but owing to the foresight of Lieut. A. Burns, Signalling Officer, in duplicating the wires communication was never lost, whilst the 8th Regiment, using single wires, were often compelled to send their messages through our lines. As the night advanced the shell fire of the enemy increased, and by midnight had reached a stage which clearly indicated that an infantry attack was pending.

Our men had made the most of the short time they had occupied these positions by building stone sangars and getting a good knowledge of the nature of the ground in their immediate front, especially with reference to points of concentration for enemy attacks.

On the 1st December, at 1.20 a.m., an enemy force of approximately 1,000 made a most determined attack. The night was very dark and strong gusty winds were blowing, thereby greatly assisting them in concealing their advance. On getting to close quarters, a sudden rush was made against the small hill held by a flank post of the 8th Regiment, who were compelled to fall back to a position about 300 yards in rear. The enemy immediately occupied the position and opened a heavy rifle, bomb, and machine gun fire on the 8th Light Horse Regiment.

"A" Squadron of the 9th were ordered to put down as heavy a barrage as possible across the front of the position held by the 8th Regiment. Fire was immediately opened and inflicted severe casualties on the enemy and also prevented reinforcements moving up in support. It also prevented the enemy advanced troops from withdrawing. Lying behind the stone sangars which had been erected across the tops of the hills held by the Regiment, the squadrons poured a destructive fire on the enemy who had advanced bravely across the open and had actually taken up positions on the small hills held by our troops. Lying as low as possible they contented themselves with throwing stick bombs, of which an enormous number had been carried forward.

Frequent calls were made on the Regiment by the 8th Light Horse for supplies of ammunition as their reserves were not at hand, and R.S.M. Aikman, who had his supplies well organized, was able to meet all demands.

A party of the 4th Royal Scots closed up to the support of the Brigade and did excellent work, their bombers being exceptionally good. Gradually the fire of the enemy died down, and all movement in front seemed to have ceased, but in spite of this all ranks remained at their posts until daybreak. At dawn the 8th Regiment moved forward and took the surrender of 150 unwounded Turks, amongst whom was their commanding officer. A large number of automatic rifles and bombs were also collected.

The determination of the Turkish attack was established by the fact that large numbers of dead were lying within 30 yards of our sangars, where they had taken cover to throw their bombs. The liberal use they made of their stick bombs, which have a cap on the handle that must be taken off before the cord which sets the mechanism in motion can be pulled, was shown by the fact that one dead Turk, who was seen to be a wearer of the famous Iron Cross, had 60 caps lying in a heap by his side. The enemy dead numbered 200, whilst 300 wounded were stated to have passed back to their dressing station.

Information was gained from an officer prisoner to the effect that their commander was determined to drive the Brigade from its position at all costs, and with this end in view had sent forward a body of picked troops, recent arrivals from the Galician Front. They were certainly a fine body of men, their physique being the best we had seen amongst the enemy forces. They were well dressed and wore the new pattern German steel helmet. Their equipment appeared to be a recent issue, and all carried the latest pattern Mauser rifle.

The enemy maintained a heavy shell fire throughout the day, whilst the Regiment cleared up the position and buried the dead. Towards evening the fire slackened and died away, the following day being spent in peace and quietness. Our casualties had been slight, but the 8th Light Horse suffered severely through being compelled to fall back, but this was unavoidable under the circumstances.

At 10 a.m. on the 3rd December the Regiment was relieved by the Warwick Yeomanry, and proceeded to bivouac about 1,000 yards south of El Burj with the Brigade who remained as Divisional Reserve.

During this period the horses were camped near Ramleh, and owing to constant and heavy rains the camp soon became a sea of mud, so that the men in charge were having anything but a pleasant time. Added to their other discomforts enemy planes made frequent visits, and flying low over the lines machine gunned and bombed them,

PADRE FINIGAN, McFARLANE, AND BURKINSHAW
with Bedouins, Belah

MAJOR T. J. DALY, D.S.O., 2nd in Command
Appointed to command 8th Light Horse Regiment
November, 1918

causing many casualties. Most of these visits took place at night when little damage was done, but during the daylight raids many casualties were incurred, especially amongst the horses of the 8th Light Horse.

On the 5th December the Regiment moved to a point 800 yards north of El Burj and took over part of the front line position. Heavy rains had fallen for some days, and as the men had no bivouac sheets they suffered great discomfort. Firewood was also very scarce, so that the men had no opportunity to dry their sodden clothes and blankets, which had been wet for days. Orders were therefore sent to the horse camp for the bivouac sheets and a supply of boots to replace those destroyed by the rocky nature of the country.

As soon as the order was received a convoy was prepared and moved out at 11 p.m., under the charge of Major T. H. Darley. Marching all night through the pouring rain and on roads which appeared to be rivers of mud the convoy arrived at 9.30 a.m. on the following day, much to the delight of all concerned.

At 8 a.m. on the 8th six officers moved out on a reconnaissance towards Nalin-Kuddis and Khurbetha-Ibn-Harith to discover possible lines of advance in readiness for an attack on those places, and on the following day the Regiment moved to Kh-Daty, rain falling heavily during the move. Information came to hand during this move to the effect that Jerusalem had been surrendered to General Allenby at 11 a.m. on the 9th.

On the 12th December the Regiment took over the position in the Suffa sector from the 5th Light Horse Brigade, the 10th Infantry Division (Irish) being on our right, and the 8th Light Horse on the left. The country in the vicinity was a mass of steep and rocky hills, densely covered with olive trees. On the 14th the advance was continued, Belain being occupied without opposition. From now on to the 25th this line was held, but owing to the rocky nature of the country trenches could not be dug and stone sangars had to be erected.

The continuance of heavy rains was causing much trouble in the transporting of supplies and munitions, and the horses were shifted to Katra. The railway had been brought forward as far as Esdud, but between that place and Gaza many washouts had occurred, the rails hanging loosely across the gaps. All supplies had to be transported by road from Esdud to the troops in the Judean Hills, and owing to the wretched state of the roads motor convoys became bogged and could not be moved for days. Wagons with five-horse teams were therefore brought into this service and large numbers of camels were employed.

Information came to hand that a large supply of Christmas gifts from Australia had been despatched from Egypt, but owing to delays caused by washouts, etc., on the track it was doubtful whether they would reach the front line for some time to come. Never were the troops in greater need of gifts than at this particular time, and the wires were set going to coax the various railway transport officers into seeing that this important consignment would be hurried along.

At midnight on the 23rd word came through that they had arrived at Esdud. To get these stores through to the Regiment by Christmas morning appeared to be impossible, but the Quartermaster sent out a number of wagons at 4 a.m. on the 24th to collect them. A relay of wagons was kept on hand so that immediately they arrived at Katra and had been sorted the portion for the units of the Brigade in the front line could be sent off without delay.

The Esdud convoy reached Katra with the stores at 6 p.m., and by 7 p.m. the fresh convoy had moved off on its long journey to the hills.

Christmas Day of 1917 will long be remembered by all members of the Regiment who took part in the operations in the Judean Hills as being the worst they had ever experienced. Heavy rain had been falling all night, and there appeared no signs of its cessation, making it impossible to light fires, with the result that a hot breakfast was out of the question.

At 10.30 a.m. a convoy of wagons could be seen in the distance slowly dragging its way through the mud in our direction, and great was the excitement when it arrived to find that it carried the Christmas billies, etc. The convoy had marched all night in the pouring rain in order that the men in the font line should not be disappointed, both men and horses being thoroughly done up on arrival. A congratulatory message was sent through from the Brigade to the horse camp thanking those responsible for the fine work in getting the gifts through under such conditions. Had our friends in Australia been able to see how these gifts were appreciated they would have felt fully repaid for their untiring efforts to help the man behind the gun.

At 4 p.m. on the 26th orders were received for the Brigade to advance and occupy a line running along the Wadi Malake in conjunction with the 4th Light Horse Brigade. During this move the Regiments presented a queer sight, as nearly every man had a billy can hanging on his rifle and parcels under his arm. Having no transport in the front line each man had to carry the whole of his belongings, which invariably included one or two cooking pots and a small bundle of firewood, which, owing to its scarcity, could not be left behind.

At 5.45 a.m. on the 27th the 10th Infantry Division commenced its attack, covered by a heavy barrage, on Camel's Hump, Shubany, and Kefr Namah, the 3rd Light Horse Brigade on the left of the 10th Division advancing with them. The advanced patrols of the Regiment met with strong opposition, but the enemy were beaten off and the 10th Division gained its objectives, the attack on Camel's

Hump presenting a splendid sight. At 5.30 p.m. the advanced patrols were withdrawn and the units bivouacked on the ground gained during the day.

On the 28th a patrol under Lieut. Wagg entered Khur-betha-Ibn-Hareth and found that it had been evacuated. At 4.30 p.m. one officer and two troops of each squadron, under the command of Major Brinkworth, moved forward and occupied a line half a mile south of Ibn Harith for the night, and on the following day the remainder of the Regiment moved forward to this line. A little later the line advanced to a position 500 yards north of the village, meeting with slight opposition during the move. The country passed over was very rough and broken by numerous wadis, so that pack horses had to be requisitioned to convey the reserves of ammunition and stores.

December 30th was spent in making roads and building sangars, the old year being brought to a close by a move to Kafa Rut, after having handed over the line to the 5th Royal Irish Rifles and the Leinster Regiment.

CHAPTER XXIII

BELAH CAMP

The Regiment had completed 33 days continuous dismounted duty in the hills, days filled with hard toil, and under the most severe climatic conditions. Since the days of Gallipoli this was the first time it had done infantry work, but in spite of the fact that on occasions rations were scarce and the nature of the work very exhausting, the men kept in excellent health.

New Year's Day, 1918, was spent in bivouac at Kafr Rut, heavy rain falling during the whole day. Orders were sent to the horse camp to the effect that the Brigade was being relieved and that the necessary horses were to be sent forward. These were immediately despatched and arrived at Kafr Rut at 10 a.m. on the 2nd. At 12.30 p.m. the Brigade moved to Latron, and on the following day proceeded to Katra, where it bivouacked for the night.

The Brigade was ordered to proceed to Belah, a few miles south of Gaza, for a spell, and preparations were immediately made for the move. At 7 a.m. on the 5th the Brigade marched to Esdud, and on the following day to Medjel. This march was the worst ever experienced, as the country was flooded for miles around. Torrents of rain fell during the journey, and the strong head wind added to the general discomfort by blowing the rain in our faces the whole day.

On the 7th the march was continued, the objective being Gaza, which was passed through at mid-day. All ranks had a good opportunity to see the damage done by the furious bombardment during the Gaza-Beersheba operations. The town was a mass of ruins, the streets being piled high with debris, and very few natives could be seen. Bivouacking for the night on the outskirts of the town, the Brigade moved on the following morning to Belah, where a camp site had been selected in the sandhills.

During the stay at this camp parties were sent out daily to salvage stores which had been abandoned during the October operations, and huge quantities were soon accumulated, the dumps being handed over to the Engineers and stored ready for future operations.

All ranks not engaged in salvage operations underwent a comprehensive course of training. In view of the success attending the occasions on which the Light Horse had charged mounted, with only their rifles and bayonets as weapons of offence, instruction was given in the method of using the bayonet as a sword when mounted. Instruction was also given by special instructors from the base in bayonet fighting dismounted, good progress being made by all ranks. The recreation side was by no means neglected. It was decided by the General Officer Commanding the Australian Mounted Division, of which we formed part, that a championship sports and athletic meeting should be held, and a committee was formed to arrange the details. A splendid programme was arranged and submitted to the various Brigades. As soon as the programme was adopted each Regiment set about the task of selecting its competitors for the Brigade meeting. To do this a Regimental meeting had to be held, the winners and runners-up being eligible to compete at the Brigade meeting.

The 4th Light Horse Brigade, who were camped close at hand, were the first to hold their meeting, the events being well contested. Open invitations were given to all units of the Division, and large crowds attended.

Several sub-committees had been assembled to arrange the various matters connected with the 3rd Light Horse Brigade meeting, and the ground committee set to work with a will to make the event a great success.

The Regiments having decided the various events, sent their representatives to compete at the Brigade meeting. A splendid day's sport was the result, the competitions being keenly contested. The Regiment came out at the top of the Brigade on the points allotted for 1st, 2nd, and 3rd prizes won. The events won by the Regiment were as follows:

Wrestling on Horseback	1st
Tug of War (Mounted)	1st
Hotchkiss Rifle Competition	1st
Mounted Bayonet Competition (Officers)	1st and 2nd
Mounted Bayonet Competition (Other ranks)	2nd
Officers' Chargers (Light)	2nd
Officers' Jumping	1st
Wagon and Limber Competition	2nd
Champion Troop Competition	1st

The committee who prepared the ground deserved special mention for the splendid results obtained, the members being Capt. McDonald and Lieut. J. K. Lyall, M.C., 10th Light Horse, and Lieut. W. E. Pascoe, 9th Light Horse. Major T. H. Darley was appointed ring-master and conducted the various events.

It now remained to settle all doubts as to who were the champions in the various events from amongst the Brigade winners. Large parties had been working for some time in preparing the ground for the Divisional meeting. This consisted of three rings, the chief of which was constructed at the foot of a fairly steep hill. Each ring was well roped in, and a stand erected on the slope of the hill, the material used being part of the stores salvaged from the Gaza defences. Large refreshment booths were erected in various parts of the ground and a liberal supply of liquor had been obtained for the thousands who were sure to be present.

Major Watson, second in command of the Warwickshire Yeomanry, was responsible for the arrangements, and carried out his arduous duties in a most capable manner. Separate committees were appointed to judge the various events, and Major T. H. Darley was appointed ring-master of No. 1 ring.

The athletic events were contested on the first day of the meeting and provided good sport, but the chief interest centred on the mounted events. Early on the second day a huge crowd assembled round the various rings, amongst whom were Lieut.-General Sir H. G. Chauvel, Major-Generals Barrow and Hodgson, Brig.-Generals Wilson, Grant, Rome, Kelly, Fitzgerald, and many other officers of high rank.

Tea and luncheon for the officers were provided under the supervision of Lieut.-Colonel Todd, 10th Light Horse, and tea was provided for about 4,000 men. The various booths were well conducted and much appreciated by the men present, the committee responsible for their management being warmly thanked by the Divisional Commander for their excellent work.

Looking down from the hill the three rings presented a splendid sight, events proceeding simultaneously in each. The chief events took place in No. 1 ring, which was placed at the foot of the hill and contained a fine set of jumps. Each event was keenly contested, but the final of the troop competition caused the greatest interest. The competitors in this event were one troop of the 4th Light Horse representing the 4th Light Horse Brigade, one of the 9th representing the 3rd Brigade, and a troop of the Worcester Yeomanry representing the Yeomanry Brigade.

The troops formed up in single file down the centre of the ring for the inspection, which was conducted by a committee consisting of Generals Rome, Kelly, and Fitzgerald, and Major Dangar.

A great deal of labour had been expended in the cleaning of equipment, etc.; even the cartridges in the bandoliers being carefully polished. The two Light Horse troops held their own easily as regards the general turn-out, but both dropped a heap of points in regard to the grooming of their horses, whereas the horses of the Yeomanry troop had been groomed to perfection.

On the completion of the inspection each troop in turn was formed up and put through a test of drill. The 9th Light Horse troop, commanded by Lieut. Muller, were 49 points to the bad when this portion of the competition was begun. Drilling like clockwork they rapidly gained points on the leaders, and but for a slight mistake, evidently due to a misunderstanding on the part of their leader, would no doubt have won, being only $4\frac{1}{2}$ points behind the Yeomanry troop at the finish, and gaining second place.

In the general service and limbered wagon contest, wagons which a few days ago had come from the front line a mass of mud and rust, were found on parade to look as though they had just been turned out by carriage builders, and nothing better was ever seen in a show ring. A keen tussle between the Warwickshire Yeomanry and the 10th Light Horse resulted in the latter being declared the winners, to the great satisfaction of all the Australians present.

At the end of the day a summary on a 3, 2, 1 basis for the whole of the events showed that the 3rd Light Horse Brigade were winners of the championship, the points being as follows:

3rd Light Horse Brigade	48 points
5th Mounted Brigade	41 points
4th Light Horse Brigade	39 points
Divisional Troops	22 points
19th Brigade, R.H.A.	17 points

A few days later the 22nd Mounted Brigade (Yeomanry) organized and held a race meeting on the outskirts of Gaza. All officers and men of the Division were invited to attend by Brig.-General Fitzgerald, D.S.O., and large numbers rode out to witness the sport. Many fine shows had been given in the past by the Yeomanry, but this meeting easily beat anything previously seen in the field.

At the foot of the famous Ali Muntar, the scene of the fierce fighting in the three Gaza battles, a splendid flat and steeplechase course had been laid out, with tents and marquees of all kinds erected at various points so that they would not obstruct the view. A tote had been provided, but this did not keep away the large number of amateur bookies who had laid the odds at previous meetings.

Good fields were the order of the day, and some splendid finishes were seen. Lieut. Hargraves came a cropper and was badly knocked about, but this was one of the risks that a would-be steeplechaser must take. The representatives of the Regiment won a couple of the events, and all present enjoyed the best day's sport seen since leaving Australia.

Information was issued to all concerned that H.R.H. the Duke of Connaught would inspect the Division on the 14th March, and a general clean up was ordered. All ranks set to work with a will, and the turn-out of the Regiment soon presented a very creditable appearance. The wheeled transport vehicles were all repainted, the harness cleaned, and all metalwork polished, with the result that on the first rehearsal parade the G.O.C. at the conference of commanding officers said that the transport of the 9th Regiment was the only clean transport on parade.

After three rehearsals the Division paraded in line of Brigade mass on the morning of the 14th, the whole Division presenting a splendid sight. Transport was placed in line in rear of its own Regiment, with the Divisional Train (transport) and Field Ambulances in a line in rear.

On the arrival of H.R. Highness the Royal salute was given, after which he passed along the lines and inspected the various Regiments. The inspection was followed by a march past by squadrons in the following order:

        19th Brigade Royal Horse Artillery
        5th Mounted Brigade
        3rd Light Horse Brigade
        4th Light Horse Brigade
        Signal Squadron Engineers
        Field Squadron Engineers
        Field Ambulances of each Brigade
        Divisional Train, Army Service Corps.

On the conclusion of the march past the Division formed up as a hollow square to witness the presentation of decorations and medals by His Royal Highness. The Duke shook hands and congratulated each recipient after which they rejoined their units, and the Division dispersed and returned to camp.

The remainder of the stay at Belah was devoted to special training in various subjects, and to refitting ready for the operations which were expected to take place in the near future.

CHAPTER XXIV

JAFFA

On the 1st April, 1918, the Brigade moved from the sandhills of Belah and proceeded by march route to Selmieh, near Jaffa. The march was not commenced until 3 p.m., as it was intended to bivouac that day about one mile south of the famous Ali Muntar hill. It was found that the whole of the Division was moving forward to take its place in the line near Jaffa, and it was rumoured that a break through the Turkish line was to be attempted near the coast, thus turning the enemy's right flank.

The ground passed over in the first day's march presented a vast difference from the spectacle seen during the march through to Belah. Much clearing-up had been done, and good roads prepared. The dead had been collected and reburied, each grave being marked by a neat cross.

The second stage was from Gaza to Mejdel, and from there in daily stages to Wadi Sukhreir, north of Esdud. The country for miles on either side of the line of march was covered with good standing crops of wheat and barley and presented a fine appearance. Passing through Yebnah to Nebi Kunda near Deiran, one of the old Jewish settlements, many fine vineyards and orange groves were seen, and all appeared to be in a flourishing condition.

On the 5th the march was continued *via* Richon-el-Zion to Selmeih where the Brigade bivouacked. On this march the ramping of trenches, cutting through wire entanglements, passing of defiles and march discipline were practised for the big operations about to take place. Contact signalling with aeroplanes was also practised by means of canvas shutters spread on the ground, the signals from which were answered by the pilot by means of the claxton horn attached to the plane.

A clean, comfortable camp was laid out on a long hill, one mile south of Selmeih. Preliminary orders for the impending operations were received and carefully studied by all concerned, the country to the north and towards Mejdel Yaba being reconnoitred daily by small parties of officers to note the features of the ground. From a high knoll known as Bald Hill, just south of the large Jewish village of Mulebbis could be clearly seen the long rugged line of hills which marked the Turkish position on that flank.

During the stay at this place leave to visit Jaffa was granted to all ranks. The town is flanked by magnificent orange groves which were in full bearing at this time. A special luxury was available for these leave parties, as the staff of the 21st Army Corps (Lieut.-General Bulfin) had taken over a dilapidated building and turned it into a bathing establishment, where hot or cold baths were available at all hours of the day. Needless to say, the members of the Regiment took full advantage of this privilege, and keenly appreciated the kindness of the British Commander in placing the baths at their disposal.

Preparations for the coming attack were pushed forward, and the transport echelons were rearranged. Thousands of camels were brought forward to assist in the move, and all ranks were looking forward to a sudden dash through the enemy line and the hasty retreat of our old friend, the Turk. In this they were doomed to be disappointed, as just when final orders were expected news came to hand that the operations were indefinitely postponed. It was at once surmised that General Allenby had been indulging in pulling the leg of the Turkish commander, and giving him a bit of a fright.

On the 18th April orders were received for the Brigade to move across country and concentrate in the vicinity of Jericho. The march was commenced on the 19th, the Brigade moving *via* Kubeibeh, Akron Abu Shusheh, to Latron, which was reached on the evening of the 20th. An early start was made on the following day into the Judean Hills to Enab, which was reached at 3 p.m.

Leaving Enab at 7 a.m. on the 22nd the Brigade moved to Jerusalem, on the outskirts of which the horses were watered and fed. After a short halt, the march was continued through the outskirts of the city. Moving alongside the ancient north wall, past the Damascus and St. Stephen's gates, the Regiment passed by the Mount of Olives and through the Garden of Gethsemane to the Valley of Jehosophat.

The winding road from Jerusalem soon led to the plain below by a series of hair-pin bends, the grade being exceptionally steep. A long and tedious march *via* Bethany and past the Good Samaritan Inn brought us to our new bivouac, Talat-et-Dum (the hill of blood), so called from the peculiar colour of the rocky ground in the vicinity.

Prior to the move we had been informed that our destination was one of the worst spots that could be imagined, but that description was far from the mark, as no one could possibly imagine such a spot. The whole of the surrounding country presented a most forbidding aspect, consisting of a series of absolutely bare, rocky hill tops, very hot, and smothered in fine dust. The ground which had recently been occupied by the enemy, whose departure had been somewhat hurried, at the request of our Infantry, was in a filthy state.

Water was a serious problem in this locality, the horses having to be sent a distance of three miles to troughs erected by the Engineers. From a hill near this watering place a good view could be obtained of the Jordan Valley, Jericho, and the Dead Sea. After spending two days cleaning up the camp area, orders were received for the Brigade to move *via* the old road, to the plains of Jericho.

The Brigade was soon on the move, all being anxious to leave this place behind, and, passing down the steep winding road along the rugged side of the Wadi Kelt, reached the plain about one mile west of Jericho.

The transport of the Brigade experienced great difficulty in descending this hill road, which had great gaps torn in it by recent heavy rains, and was altogether unsuitable for wheeled vehicles. In addition to having the brakes of all vehicles jammed full on, the rear wheels were lashed with stout rope. In spite of this, one G.S. wagon of the 8th Regiment capsized over the cliff, but fortunately the drivers escaped. The last vehicle to descend was the Maltese cart belonging to the Regiment, and just as it reached the bottom both wheels struck a deep rut with the result that both shafts broke clean off, causing the cart to tip forward and throwing the driver underneath. The startled mules immediately bolted, dragging the cart after them, but although they were stopped within a few yards of the scene of the accident, the driver, Pte. Learmouth, was so badly injured that he died a few minutes later in the dressing station at the foot of the hill.

Turning north, the Brigade moved parallel with the foothills for about three miles, and at mid-day bivouacked on the right bank of the Wadi Nuameieh, near the foot of Gebel Kuruntul (the Hill of Temptation).

The Wadi Nuameieh is a rapidly-running creek which rises in the Judean Hills and carries a permanent stream of good water across the desolate plains of Jericho to the Jordan River. On the eastern face of the Hill of Temptation, which is almost perpendicular, is built an ancient monastery with rooms and church cut in the solid rock and with a balcony hanging over the precipice. On top of the hill, a climb of some 400 feet, the monks are building a church on the actual spot where Christ is stated to have been tempted by his satanic majesty. As this is being built of huge blocks of granite, each of which has to be carried up the face of the cliff by the workmen, it can readily be seen that it will be some considerable time before the building will be completed.

The troops were allowed the privilege of visiting the ancient church, and those who went were well repaid for their trouble, as the interior was of great interest and contained many old relics.

CHAPTER XXV

THE ES-SALT OPERATIONS

During the few days spent in the camp at the foot of Mount Forty, the Hill of Temptation, reconnaissances were made daily across the River Jordan and of the various fords. Preparations were also pushed forward for operations in the hills east of the river.

Capt. A. H. Nelson was appointed Administrative Commandant of Jericho.

The view from the camp site looking east was most forbidding. A dreary plain, thickly studded with the skeletons of camels, spread for miles, and about seven miles away the Jordan wound its way south to the Dead Sea. Across the river, six or seven miles of gently sloping ground led to the foothills of the land of Moab.

Away to the left, on the plateau, could be seen the outskirts of the town of Es-Salt, supposed to be the ancient Ramoth Gilead. This town has a population of about 20,000, half of whom are Christians, and is connected with Amman, 20 miles distant, by a very good metalled road. This road is identical with the one running south-west across the hills of Moab, to emerge on the Jordan Plain near Shunet Nimrin, and thence across Ghoraniyeh Bridge to Jericho.

Es-Salt lies at the head of a valley, the buildings rising one above the other on the slopes of the hills. On its western and southern sides it is protected by a system of steep terraced hills, the chief of which is Kefr Huda. It was in effect the key to the whole land of Moab, and upon its retention much depended. The chief approach to Es-Salt was the metalled road through Shunet Nimrin, but there were two tracks up the hill side, one being from Umm Shert and the other from Jisr Ed Damieh.

The situation at the time was briefly as follows: The British line ran from Jaffa through Nablus to the junction of the Rivers Auja and Jordan. It then followed the banks of the Jordan south to the bridgehead at Ghoraniyeh.

The left flank of the enemy's line rested in the nest of hills at Shunet Nimrin, guarding the road to Es-Salt and Amman, where strongposts had been established. From this point the line ran across the Jordan Valley to Nablus, where strong enemy forces were quartered ready to reinforce either flank at short notice, and from there the line stretched to a few miles north of Ludd and Jaffa, with supports at Besan, Jenin, and El Afuleh.

THE ES-SALT OPERATIONS

The Anzac Mounted Division had by their capture of Jericho and the crossings of the Jordan extended the right flank of our force, but the difficulty of supplying this force had held up any further advance. Headquarters, however, fearing the effect of the coming summer on the troops holding the Jordan Valley and Plains of Jericho, were anxious to further extend the line into the hills of Moab, where the summer could be spent in a clear and healthy climate.

The army of the King of Hedjaz was reported to be steadily working its way north along the railway from Medina, and a junction of our forces was of great importance, as it would have a disastrous effect on the enemy.

With this object in view the Anzac Division, in February, made a sudden dash on Es-Salt and Amman, both of which were captured, but had to be abandoned a few days later, owing to the lack of support and the heavy reinforcement of the enemy line. In this affair the Anzac Mounted Division were roughly handled, and the folly of making such an important move with so small a force was clearly apparent.

With a view to retaking these important points and holding them against all possible counter-attacks a much larger force of troops had been brought into the valley and placed at the disposal of Lieut.-General Sir H. G. Chauvel, who was to command the operations. The force available was as follows:

The Anzac and Australian Mounted Divisions
A composite Brigade of Yeomanry
Two Regiments of Indian Cavalry (with British and Indian Officers)
The Imperial Camel Corps
The Royal Horse Artillery of the 4th Cavalry Division
91st Battery (Heavy) Royal Garrison Artillery
383rd Siege Battery, R.G.A.
9th Mountain Artillery Brigade
Hong Kong and Singapore Mountain Battery
Two Light Armoured Car Batteries
20th Indian Infantry Brigade, and the
60th British Infantry Division (less one Brigade).

At 9.15 p.m. on the 29th April the Regiment, less transport, with the remainder of the Brigade moved from bivouac through Jericho and at midnight crossed the Ghoraniyeh Bridge. Turning north, the Brigade moved parellel with the river for a distance of three miles and halted, moving forward again at 2.30 a.m. on the 30th, with two troops from the Regiment as advance guard to the Brigade. Following in the rear of the 4th Light Horse Brigade, the column moved along the valley as fast as the rocky nature of the country would allow.

At 4.45 a.m. the column came under heavy shell fire, but the ranging was far from good, and no casualties were incurred. As daylight broke the valley presented a wonderful sight. From the slight rise on which we were moving the 4th Light Horse Brigade could be seen pushing forward at a steady trot, whilst in our rear could be seen troops of all arms of the service moving to their allotted positions.

The role of the 4th Light Horse Brigade was to hold the valley from the banks of the river to the foothills, whilst the 3rd Light Horse Brigade pushed on *via* the goat tracks up the hill side to Es-Salt. By this time the Infantry attack on Shunet Nimrin had developed, heavy gun and rifle fire being heard from that direction.

At 6.30 a.m. the Regiment had reached the Damieh-Es-Salt track about 5,000 yards east of the Jordan, and orders were received from the Brigade to push forward by this track to Es-Salt. "A" Squadron was sent forward to secure the first sector of the heights, and the remainder of the Regiment followed. Advance patrols were pushed forward with strong supports to cover the advance of the remainder of the Brigade, and patrols were sent out to either flank to give timely warning of any enemy forces which might be approaching.

The road on which the advance was made consisted of a rough goat track, the Brigade being forced to move in single file, and even in this formation the track presented innumerable difficulties. No opposition was met for the first two hours, when an enemy post of three men was encountered. One of these men was killed and the others captured. A little later a second post was seen, but these immediately retired, and all efforts to capture them failed.

The Regiment were now about 4,000 feet above the valley, and about two miles from Es-Salt, and came in contact with a strong force of the enemy, holding a strong position astride the road. Dismounting, the Regiment advanced in extended order. An enemy cavalry patrol was observed about 1,200 yards to the east, and a patrol was despatched to deal with it. On our men opening fire the enemy abandoned their horses and retired.

The enemy position appeared to be as follows: His main force was occupying a ridge about 1,000 yards long at a distance of 600 yards in front of "B" Squadron, with detached hills strongly held on both flanks, at distances of from 12 to 1,400 yards. These positions had been strengthened by the erection of stone sangars and were heavily manned with rifles and machine guns.

The position occupied by the Regiment covered a small basin under cover from enemy fire, and in this position the Brigade concentrated at 2 p.m. "A" Squadron, which had been left in rear, rejoined the Regiment. One squadron of the 10th Light Horse was sent forward to the attack, supported by the fire of the machine guns and of the Hong Kong and Singapore Battery, and succeeded in driving the enemy from his left flank position.

During this move "B" Squadron, supported by a section of the 3rd Machine Gun Squadron, had kept up an incessant fire on the enemy's central position at a range of about 600 yards, whilst "A" Squadron moved to deal with the right flank position. This position was carried by a determined rush, and the squadron was thus enabled to bring a very heavy enfilade fire to bear on the central position, making things decidedly uncomfortable for the occupants. The remainder of the 3rd Machine Gun Squadron had moved to and occupied a position 800 yards south of "B" Squadron, whilst the Mountain Battery had brought up more guns into a position suitable for supporting the further advance of the Regiment.

At 4.30 p.m. orders were received for every available man of the Regiment to join forces with two squadrons of the 10th Light Horse in a dismounted attack on the main enemy position. At 5.15 p.m. the attacking troops were formed up in three lines in rear of "B" Squadron, awaiting orders. For the purpose of the attack the troops would have to race down a steep and rocky hill, across a valley, and up a steep slope to the enemy trenches; but this ground presented an unusually favourable opportunity for covering fire, allowing our men to get within 20 yards of the enemy position before it would have to cease.

At 5.30 p.m. the first line jumped to their feet, and with loud cheers dashed over the hill and down the slope, and at the same moment heavy supporting fire was brought to bear on the enemy position from all available points. At the bottom of the slope the line paused for a breather and then pushed forward with great determination, supported by the second and third lines. The final charge was carried out with great spirit and dash, the enemy force being driven from their trenches in disorder, and the captured position at once consolidated.

The 8th Light Horse Regiment, who had been held in readiness in rear of "B" Squadron, were now ordered to advance, mounted, and seize Es-Salt. Pushing forward rapidly they cut off and captured 200 of the retiring enemy force. These were sent back under escort, and the Regiment rode forward on its mission.

At 7.45 p.m. the Regiment concentrated at the captured position and moved to Es-Salt, which had been taken by the 8th Regiment. Throwing out a light outpost line, the Regiment bivouacked for the night.

The casualties of the Regiment during the day had been as follows: Killed, Lieut. M. O. Farmer and No. 1216 Signaller N. M. Fleming; Wounded, Lieut. J. F. Kildea, Sgt. Gandy, and Ptes. W. N. Hankin, S. Dickson, and H. L. Brooksby; a surprisingly small list in view of the nature of the operations conducted and the heavy casualties inflicted on the enemy.

At 4 p.m. on the 1st May orders were received from Brigade to move immediately and occupy the high ground north and west of

Es-Salt. A section of the Machine Gun Squadron moved with the Regiment, which took up a line, the right resting 2,000 yards north of Es-Salt, and the south 2,000 yards south-west of Kefr Huda. This last-named place is a large tomb on a point 3,597 feet above sea level, and is the traditional burial place of the prophet Hosea.

A patrol which had been sent out under Lieut. Sharp captured one Turkish officer and two N.C.O.'s. Regimental Headquarters and two troops of "A" Squadron were held in reserve in a large cave 1,200 yards north-west of Es-Salt. A Turkish prisoner was taken at this place, he being rescued from the natives, who were handling him very roughly. The natives in the locality were of a type very different from those on the other side of the Jordan. They were nearly all armed with modern rifles of both English and German pattern, and in moments of excitement or as a sign of rejoicing were wont to discharge their rifles in the air. This was first looked upon by our men with a certain amount of suspicion, but it was soon seen to be quite a friendly demonstration in our honour. Still, it is very doubtful whether they could be trusted by friend or foe.

The country hereabouts was fairly thickly populated, although few houses were seen outside the town area. The hillsides had been cut into a series of steps, each of which was cultivated with good standing crops and lovely vineyards. Several good wells were located in the area occupied by the Regiment.

At 8 a.m. small parties of the enemy were located on a ridge 2,000 yards north-west of our line, and at 9 a.m. information was brought in by natives to the effect that 20 Turks, with 50 camels and 40 pack mules and a dump of ammunition, were hidden in a vineyard two miles to the north. Lieut. P. Teesdale Smith with his troop was sent to verify this statement and reconnoitre the position with a view to its capture.

At 11.30 a.m. word was received from Lieut. Smith that he had located the party referred to, but that it far exceeded in numbers the first information. He asked that a second troop be sent to his support, as he felt confident that with two troops he could effect their capture; but before the second troop could be despatched word was received that the enemy force had retired to the north.

A very heavy mist had now settled over the hills, making it impossible to see more than a few yards. This was of great value to the enemy, who knew the ground to perfection, and under its cover a patrol of Turkish Cavalry moved to within short range of "A" Squadron post, which was east of Kefr Huda. As soon as they were seen the post opened fire, killing one horse and wounding one man and one horse, the remainder of the patrol retiring at a gallop.

During the day a large number of natives passed through the lines, driving their cattle, to Es-Salt. As night approached, our line was shortened, and an outpost line established, "B" Squadron being

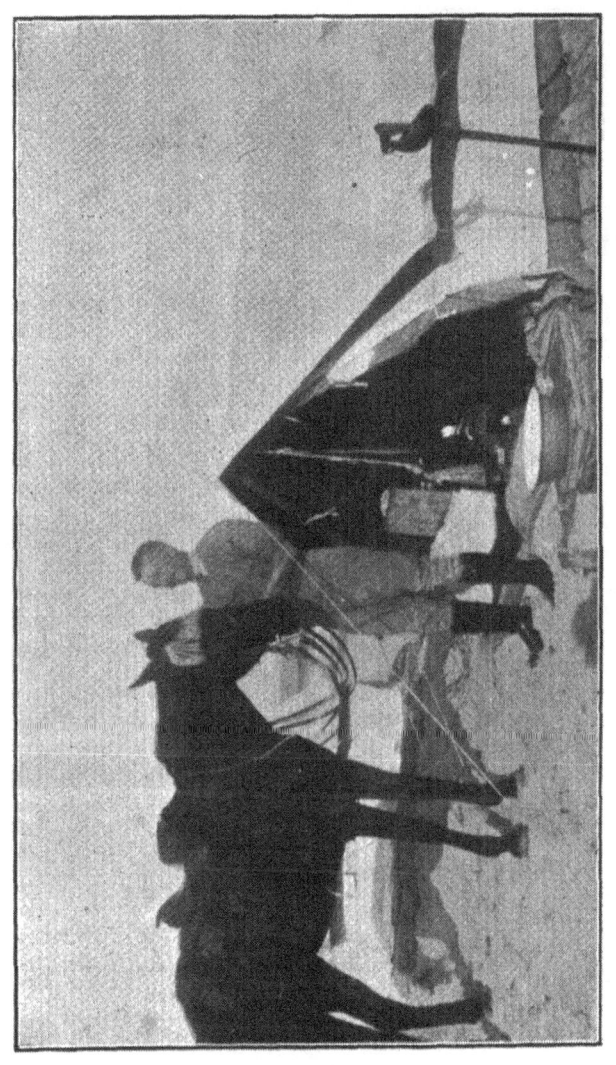

THE AUTHOR AND "BILL" AT MARAKEB

THE JEWEL OF THE EAST—DAMASCUS

in touch with the 8th Light Horse on our right. The left flank was very insecure, as "C" Squadron failed to gain touch with the 10th Regiment, who should have linked up with our left.

All roads passing through our line were patrolled throughout the night, which was very misty and bitterly cold. The intense cold was severely felt by our men, who were without their greatcoats and blankets, whilst the heavy mist, through which objects could only be seen at a range of four or five yards, made the work of the sentries very difficult. No enemy movement was detected throughout the night.

At 4 a.m. on the 2nd May dismounted patrols reconnoitred the country 1,000 yards north of the line, and on their report of "all clear" the line advanced to the position held the previous day. At 6 a.m. information was received to the effect that late the previous night the 10th Light Horse had been sent to intercept an enemy force stated to be moving on Es-Salt, *via* the Damieh Road.

At 6.45 a.m. the 10th Regiment reported having gained touch with a force of 200 Turkish infantry, and at 7 a.m. Lieut. Sharp, with two troops of "A" Squadron, was sent forward to close the gap between the left of our line and the 10th Regiment.

The line now held by the Regiment was about 5,500 yards in length, and as the total number of men available was only 300, it can be clearly seen that only slight opposition could be made against any determined advance of the enemy. At 10 a.m. Capt. Luxmoore, commanding "B" Squadron, reported that a force of approximately 1,000 enemy, with guns, was moving towards our position from the direction of Amman, and was at that time about five miles distant. "A" Squadron also reported a further force of 200 enemy infantry and cavalry to be advancing from a north-westerly direction.

At 11 a.m. the force reported by Capt. Luxmoore was stated to be moving northward, and a little later, that it was moving eastward, which made its movements appear a little confusing. At 2 p.m. information came through to the effect that the enemy was making a determined attack on the sector held by the 2nd Light Horse Brigade, which were on our right, astride the Amman-Es-Salt road.

At 3 p.m. enemy artillery opened a heavy shell fire on our line, and continued this fire throughout the afternoon. At 7 p.m. information was received that the 4th Light Horse Brigade, who were holding the Jordan Valley from the river to the hills in the vicinity of Damieh and Umm Shert, had been driven back, thereby losing control of the Damieh-Es-Salt road, and giving the enemy a clear run to the position held by the 3rd Brigade, north and west of Es-Salt.

The Regiment was still hanging on to its extremely long line, and had to hold it through the night, which fortunately was free from mist. The night passed quietly, but was very trying, as large numbers of the enemy were known to be in the vicinity. The hilly and rocky nature of the country favoured surprise tactics for an active enemy, and had the enemy taken this action, it is doubtful whether they could have been held up at any point.

Another problem now faced the G.O.C. The troops had marched out carrying two days' rations, also an emergency ration for men, and two days' grain for horses. These had been consumed, but owing to the tactical situation, the ration convoys had not been allowed to move forward. Luckily there was plenty of good grazing for the horses, and a small quantity of barley had been requisitioned by the Brigade, so that the horses did not go without a meal.

At 4 a.m. on the 3rd May "B" Squadron moved forward 1,000 yards and occupied a line running east and west above Tel-el-Jaludi. Information was received that the enemy were making a strong attack on the position held by the 8th Light Horse on the Amman road, and two troops of "B" were sent to reinforce that point.

At 6.40 a.m. Lieut. Hargrave reported a strong enemy movement on his immediate front, the enemy endeavouring to move round his left flank towards Kefr Huda. One troop of "A" was withdrawn from the line and sent to his support, and a little later Capt. Luxmoore reported that the attack against the 8th Regiment had been repulsed and 320 prisoners taken.

At 9.15 a.m. the enemy commenced an attack against the flank of "C" Squadron, about 400 yards north-east of Kefr Huda. The attack was pushed with great determination, enemy bombers advancing to within 15 yards of the position held by Lieut. (Jerry) Masson and 15 other ranks with one Hotchkiss rifle. This small force put up a most determined resistance and suffered severely, most of the casualties being caused by bombs. Lieut. Masson was slightly wounded, Cpl. Baker and Pte. McGinty killed, and five other ranks severely wounded. Sgt. Smith was also badly wounded and taken a prisoner, and the Hotchkiss rifle blown to pieces by a grenade.

On enemy reinforcements being pushed forward, this gallant band were forced to retire, L.-Cpl. Morrison with great gallantry covering the withdrawal of the wounded. When the attack commenced the commanding officer was at Brigade Headquarters, half a mile west of Es-Salt, and Major Daly, second in command, moved forward to the front line, arriving as the withdrawal was taking place. He immediately ordered the flanking troops to conform to the movement, and sent up one troop of "A" Squadron as support. The enemy's advance was thus checked, and they were forced to fall back leaving 12 dead on the ground.

During the attack the enemy had brought up a large number of machine guns and opened fire on our posts from all directions. A small party of the Sherwood Rangers arrived to strengthen our line, and a reconnaissance was made with a view to driving the enemy

THE ES-SALT OPERATIONS

force back, but on full reports as to the strength of the various enemy forces, the task was found to be impossible without further assistance, which was not at the time available.

Late in the afternoon orders were received to withdraw to a position nearer the town, thus shortening the line by about 2,000 yards, and a little later word came through to the effect that the whole of the Division would withdraw after dark *via* the Umm Shert track to the Jordan Valley. The Regiment was ordered to cover the withdrawal of the 2nd Brigade and all troops east, and to guard all exits to the north of Es-Salt till midnight.

The advance on Es-Salt had been a difficult undertaking, but it was a trifle compared with the difficulties attending the withdrawal.

The method to be adopted in this connection was as follows: Absolute silence was to be maintained in the outpost line. The 2nd Light Horse Brigade were to withdraw at 9 p.m. to a position covering the exits of Es-Salt to the east. At 11.15 p.m. "B" Squadron was to fall back 1,000 yards, and the Sherwood Rangers were to take up a position 600 yards north of the town, holding this line until the whole of the Regiment had passed through. At 10 p.m. all pack horses except Hotchkiss gun packs were concentrated at Brigade Headquarters and sent under the charge of Lieut. Stevens down the Umm Shert track, so as to get them out of the way before the fighting troops retired.

At 11.30 p.m. snipers were left out whilst the remainder of the mounted forces withdrew to the second position just north of the town, and at midnight the head of the 2nd Light Horse Brigade passed through the town on their way down the track. Half an hour later the Regiment, less "B" Squadron, who were to act as rear guard, followed in rear of the 2nd Light Horse Brigade, and at 1.30 a.m. on the 4th passed through the 2nd Brigade, who had taken up a line astride the track two miles south-east of the town. As the last party withdrew the enemy were seen to be making a bombing attack on the sangars which had just been evacuated.

The most critical portion of the withdrawal had now been completed; and up to this everything had gone smoothly, but all ranks fully realized the difficulties still to be met in withdrawing from the presence of a resolute enemy and handicapped by having to travel down a rocky slope on which movement could only be made with difficulty, in single file. The drop from Es-Salt to the valley represented a fall of approximately 4,000 feet in a distance of 10 miles.

At 4 a.m. the Regiment arrived at the point where the Umm Shert track leads down the final slope to the valley, and as this descent was commenced enemy artillery opened a heavy shrapnel and high explosive shell fire from the direction of Umm es Shert and Red Hill. Fortunately their ranging was faulty, and no casualties were incurred. At 6 a.m. the tail of the Regiment cleared the foothills and proceeded to a point about one mile south-east of the Auja ford, where it bivouacked.

Horses and men were feeling the strain of the strenuous work of the past six days, both having been without rations for the last two. Ration convoys which had been held in readiness ever since the operations were commenced were now rushed forward, and a good meal soon put all ranks into their usual good spirits.

At 7.30 p.m. the Brigade marched *via* the Ghoraniyeh Bridge and Jericho to the bivouac site at the foot of Mount Forty, arriving at 9.30 p.m., and settling down for a much-needed night's rest.

During the operations aeroplanes were used to carry comforts to the wounded in the hills.

These operations could be classed as a very successful raid, as in the vicinity of Es-Salt some 1,200 Turks and Germans had been killed or captured, with small loss to ourselves, besides which 30 machine guns, five motor lorries, and large quantities of war material had been captured.

CHAPTER XXVI

THE AUJA BRIDGEHEAD

All visions of a good long rest at Jebel Kuruntul after the extremely hard work of the past week were soon dispelled, as at 1 p.m. on the 5th May orders were received that the Brigade would move in one hour's time to reinforce the New Zealand Mounted Rifles, who were digging a position to protect the Auja bridgehead.

The Auckland Mounted Rifles were holding the left bank of the Jordan near the junction of the two rivers, and handed over this position to the Brigade on its arrival about 4 p.m.

The commanding officers of the Light Horse Regiments, together with Lieut.-General Sir H. G. Chauvel, made a reconnaissance of the proposed position, and decided on the defence lines to be taken up. The 9th and 10th Regiments were ordered to take over the outer line, the 9th on the right, whilst the 8th Regiment was sent along the right bank of the river to watch the Wadi Mellahah.

The Regiment moved from bivouac at 1.45 p.m. and proceeded at a trot to the bridgehead. On arrival the New Zealanders reported that earlier in the day much enemy movement had been observed along the foothills, but that the situation was then quiet. The Regiment dismounted and put down horse lines on the right bank of the river, and after having detailed a party to stay with the horses paraded dismounted and carrying all available entrenching tools.

Crossing the river by the pontoon bridge, the dismounted party proceeded to climb the steep bank on the opposite side. A few minutes after the top was reached working parties could be seen in all directions, every man putting his best efforts into the task, as the need of good cover was clear to all. It was expected that the enemy would lose no time in trying to drive us from this important position, so all hands were kept at work throughout the night, and by morning a good line had been prepared and protected by wire entanglements.

The defence system consisted of a front line of isolated trenches, each trench being about 100 yards from those on either hand, and with the line running in a semi-circle about 1,500 yards from the bridgehead. A support line was dug 200 yards in rear, and a third line consisting of strongpoints 100 yards in rear of the supports. At 7 p.m. all except three men per troop were brought up from the horse lines to assist in the work, and patrols were sent out during the night to watch for enemy movement.

This turned out to be the commencement of a period which will never be forgotten by those who shared it, viz., the long and monotonous defence of the Jordan Valley, which lay 1,292 feet below sea level, and was infested with millions of mosquitos. It was said to be unfit for human habitation during the long, weary months of summer, but that point did not prevent our force from holding these important points. The whole aspect of the place was forbidding, whilst the atmosphere was heavy and depressing on account of the extreme heat which often reached the vicinity of 130 in the shade.

Scorpions, spiders of the tarantula variety, snakes, and sand flies were plentiful and helped to while away one's leisure moments. It was some small consolation to know that the Turks would have their share of these blessings, but they had the advantage of being able to send parties of men into the hills of Moab for a cool change, thus giving them a respite from the tortures of the valley.

By the 6th the troops had thoroughly settled down in their new position, which was steadily improved by working parties day and night. The usual precaution of standing to arms one hour before daylight each day was observed, and patrols sent out. These patrols came in contact with enemy cavalry in the direction of Umm Shert, with whom they exchanged shots. A battery of enemy mountain guns shelled our position frequently, but did little damage.

About 10 p.m. on the 6th word came through that about 300 of the enemy had broken through the right flank of the 5th Mounted Brigade, who were stationed about two miles along the river to our left. The 8th Regiment was therefore withdrawn from the line and sent along the Wadi Mellahah, and shortly afterwards the enemy were reported to have retired. Working parties were sent to the right bank of the river to cut a road down the steep bank in order that the wheeled transport could reach the horse lines. This work was very trying, as the drop was about 200 feet, and the task a difficult one. Great credit is due to the engineer who surveyed the route and superintended its construction.

Shortly after dawn on the 7th six enemy planes, under cover of the heavy mist, flew over the lines and dropped a number of bombs. The enemy artillery also showed great activity during the day, subjecting our lines to constant shelling, but again little damage was done and the working parties were not interrupted. As a precaution against hostile air raids all ranks were ordered to dig narrow trenches alongside their tents, about 4 feet deep. Orders were issued that on the signal being given all ranks would immediately go to ground in their trenches, commonly known as "funk holes."

On the 9th May the Regiment took over the bridgehead defences, which now included a position about one mile north of the bridge, and between the River Jordan and the Wadi El Mellahah. Two troops of "C" Squadron, with three Hotchkiss rifles were detailed to hold this position, whilst the remainder of the Regiment held the

THE AUJA BRIDGEHEAD

main position. Four sections of the 3rd Machine Gun Squadron were also sent into the main position, and the remainder of the Brigade remained in reserve. The trenches were completed by the installation of a complete telephone system, connecting all points; and the Artillery on several occasions practised barrage fire over the front of the trenches.

On the 17th May the Regiment was relieved by the 10th Light Horse, and all ranks returned to the horse lines on the west bank of the river. The Regiment continued to find working parties as required, and sent out patrols daily. Several prisoners were captured by these patrols, who were not interfered with except that they were occasionally shelled by enemy artillery.

Towards the end of May the enemy brought into position a gun of much longer range, using an aeroplane for observation purposes. Examination of one of these shells proved the gun to be a 4.1 naval gun, a piece of ordnance capable of outranging any gun we had on that portion of the front. Constant shelling from this gun caused a great amount of inconvenience, but although the shelling was good the damage was slight. The shells used were naval, armour-piercing, and in most cases buried themselves in the ground without exploding.

At night the enemy were noticed to be making a great display of "Very lights" (coloured lights fired from a pistol) which gave one the impression that they were celebrating some great event. The lights were accompanied by great bursts of rifle and machine gun fire and caused much speculation as to its meaning, as no British troops were near enough to be the cause of it. Information from prisoners, who were captured in small parties daily, on this point was to the effect that the enemy were in dread of another raid by our force, which was probably correct.

On the 31st Sgt. E. P. Lee, with "D" Troop of "A" Squadron, when patrolling the east bank of the Jordan at 5.30 a.m. was attacked by a party of the enemy 50 strong, who had advanced from the north, and at the same moment another patrol attacked from the north-east. Sgt. Lee therefore withdrew to a position about 700 yards to his rear, and sending his horses to cover, opened a brisk fire on the enemy. The enemy forces, taking full advantage of all available cover, endeavoured to cut off the troop, and several times made an attempt to close in with the bayonet, but the steady fire maintained by the troop held them up, and at 1.30 p.m. they withdrew. Sgt. Lee then completed his patrol and returned to Headquarters.

On the 1st June orders were received to the effect that the 22nd Yeomanry Brigade would take over the position on the 4th, and parties of officers from that Brigade arrived to make themselves conversant with the defences, 130 men were employed in narrowing the bed of the Wadi in order to make the steam move more swiftly, thereby preventing the mosquitos from breeding in it.

On the 2nd all ranks stood to arms at 3.30 a.m., but there was no indication that anything unusual was about to happen. A heavy mist had settled over the valley, with not a breath of wind to disturb the low-lying clouds, and the silence seemed uncanny.

Shortly after 5 a.m. the drone of aeroplanes could be heard over the lines, but nothing could be seen, although it was evident that they were flying exceptionally low. A few minutes later planes could be distinctly heard coming along the valley, and orders were given for all ranks to retire to their "funk holes." This proved a wise precaution, as a few seconds later a perfect hail of bombs was showered on the lines, whilst at the same time each airman opened fire with his machine gun.

The units of the Brigade were bivouacked in a small clearing near the bridgehead, and were therefore much closer together than was usually the case. Under these circumstances they presented a target no enemy airman could resist, as such opportunities were few and far between, but this could not be avoided under the circumstances. Actually flying lower than the tops of the banks on either side of the depression the planes circled over the camp dropping their bombs wherever they thought troops were likely to be, and after raking the whole area with machine gun fire, they flew off to bomb the 4th Brigade.

The timely warning to take cover had been complied with by all except two men of the Regiment, and these two were our only casualties, as both were hit. The horses, however, which were compelled to stay in the open, were not so fortunate, three being killed and 11 wounded. The casualties of the Brigade during the raid amounted to 10 men wounded and 103 animals wounded or killed.

It was stated that the planes, between 12 and 16 in number, had recently arrived from Germany under the command of one of their most famous airmen, and during the raid had dropped about 100 15-lb. bombs. Four Hotchkiss guns, specially mounted by the Regiment to deal with aircraft, were brought into action, but owing to the invisibility could not claim to have done any damage.

At 8.30 p.m. on the 3rd the Regiment moved to Ain ed Duk, arriving at 10.45 p.m. This place is named after a fine spring of beautiful fresh water running out of the foothills, about one mile north of the Mount of Temptation.

At 6.30 p.m. on the following day the Regiment took over the front line of this sector from the 7th Light Horse Regiment. A camp was formed near the spring for the remainder of the Regiment, from which supplies were forwarded daily to the front line, which consisted of a series of posts named Wood, Wild, Wain, Wart, and Wax. One squadron held these posts by day, a second squadron being sent in at night, whilst the third squadron acted as a support.

The work of improving these strong points was pushed rapidly forward, but owing to the rocky nature of the country the work was exceptionally heavy. Patrols were sent out daily in the direction of Tel el Truny which was usually held by the enemy in force.

On the 16th June the Wellington Mounted Rifles took over the defences, and the Regiment moved to Brigade bivouac at Tel es Sultan. On the following morning the Brigade moved to a point two miles east of Jericho where it remained as a reserve, whilst the Anzac Mounted Division made a reconnaissance towards Shunet Nimrin. An enemy long-range naval gun, firing at a range of 17,000 yards, bombarded Jericho for two hours, but although the shells fell close to the town they did little damage beyond giving the natives a big fright.

At 7.30 p.m. the Brigade, less 10th Regiment, proceeded *via* the Roman road to Talaat ed Dumm, arriving there at 10.30 p.m. In spite of the bad impression this place had made on all ranks during their first visit to its barren hills, it was a welcome change after the heat and dust of the valley. This move was a prelude to a more welcome change, lasting for close on three weeks, in the Judean Hills.

On the 21st the Brigade marched out on the Jerusalem Road, halting at kilo 12 for three and a half hours to allow the 2nd Light Horse Brigade, who were returning to the valley, to pass through. At midnight the march was resumed, Jerusalem being passed in the early hours of the morning. Moving along the Beersheba Road, the column marched to a point a few miles south of Bethlehem, known as Solomon's Pools. These wonderful reservoirs, supposed to have been constructed by King Solomon, were close alongside the white limestone road, and contained a plentiful supply of fresh water.

They had been constructed at the head of a deep ravine and splendidly sited. Below the pools could be seen the roof and spires of the Monastery of the Closed Garden with its wonderful orchard enclosed by high walls. The surrounding country was extremely hilly, the hillsides being terraced and cultivated with vineyards in all directions. The Regiment bivouacked on the lower terraces near the pools, and after the loose stones had been removed a comfortable camp was laid out.

All ranks soon settled down to enjoy the change, the cool and beautiful climate being a big contrast to the stifling atmosphere of the valley. Canteens were organized and well stocked, and a supply of beer was obtained.

Training was commenced shortly after arrival to keep the men in condition, but this was mostly of a light nature. Parties of men under the charge of an officer were allowed leave to visit Jerusalem and Bethlehem, all ranks taking the opportunity to visit the holy places, and do some shopping, mostly consisting of the purchase of presents for the dear ones in the homeland.

The Brigade Band, which had been rusticating at Port Said, was brought forward, and several good concerts were arranged, the Brigade also being visited by the theatrical companies of several

British units camped in the area. Many of these shows were of a first-class nature, being complete with dresses and scenery fit to put on the boards of any theatre, whilst the singing and make-up of the men in female attire was a surprise to all.

In view of an early return to the valley all ranks were again inoculated against cholera and typhoid. On the 9th July orders were received, and on the 10th the Brigade moved out on its way to Talaat ed Dumm, en route for the valley. The short rest amidst such beautiful surroundings, and the wonderful climate of the hills, had worked wonders with all ranks, and it was in the highest spirits that the Regiment set out on this march, caring nothing for what lay ahead.

CHAPTER XXVII

THE RETURN TO THE VALLEY

On the 10th July, 1918, at 5.30 p.m., the Regiment, with the remainder of the Brigade, moved to Talaat ed Dumm, arriving at that place at 1.15 a.m. the following day. The night was very dark and the descent of the steep hill, with its hairpin bends, presented a difficult problem for the transport. Two G.S. wagons went over the bank at the roadside, Driver Whelan being badly bruised and sent to hospital.

On the 11th orders were received from B.H.Q. to lay out the present position as a permanent bivouac. Tents were therefore issued and pitched and roads constructed; but this proved slow work, owing to the rocky nature of the country. The prospect of making a lengthy stay at this bivouac was regarded with anything but pleasure. Great was our joy, therefore, when at 6.20 a.m. on the 14th word came through to the effect that the Anzac Mounted Division were being heavily attacked by a force of German infantry at the Mussal-abeh and Abu Tellul positions, and that the Brigade would march immediately to their support.

The Regiment, less transport, moved immediately, *via* the Roman road to the valley, arriving at Imam Aly at 11.15 a.m. Information reached the Regiment at this point to the effect that the 1st Light Horse Brigade had the situation well in hand. A Jaeger (German) battalion, 1,400 strong, with two divisions of Turkish infantry, had made a sudden and unexpected attack on the line held by the 1st Light Horse Brigade, and one Regiment of the 2nd Brigade. The Germans in the centre of the attacking line had broken through two strongposts and succeeded in completely isolating the post on Mussalabeh. Although completely cut off, the defenders of this post gallantly held on until the units of the Brigade had reorganized, when a splendid counter-charge by the 3rd Light Horse Regiment resulted in the complete repulse of the German force, practically all of whom were either killed or captured.

In the first rush the German infantry had swept all before them and succeeded in entering the camp of the 1st Light Horse Brigade, which they passed through like a swarm of locusts. The Brigade had just received a supply of English bottled beer, and as the Germans were experts at mopping up captured positions, they promptly mopped up the Brigade's beer, thus venting their spite on the detested English. No doubt had they been given time they would have obliged with a few bars of their "hymn of hate," but the counter-attack by the 3rd Regiment, made doubly vigorous at the thoughts of the lost beer, completely settled all future efforts on their part.

The prisoners when collected proved to be a fine body of men, and were evidently picked troops. They complained bitterly that the Turks who should have supported them had failed miserably, and had not advanced to close quarters. Documents subsequently captured referred to the unfortunate attack on the Auja line, where the Germans and Turks lost close on 1,200 men.

At 4 p.m. the Regiment was ordered to remain in support of the N.Z.M.R. Brigade, and reported to the G.O.C. near Wart post. The New Zealanders moved out on minor operations, and encountered very heavy artillery fire when crossing the Auja. On return they reported "all clear" for 2,000 yards in front of the line of posts, and the Regiment returned to Makam Imam Aly, where it bivouacked and was joined by the transport.

On the 16th the Brigade was ordered to relieve the 1st Brigade on the Mussalabeh position, and proceeded to the bivouac site at Madbeh for this purpose, taking over the lines of the 1st Light Horse Regiment. As enemy artillery had been particularly active in shelling the horse lines, the horses of the 8th and 10th Regiments were sent back to the Wadi Nueiameh, whilst those of the Regiment were placed in the wadis near Madbeh.

"B" Squadron took over the central position on Abu Tellul, whilst "C" were engaged in burying 30 Germans who had been killed in the recent attack, and whose bodies had just then been located. As "B" returned to the lines on the following morning they were subjected to a severe shelling, sustaining two casualties, one of whom, Cpl. Fletcher, died shortly afterwards. "A" Squadron moved out to the relief of "B" on the 21st, remaining there as a dismounted unit for the remainder of the period, whilst "B" and "C" provided working parties for the strengthening of Vyse, Vale, Vane, and View posts.

Owing to the proximity of the swamps which were infested by millions of the deadly malarial mosquitos, nets were issued on the scale of one per bivouac tent, also veils and mosquito gloves. The heat was intense, and this period proved to be extremely trying. The ground in the valley had been churned into a fine powder, the least movement causing it to rise in clouds. This had a twofold effect, as it not only caused intense irritation and thirst, but gave the enemy a good idea as to the amount of movement in our lines.

On the 30th working parties were cancelled, one squadron being detailed each night for outpost duty, and for patrolling in front of G sector. The first patrol sent out encountered a party of the enemy, who were moving towards the posts. This party was at once fired on, one man being killed and the remainder forced to retire. The body of the dead Turk was searched for papers, but none of any

THE RETURN TO THE VALLEY 141

importance were found. On the 6th August, at 1 a.m., the patrol from "C" Squadron were attacked and forced to retire. Lieut. J. M. McDonald immediately led the patrol back to the position which was re-occupied, L.-Cpl. McIntosh being wounded by a bomb during the movement.

On the 8th a successful reconnaissance was carried out by a special patrol under Lieut. J. M. McDonald. The patrol had to report on the nature of the country in our immediate front, also as to the nature of the enemy defences between El Baghalat and a point on the west bank of the Jordan, about three miles north of Maskerrah. This task was carried out in a most creditable manner, Lieut. McDonald and the members of his patrol being congratulated by the Brigadier on their fine work.

During the following night Lieut. Bridger Lane took another patrol into the enemy country, making a reconnaissance to the east of that made by Lieut. McDonald's patrol. In spite of the fact that the enemy were very active at this time, this patrol was also successful in carrying out its object, and returned safely to our lines, being congratulated on its performance.

On the following day the Regiment took over the line of posts, Maskerrah, Mussalabeh, and Vyse, with "A" Squadron holding the Bluff and Abu Tellul. Maskerrah was close alongside the big swamp with its millions of mosquitos, and it cannot be denied that they took a very active part in the Great War. It is certain that the Turks, who took little, if any preventive measures against these pests, suffered severely, as in spite of all precautions taken, over 80 per cent. of the men who did duty in that area were infected by malaria, several of the cases proving fatal.

On the 12th a heavy bombardment was observed to the north-east, which proved to be an attack by the 60th Division, who gave the enemy little rest. On the following day word came through to the effect that the attack had been entirely successful, a number of enemy trenches being captured at small cost to ourselves, whilst the enemy were roughly handled and lost a number of prisoners.

At 3 p.m. on the 13th orders were received to hand over the positions to the 1st Battalion of the British West India Regiment, commonly known as "The Gollywogs." These men were somewhat of a puzzle to our troops at first, for although they were black as jet they all spoke perfect English and appeared to be well educated, and good soldiers.

The relief being carried out, the Regiment concentrated at No. 1 crossing of the Wadi Auja, to which place the horses had been brought from the Wadi Nueiameh. After mounting, the Regiment moved to Ain ed Duk, which was reached at 2.30 a.m. on the following day, and remained as a support to the West India Regiment. Major Bleechmore and 35 other ranks were left with the 1st Battalion, B.W.I. Regiment as a support, and Lieut. Hargrave with 41 other ranks was sent to the 2nd Battalion on similar duty.

From Ain ed Duk a patrol was sent out daily to Tel el Truny. This patrol was always fired on from Tel el Risheh at long range, but no casualties resulted. Tel el Truny was a charming spot at the foot of a deep gorge, the luxuriant growth in the locality being a great contract to the bareness of the Jordan Valley.

On the 22nd August, the parties under Major Bleechmore and Lieut. Hargrave were recalled, and arrived at Regimental Headquarters at 6.30 p.m. At 7.30 p.m. the Regiment, on being relieved by the 1st Light Horse Regiment, moved *via* the old road to Talaat ed Dum, arriving there at 11.45 p.m. During the first portion of the march the dust was so thick that it was impossible to see the man riding at one's side, although actually moving knee to knee.

This was accounted for by the fact that as one Brigade moved out along the valley the other Brigade was moving in, and there was not a breath of wind to shift the clouds of low-lying dust. Needless to say, all ranks were delighted to reach the plain and get a breath of fresh air.

CHAPTER XXVIII

LUDD

When the order for the move to Talaat ed Dum was received it was not thought that we were parting from the Jordan Valley for good, but that it was simply for a few days' spell in the cool breezes of the hills. There had been many indications that in the near future every effort would be made to deal a crushing blow to the enemy, and the time of the year to conduct such operations was fast approaching, still there had not been the numerous rumours that usually preceded such movements.

It was expected that the General Officer Commanding-in-Chief, General Allenby, himself an old cavalry soldier, would make the most of his mounted force during the next operations, as the country was suitable, and there was an abundance of water.

On arrival at Talaat ed Dum the Regiment bivouacked, the following day being spent in rest. Orders arrived to the effect that the Brigade would march *via* Jerusalem, Enab, Latron, and Ramleh to Ludd.

At 7.30 p.m. on the 23rd the Regiment marched out and passing through Jerusalem at 11 p.m. reached Enab at 3 a.m. Lieut.-Colonel Scott assumed command of the Brigade, and Major Charley took over the command of the Regiment. Resting by day and marching by night, the Regiment arrived at Ludd at 1 a.m. on the 26th, and formed a camp in an olive grove.

The following day was spent in laying out the lines and making everyone comfortable after the strenuous months spent in the heat the dust of the valley, the beautiful surroundings of this camp being appreciated by all. All ideas of a long rest were quickly dissipated by the receipt of orders for intense training, and this was carried out to the letter.

To the delight of all ranks it became known that the Brigade was to be armed with swords and used as cavalry in the coming operations. The Quartermaster drew swords from Ordnance on the following day, and these were immediately issued to the troops. The prospect of carrying out a charge under cavalry conditions appealed strongly, and the keenest interest was taken in the new instruction.

On the following day classes of instruction in sword drill were commenced under the supervision of Major Kavanagh, G.S.O., of the Australian Mounted Division. Instruction was also given in cavalry drill, which differs considerably from light horse drill, and owing to the short time available for the amount of training necessary, reveille was sounded at 4.30 a.m. daily, the troops parading for drill at 5 a.m.

On the 3rd September an epidemic of influenza broke out in the Regiment, and 40 men were placed on the sick list. The health of all ranks had suffered considerably by the conditions of life in the Jordan Valley, and in a few days practically the whole of "A" Squadron were on the sick list, as well as a number of men from other squadrons. The medical officer, Captain Shelly, had a particularly strenuous time looking after this abnormal number of patients, but rose to the occasion in splendid style, and soon had them back at duty.

On the 6th Major Daly arrived from hospital and took over command of the Regiment, Major Charley returning to duty with "C" Squadron. On the 11th Colonel Scott returned and took command of the Regiment.

As most of the men were now fit, the special training was pushed rapidly forward. Several changes took place in the equipment of the Regiment. Consequent on the men being issued with the sword it became impossible for them to carry the rifle slung, and cavalry rifle buckets were issued. The amount of ammunition to be carried on the person was reduced to 90 rounds, a second bandolier to be carried round the horses' necks being issued.

Other changes included the Chursa water-lifting apparatus, for drawing water from the deep wells, and portable troughs made of rubberized canvas with brackets and pegs. Explosives for demolition purposes, hand and rifle grenades, parachute smoke signals, and Popham pannels for signalling from the ground to aeroplanes were also issued, as was an additional supply of entrenching tools.

As it was expected that during the coming operations the wheeled transport might have to be abandoned, every offside horse was issued with a complete set of pack saddlery. Load tables were so arranged that in this event the load could be quickly transferred to the packs.

All surplus kit had to be dumped at Divisional Headquarters, and all stores that could possibly be done without were returned to Ordnance. This entailed an enormous amount of work, and it is no exaggeration to say that the busiest man in the Regiment at this time was the Quartermaster, who was responsible for the carrying out of these alterations.

On the 12th a Regimental tactical scheme was carried out, on the 13th a Brigade scheme, and on the following day the whole of the Division, including packs and wheel transport paraded for inspection by the G.O.C. Major-General Hodgson. During this parade the transport had to abandon their wagons and convert to packs. The smartness with which this was done by the transport of the Regiment was specially commented on by the G.O.C.

On the morning of the 17th the following officers of the Division assembled at Headquarters to meet the Commander-in-Chief, General

THE BARADA GORGE, DAMASCUS
Copyright by Australian War Museum

THIRD LIGHT HORSE BRIGADE CAMP AT TRIPOLI
9th Light Horse Camp in foreground.   *Australian Official Photograph*

Allenby: Lieut.-General Sir H. G. Chauvel (Corps Commander), Major-General Hodgson (Divisional Commander), Brig.-General Wilson (3rd Brigade), Lieut.-Colonel Bourchier (4th Brigade), Brig.-General Onslow (5th Brigade), Lieut.-Colonel McLaurin (8th Light Horse Regiment), Lieut.-Colonel Scott (9th Light Horse Regiment), Lieut.-Colonel Olden (10th Light Horse Regiment), Lieut.-Colonel J. W. Parsons (11th Light Horse Regiment), Lieut.-Colonel Cameron (12th Light Horse Regiment), Lieut.-Colonel Langley (14th Light Horse Regiment), Lieut.-Colonel Mills (15th Light Horse Regiment), and Colonel Blanc (commanding a French Cavalry Regiment, 3rd Spahis), and the officers commanding the technical units of the Division.

General Sir E. H. Allenby, after cordially greeting each officer present, said: "I came here, gentlemen, to wish you good luck, and to tell you that I consider you are on the eve of a great victory. Practically everything depends on the secrecy, rapidity, and accuracy of the cavalry movement." The Commander-in-Chief then briefly outlined the strategical situation as it existed at that moment, giving his reasons why the prospects of victory seemed so bright, and indicating that the hoodwinking of the Turkish Commander-in-Chief, Limon von Sanders, was already apparent. He concluded his terse and soldierly address with these words: "You have trained strenuously and devotedly at a time when you should have been enjoying a well-deserved rest, after your long and trying summer in the Jordan Valley; but I hope, and feel confident, that you are at last about to reap the reward of your devotion."

Following General Allenby's visit a conference was held at which the Divisional Commander, Major-General Hodgson, explained the role of our Division in the first phase of the forthcoming operations.

The intention of the Commander-in-Chief was briefly as follows: The Turkish line at this time was much the same as it was in April and May, 1918, but had been considerably strengthened by incessant labour, particularly in the centre, or Nablus sector, and the left flank covering the Jordan Valley and the Hills of Moab. It extended in a continuous line from the sea, north of Jaffa, through Tabsor, in a general direction south-east to the Jordan, 10 miles north of the Ghoraniyeh Bridge, thence across the plain through the Moab Hills to Amman to the Hedjaz Railway.

From the sea to the Jordan Valley their line was held by the 7th and 8th Turkish Armies, whilst the 4th Turkish Army, commanded by Djemal Pasha, the younger, commonly known as "Petit Djemal," held the Moab Hills and railway.

By various ruses the enemy had been led to believe that the main offensive would be directed against his left flank, whereas General Allenby's intention was to break the Turkish line near the sea, by concentrated artillery fire, followed by a quick rush of infantry. By this means a gap, sufficiently large to allow the passage of three

Divisions of Cavalry to pass through was to be created, and this cavalry force were then to push on, along the coastal sector, with all possible speed until the Nahr Iskanderun was crossed at, or near, Sheik Mohammed.

The 4th and 5th Cavalry Divisions and the Australian Mounted Division were the troops selected for this part of the operations, whilst the Anzac Mounted Division, with four Infantry Battalions, an Indian Infantry Brigade, and Artillery, under the command of Major-General Chaytor, were to operate against the 4th Turkish Army in the Jordan Valley.

The remainder of the Infantry, comprising the 20th and 21st Army Corps were to hold their present line, and be ready to join in the general advance, with Nablus as their main objective.

The 5th Cavalry Division were to cross the Nahr Iskanderum and move along the cost, their ultimate objective being Nazareth, whilst the 4th Division were to push through the pass to the plain of Esdraelon, near Megiddo. The Australian Mounted Division were to follow the 4th Division as far as Megiddo and operate from this point as ordered. It was expected that the 4th Division would, by its rapid advance, capture El Afuleh and Beisan, whilst the Australian Mounted Division held the pass, thereby preventing a break through. They were also to send a force to outflank and capture Jenin, thus cutting off the Turkish troops retiring from the direction of Nablus.

As a precaution, none of these instructions were committed to writing. Orders relating to the supply and transport and such other matters as may be generally known were issued in the usual printed form, but these documents were ordered to be destroyed before the operations commenced. These precautions were necessary owing to the presence of enemy agents who were known to mix with our forces. The large number of natives employed by our force, also the inhabitants, could never be trusted, but prior to and during these operations, it is safe to say, none of the intentions of the higher command leaked out.

The 3rd Light Horse Brigade were detailed to act as advance guard to the Division, so it was clear that our Brigade would get its fair share of the work in view. The Commanding Officer called his officers together and explained the particular part set down for the Regiment, they in turn making it clear to the members of their respective troops.

On the morning of the 18th September, all was bustle and excitement. All camp gear, surplus clothing, bivouac sheets, blankets, cooking utensils, etc., had to be packed and carted to the Brigade dump, to be left under a guard until required, and the camp site thoroughly cleaned.

After the evening meal the Regiment, 388 strong, paraded ready to march, and at 7 p.m. mounted and moved to the place of assembly, the Divisional parade ground near the Jaffa road. All ranks were in the best of spirits at the prospect of taking part in one of the greatest adventures cavalry ever undertook.

CHAPTER XXIX

THE DASH THROUGH. JENIN

At 10 p.m. on the 18th September, 1918, the Regiment reached a point near Sarona and bivouacked. All ranks were advised to get as much rest as possible in view of the hard task in front of them, and to be ready to march at 6.30 a.m. on the following morning.

At 4.30 a.m. on the 19th a furious bombardment to our left announced that the great offensive had begun. The roar of the masses of guns was deafening, and it was clear to all that this particular position would soon be taken.

Horses were saddled and all ranks hastily prepared to move. Some anxious moments ensued before the great tidings came through to the effect that the Infantry had broken the enemy line at Tabsor, and a few minutes later orders were received for the Regiment to move to the point of assembly two miles east of Jelil. After watering the horses the Regiment moved towards Tabsor.

About one mile south of our wire a halt was made to feed, after which the Brigade moved through the enemy's wire in the vicinity of Tabsor, and continued north along the sandhills. Few traces of the morning's fight could be seen, but two or three small parties of prisoners were met and a few captured guns which were awaiting removal.

Nothing was seen of our Infantry who, after smashing their way through the enemy line had, in accordance with pre-arranged plans, swung to the right in an easterly direction. The Brigade passed through Khurbet es Zerkie and El Mughair to the Nahr Iskanderun near Sheik Mohammed, which was reached at 7 p.m.

The wheeled transport of the Division had been formed into three echelons, "A", "B", and "C", for the operations, "A" consisting of ammunition, water and medical carts accompanied the troops; "B" consisting of supplies (about 100 wagons) followed in rear of the Division, whilst "C" (baggage) brought up the rear. The supply echelon of the Division, 3rd, 4th, and 5th Light Horse Brigades, Corps Troops, Divisional and French Troops, were placed under the orders of Major T. H. Darley, whilst the baggage echelon was placed under the orders of Capt. B. B. Ragless.

The Regiment bivouacked for the night at Sheik Mohammed and at 1 a.m. on the 20th moved off in a north-easterly direction, *via* Zeleife, arriving at Kh Shumrah at 5 a.m. The 5th Cavalry Division had continued to move along the coast, whilst the 4th Division, preceding the 3rd Brigade by about 12 hours, had moved east to El Lejjun, with orders to push on and occupy El Afuleh and Nazareth.

At Kh Shumrah, near the railway line, a party of about 100 Turkish prisoners were observed under escort of Indian Cavalry, and many enemy transport animals and vehicles were found abandoned along the road. From Shumrah the Regiment followed the metalled road leading up the valley of the Wadi Arah and passed Musmus. Shortly after passing the latter place the road passed over a steep rise from the top of which the plain of Esdraelon, with Mount Tabsor and the Nazareth Hills, could be plainly seen.

On this same road in 1479 B.C. King Thotmes III, with an army of Egyptians, marched to attack the King of Kedesh on the plain of Esdraelon.

The Brigade arrived at El Lejjun at 11 a.m., watered, fed, and off-saddled. Water was obtained from a good stream, and during the short halt all ranks enjoyed a refreshing bath and rest. It was found that one thousand prisoners had been taken at this point by the 4th Division, and a little later steady streams of prisoners, moving towards Lejjun, told the tale of the splendid work of the Indian Cavalry. Two thousand Germans and Turks who had been specially despatched by the enemy high command in a desperate effort to seize the pass, and by so doing delay our advance, were now prisoners in our hands on the very ground they had been sent to hold. Things were indeed going well, and here on the actual field of Armageddon, the Regiment was eagerly waiting orders to strike its first blow in the present operations.

At 3.30 p.m. orders were issued to saddle up, and to be ready to move rapidly and seize all northern exits of Jennin. At 4 p.m. the Brigade, less 8th Regiment, who were left to hold Lejjun, advanced on Jenin in which direction many huge fires could be seen. Small parties of enemy troops could be seen on the right flank, and were immediately charged by a troop of "C" Squadron under Lieut. Cruddas, D.C.M., the whole party being captured.

Lieut. J. M. McDonald with two troops was sent out to reinforce Lieut. Cruddas, and located a large force camped amongst the olive groves immediately north-east of Kefr Adan. Drawing swords, the two troops formed line and charged, but the astonishment of the Turks at being so suddenly confronted by our men was so great that they surrendered without firing a shot. The officers who were amongst the prisoners stated openly that they had no idea we had broken through their line.

The troops had a very busy time rounding up the stragglers, which included a number of Turkish cavalry. Prisoners on being formed up and counted were found to number 1,800, including many Germans, over 200 horses, 200 mules, and many donkeys. This small affair did not delay the Brigade, which moved on to its objective.

THE DASH THROUGH JENIN 149

The railway was crossed at 6 p.m. and by 6.30 all roads leading north from Jenin had been blocked. "A" Squadron sent out strong patrols north to the vicinity of Mukeibileh, and 29 prisoners were taken; 30 motor lorries and a number of motor ambulances were located abandoned on the Afuleh-Jenin road, and two motor ambulances, one being fitted with a combination dynamo and motor set, were located by "B" Squadron.

At 10 p.m. the Regiment concentrated north-east of the town, one troop under Lieut. Masson being left in position. Major Charley with "C" Squadron was detailed to take charge of the prisoners who were being collected at the point where the main road crossed the railway. At 1 a.m. on the 21st the Regiment moved to assist the 10th Light Horse in collecting prisoners who were surrendering in large numbers, and by daylight about 7,000 had been rounded up at Brigade Headquarters.

At 5 a.m. the Regiment moved to the west of the town and occupied the aerodrome. "A" Squadron rejoined and together with "B" were sent into the town to clear it of stragglers. About 300 were collected and sent to the concentration point near the railway. An enormous quantity of war material was captured, in spite of the fact that the enemy had set fire to their stores, but most of the aeroplanes had been destroyed. One small scouting plane was found intact on the outskirts of the town. The narrow streets of the town were choked with enemy transport wagons, most of which were in a dilapidated condition. The stores in the town had been looted, chiefly by the natives, and later in the day this matter became so serious that it was made known to them that anyone found looting would be shot.

A very fine monument to some of the German airmen who had been killed on this front was found on the north side of the town.

Armourer-Sgt. Cozens located an enemy gun, 10.4 centimetre, No. M 15, K.A.N. 342, near the railway station, and "B" Squadron made the capture of the day by taking 120 cases of champagne from a cave near the station, without a casualty. A guard was promptly mounted over this last batch of prisoners, but a large quantity of it escaped before it could be taken over.

At 11 a.m. the Regiment moved to the northern side of the town and bivouacked on the outskirts of the orchards, sending guards into the town, and patrols in various directions. Capt. A. H. Nelson was detailed to carry out the duties of Military Governor of Jenin. Many of the German and Turkish officer prisoners admitted being taken completely by surprise at our unexpected appearance across the northern side of Jenin, stating that they thought we must have been landed at Haifa, never believing it possible that we could have moved along the coast so rapidly. The Regiment moved to a position about one mile north of the town and bivouacked. The prisoners taken by the Brigade during the past 24 hours reached the huge total of 8,000.

At 4.30 a.m. on the 22nd September Major H. M. Parsons, D.S.O., with a composite squadron consisting of two troops each of "A" and "B" Squadrons, moved along the Jenin-Beisan road to endeavour to capture a large party of Turkish infantry who were reported to be retreating in a northerly direction. By 9 a.m. he had reached Tell esh Shok and sent back word that he was on a rise two miles distant from and overlooking the town of Beisan, and that he had observed our Cavalry entering that place from the direction of Afuleh.

No trace had been seen of the retreating enemy, who had evidently changed their direction. At the village of Jelbon, No. 769, Cpl. A. H. Tod, of "A" Squadron, with a small patrol on the right flank, discovered a party of the enemy concealed behind a large cactus hedge. He skilfully reconnoitred their position and manoeuvred his patrol to their flank. Drawing swords, he formed his few men in line, and made a dashing charge, capturing three officers and 28 Turkish infantry. At 2.30 p.m. the Brigade moved to a position about two miles north of El Afuleh, and Major Parsons, with the composite squadron, rejoined at 10 p.m.

In the early hours of the 25th orders were received to hold the Regiment in readiness to advance on Tiberias and to attack that place at dawn on the following day. One squadron of the 8th Light Horse was sent out to make a vigorous reconnaissance of that place. At 5 p.m. the Brigade moved out, leaving the Regiment to follow as soon as the various detached parties had returned, and at 6.45 the Regiment followed suit, passing through Nazareth at 10.30 p.m. Some delay was caused in passing through the narrow streets of this ancient city owing to the congested nature of the traffic and dust, but at 11.30 the Regiment arrived at Kefr Kenna (Cana of Galilee) and after a short halt continued the march at midnight.

At 5 a.m. on the 26th the Brigade arrived on the high ground overlooking Tiberias. The enemy were reported to have evacuated the town, and to be retiring to the Jordan south of Lake Huleh. A small party of Germans had crossed the Sea of Galilee in a motor boat and escaped into the hills on the other side. Horses were fed and the men breakfasted, after which the Brigade moved through the town along the western shore of the Sea of Galilee to El Mejdel. At this place the horses were off-saddled, and men and horses enjoyed a good swim.

At 1.15 p.m. "A" Squadron marched out, with orders to move into the hills and occupy Safed, which task was accomplished by 5 p.m. In the last 24 hours this squadron had marched close on 50 miles, mostly on metalled roads, many miles of which were through the hilly country of Galilee. Both men and horses stood the test admirably, and appeared ready for any demands made on them. The Jewish population of the various towns in this district were overjoyed at our occupation, and were astonished to learn that both Haifa and Nazareth had been captured by our troops.

THE DASH THROUGH. JENIN

At 7.45 a.m. on the following day the Brigade moved from El Mejdel to Rosh Pinnar, a prosperous Zionist town, arriving at 11.30 a.m. and halting. The Regiment was pushed forward with orders to force the crossing of the Jordan, word being received as they moved off to the effect that the bridge across the river at Jisr Benat Yakub (the bridge of Jacob's daughter) had been blown up, and that the enemy were holding the crossings in force.

Major C. Bleechmore with one squadron was sent forward to reconnoitre the crossings, and reported that the enemy were holding an entrenched position on the eastern bank, commanding the river from where it flowed out of Lake Huleh to just south of the bridge, which had been considerably damaged by explosives. The strength of the enemy was estimated at about 1,000, with one or two field guns. Strong patrols had been pushed north and south, and into the village of Mishmar Hayarden.

Lieut. E. Hannaford later reported having found a crossing not held by the enemy, about two miles south of the bridge. At 12.30 p.m. the Regiment received orders not to become involved with the enemy, as the Division intended an alteration of plans. By this time the Notts Battery, R.H.A., had opened fire on the enemy position, personally indicated to the Battery Observation Officer by Major Bleechmore. The battery made splendid practice, and succeeded in knocking the enemy gun, which had been placed in position to cover the bridge, off its mounting with its second shot.

At 3 p.m. orders were received that a combined effort would be made to force the crossing. The plan was that the 5th Light Horse Brigade would force the crossing south of the bridge, whilst the Regiment made a demonstrative attack, with its right flank resting at the bridge and its left on a clump of trees at the ford. During this movement the 10th Light Horse were to rush the ford, mounted, supported by covering fire from the 3rd Machine Gun Squadron and the 8th and 9th Light Horse Regiments.

With this object in view the Regiment and 3rd Machine Gun Squadron moved forward and took up their positions under heavy fire. By 3.15 p.m. "A" and "C" Squadrons were in position overlooking the river and ready to support the 10th Regiment with their fire. At 4 p.m. the 5th Brigade were observed crossing unopposed at El Min, but the ford in our sector was still strongly held by the enemy, who were in a good position and had the use of good cover.

At 5.30 p.m. the 10th Regiment succeeded in crossing the river, followed by the 8th, and took up a position on the high ground on the eastern bank. At 9.15 p.m. the Regiment, together with the 3rd Machine Gun Squadron, concentrated at Regimental Headquarters, then moved *via* Mishmar Hayarden to the ford at Shejerat Benat Yakub, which was crossed at 10.45 p.m. The casualties of the day consisted of one officer (Lieut. N. Wastell) and four men wounded.

After crossing the ford a halt was made for half an hour to feed the horses, after which the Brigade pushed on with the intention of surrounding Deir es Saras before dawn. This move was made across country, "B" and "C" Squadrons furnishing the advance and flank guards. The going here was particularly bad, the country being rocky, hilly, and trackless; horses having to be led up some of the steep rocky goat tracks for the first couple of miles, after which the conditions slightly improved.

At 5 a.m. on the 28th the Regiment was astride the main road, a little to the east of Deir es Saras, but the enemy were found to have retreated towards Kuneitra. At 6.30 a.m. three enemy planes, flying low, passed over the Brigade and dropped bombs near the bridge over the Jordan. At 7.30 a.m. the Brigade continued the advance along the main road towards Kuneitra, the remainder of the Division following, as each unit crossed the river. Aerial reconnaissance reports showed that the high ground covering the approaches to El Kuneitra to be held by a mixed force of roughly 1,000 of the enemy.

The country being passed through consisted of a high tableland, crossed by a solitary road, on both sides of which, as far as the eye could see, were masses of loose boulders, making progress, off the road, practically impossible. The inhabitants of these parts were Circassians, and friendly to the enemy, with whom they fought, chiefly as cavalry, on their stout little Arab ponies. Several of their patrols were seen in the distance, but these took great care to keep well out of range.

As the high ground overlooking Kuneitra was gained large numbers of Circassian cavalry could be seen retiring in the direction of Sasa; Kuneitra being occupied without resistance at 2.30 p.m. The mayor of the town with an escort came out under cover of an immense white flag and surrendered the town to Major-General Hodgson. After watering the horses on the outskirts of the town, the Brigade moved to a position two and a half miles south of Jeba, where it bivouacked.

This advance had brought the Brigade to within 34 miles of Damascus, the intervening country being open tableland, broken by deposits of lava and basalt. It was, however, abundantly watered by running streams and possessed a good main road.

CHAPTER XXX

THE DASH THROUGH. SASA

A bitterly cold night spent on the rocky ground near Jeba was followed by a dull and gloomy morning, but all ranks were in good heart at the wonderful success met with at every stage of the operations. Damascus was near at hand, and everything pointed to a successful attack, and its early capture.

The general situation on this day, 29th September, 1918, was that the Anzac Mounted Division, under General Chaytor, had captured Amman and the southern portion of the Turkish Army below Amman. The remainder of this army, still a formidable force, were retiring northwards on Damascus along the Hedjaz railway, and was being pursued by the 4th Cavalry Division and the Sheriffian troops.

The 5th Cavalry Division was now moving in rear, and in support of the Australian Mounted Division, the objective being the capture of Damascus and its garrison, and the cutting of the retreat of the 4th Turkish Army. The 7th and 8th Turkish Armies, with the exception of a few stragglers, had ceased to exist, therefore, there only remained the 4th Turkish Army and the garrison of Damascus to deal with. These troops were to be given no respite, but were to be driven as fast as possible, until finally captured, thus completing one of the most wonderful undertakings of any army.

Whilst the troops were having breakfast a distinct earthquake shock was felt, lasting several seconds. At 1.45 p.m. "B" Squadron were sent out as an escort to a party of Engineers to Nahr Mughaniye, at which place a water supply was to be developed. At 2.30 p.m. the Brigade, with the Regiment acting as advance guard, continued the advance. "B" Squadron were ordered to push forward and reconnoitre the enemy position which was reported astride the road in the vicinity of Kanakir and Sasa.

The Brigade arrived at Bahr Mughaniye at 6.30 p.m., where it watered. The Regiment now moved forward to the support of "B" Squadron, who had gained touch with the enemy in the vicinity of Khanakir. Major H. M. Parsons reported the enemy to be holding a very strong position astride the road, about two and a half miles south-west of Sasa. The position consisted of a chain of small hills, almost solid rock, and covered with huge boulders, the position having a frontage of a little over a mile.

Earlier in the evening "B" Squadron had engaged the enemy to find out his strength and disposition as to flanks, but immediately came under heavy rifle and machine gun fire, and sustained a number of casualties. A patrol which had been pushed forward was allowed to pass through by the enemy, and after a brisk fight was captured.

It was imperative that the enemy be driven out of his position without delay, as the whole of the Australian Mounted Division were being held up, and at 8.30 p.m. "A" and "C" Squadrons, under the command of Major T. J. Daly, D.S.O., moved across country to work round the left flank of the enemy position. They were instructed to fire a green flare when the hill on the extreme left of the enemy position had been taken. It was a difficult movement in the darkness, over extremely rough country, composed of lava formations, with deep crevasses from 8 to 10 feet in depth, besides, the leaders being at the disadvantage of not having had the opportunity of making a daylight reconnaissance.

"B" Squadron were ordered to clear the hill nearest the main road and to fire a red flare when the crest had been cleared of the enemy. When this flare was seen it was found that the enemy were still holding the intervening high ground on a frontage of about one mile, the least movement on our part being met with heavy bursts of fire from machine guns which had been laid on the road during daylight.

At 10.20 p.m. green flares were seen in the direction of the two squadrons, and a few minutes later Major Daly reported, by telephone, that he had gained the ridge on the extreme left of the enemy position, and that "A" Squadron were working their way along the ridge. At 11 p.m. the 8th and 10th Light Horse Regiments were ordered to attack between the flanking squadrons of the Regiment. The 8th Regiment came forward dismounted and formed up on the right of the 10th, the two Regiments moving forward in line to the attack, with bayonets fixed.

As the 8th reached the crest of the hill, the hum of motor lorries could be distinctly heard, and it was evident that the enemy had kept these close at hand, in order to get their force away at the last possible moment, and to avoid pursuit by our mounted troops.

"A" Squadron succeeded in capturing 12 Germans, some of whom stated that on seeing the green flares the German officers had realized that they had been outflanked. They had considered it impossible for mounted men to move across such country during the night, and had therefore taken no special steps to guard their flanks. They also stated that their force had commenced to retire immediately the green flares were seen. Th whole position was clear of the enemy by 3 a.m.

The operations had been hard and difficult, owing to the darkness and the state of the surrounding country. The position held by the enemy was splendidly chosen for defence, and covered a good field of

THE DASH THROUGH. SASA

fire. The enemy force was stated to have consisted of 300 German machine gunners and 1,200 Turkish infantry, with four field guns.

At dawn on the 30th as the Brigade had still to be concentrated the 4th Light Horse Brigade passed through, and were ordered to carry on with the pursuit of the retreating enemy force. From the high ground overlooking Sasa several hundred enemy infantry could be seen retiring across the open country in the direction of Damascus. These were eventually overtaken and captured by the 4th Light Horse Brigade.

The 5th Brigade followed in rear of the 4th Brigade, and at 7.30 a.m. the 3rd Brigade moved from Sasa, the Regiment forming the advance guard. As the advance continued the country opened out into a beautiful wide tableland, dotted with villages, and a fair amount of cultivation.

Away on the horizon a cloud of dust marked the advance of the 4th Cavalry Division, who were in hot pursuit of Djemal Pasha's 4th Turkish Army, but the wonderful mobility of the retreating Turks enabled them to reach Damascus.

Pushing forward at a good pace the Brigade reached Khan esh Shiha at 9 a.m., and from this place the first sight of Damascus was obtained. It was reported that a force of approximately 4,000 enemy were in the vicinity of Kaukab.

Orders were received for the approaching march on Damascus by the Australian Mounted Division. The 5th Light Horse Brigade, closely followed by the 3rd Light Horse Brigade, were to outflank the city by moving *via* Katana north-easterly along the foothills to Kalabat el Mezze, whilst two Regiments of the 4th Light Horse Brigade, under Lieut.-Colonel Bourchier, D.S.O., were to move directly on the city *via* Daraya. Each unit moved towards its objective at a trot, and as the rising ground was reached a distant glimpse of the ancient city came into view.

The advance of the Division made a splendid sight, the 4th Brigade on the right, the 5th on the left, and with the 3rd in rear. About two miles south-west of Kaukab the 5th and 3rd Brigades turned slightly to the left and advanced rapidly along the foothills. The 4th Light Horse Brigade were meeting much opposition in the direction of Kaukab, and two batteries of artillery unlimbered and commenced to shell the enemy position.

Under cover of this fire one Regiment of the 4th Brigade were seen to draw swords and clear the position by a splendid charge. The 5th and 3rd Brigades continued their advance until about one mile south-west of El Mezze, when their further advance was checked by the leading Regiment, the French Cavalry, coming under heavy rifle and machine gun fire. The fire was directed from the high walled gardens surrounding the village, and the guns of the R.H.A. were again brought into action. The German gunners were in a well concealed position, and held on grimly, any attempt at movement by our force being met with a storm of bullets. At 2 p.m. the French Cavalry were observed to move west into the hills, followed shortly afterwards by a portion of the 5th Light Horse Brigade.

At 4 p.m. the 3rd Light Horse Brigade moved off, the Regiment being in advance, with orders to cross the Damascus-Beirut railway and endeavour to get astride the main road in the vicinity of Jobar. Progress was slow owing to the terribly rough and steep hills to be crossed.

At 4.45 p.m. "A" Squadron had seized the high ground overlooking Dumar and the Damascus-Beirut main road and railway. The only means of entering the village from this point was by a narrow rocky track. "A" Squadron made two attempts to force this route, but found it to be strongly defended by a number of machine guns placed in and around the village.

The squadron with a section of the 3rd Machine Gun Squadron attached took up a position on the high ground overlooking the village, main road, and railway. Large numbers of the enemy, in great disorder, were attempting to escape in the direction of Beirut, the road being choked with transport of all descriptions. The squadron immediately opened fire on this party, and inflicted heavy casualties. On the arrival of the remainder of the Regiment a few minutes later "B" Squadron and all available machine and Hotchkiss guns were put into the line, concentrating their fire on the road and railway.

The enemy forces were making desperate efforts to escape, and opened a fierce fire on our position. Thousands of the enemy were pushing forward in their endeavour to get through the pass, in spite of the deadly fire brought to bear on them, just one great mass, without order or leaders, each striving to save himself at the expense of his neighbour. Refusing to surrender, they were shot down in scores, and eventually seeing the hopelessness of their attempt, they retired in the direction of Damascus, leaving the Gorge piled with bodies of men and animals.

At dusk a fresh attempt was made to force the track to the village, but as it was strongly held and was likely to lead to heavy casualties, it was decided to wait for daylight. Orders were received at 6.30 p.m. to hold the present position, commanding the main road and railway for the night, and that the advance would be continued at 5 a.m. on the following day.

The Regiment was detailed to send two troops, dismounted, to reconnoitre the road and village as early as possible. Two troops of "C" Squadron, under Lieuts. Hargrave, M.C., and Masson moved out for that purpose at 7.15 p.m. It was a difficult task, but was accomplished without casualty, the troops returning at 9 p.m. Lieut. Hargrave reported that the village had been evacuated with the exception of a few stragglers, and that six hospitals had been located,

THE DASH THROUGH. SASA

these being full of sick and wounded. The main road was blocked by enemy transport, and a Turkish guard was on duty at the railway station. Great credit is due to these two troops for their boldness and daring in successfully reconnoitring the position.

The Regiment held its position during the remainder of the night, intermittent fire being maintained on the road and railway at the entrance to the Adana Gorge. At this point the main road, railway, and the Barada River run side by side through the Gorge. It was estimated that the enemy suffered 700 casualties at this point, besides which hundreds of animals of all descriptions were killed. During the night an enemy train from Beirut passed through the Gorge and was captured by the Brigade when the advance was continued the following day.

CHAPTER XXXI

THE FALL OF DAMASCUS

As day broke on the 1st October, 1918, the beautiful city of Damascus, the Jewel of the East, came into view. Many splendid buildings could be seen, including the main railway station and the military barracks, now used as a hospital, from the staff of which the red crescent was flying. The Barada River wound like a silver thread through the town and surrounding country, with numerous small water channels passing through the beautiful orchards and vineyards which enclosed the city on all sides.

At 5 a.m. the Regiment, with the remainder of the Brigade, crossed the river by the bridge at Dumar and proceeded along the main road towards Damascus. As the advance continued the terrible execution of the previous day became apparent, the road being completely blocked with piles of dead and dying men and animals, and disabled transport. The advance troops reported that for nearly a mile ahead the road was practically impassable, and parties were sent forward to clear a track. It was gruesome task. The wounded Germans and Turks were carried, with as much care as possible, to the grassy bank of the river, where they were left to be collected by our ambulances, which were in rear of the Brigade, whilst the dead were removed to the side of the road to await burial.

Wounded animals were shot and dragged to the side of the road, as were also the vehicles. Many of the vehicles had overturned into the river during the attempt to break through, and had been abandoned.

The advance Regiment, 10th Light Horse, pushed forward and captured the railway station together with the train which had passed through the previous night. About 1,000 prisoners were also taken at this point. A few Germans made an attempt at resistance, but were soon overpowered and taken prisoner. At the barracks a huge force of Turks could be seen on the parade ground, and appeared to be in a state of great confusion. After a slight show of resistance they surrendered to the advance guard.

As the column reached the centre of the city dense crowds filled the streets and squares. A large number of these people carried firearms of some description, and as a sign of rejoicing they proceeded to discharge them into the air, so that what was really a peaceful entry sounded more like a desperate battle. The crowds were composed of all classes: Arabs in their long galabiehs, Syrians mostly in

THE FALL OF DAMASCUS

European dress, Greek and Turkish civilians, Jews, Armenians, and French. Cheering wildly they lined the streets and offered gifts of fruit and cigarettes to the passing troops.

This wonderful welcome was somewhat difficult to understand, and many doubted its genuineness. It was, however, ascertained from a guide that a rumour had been circulated the previous afternoon to the effect that in the event of the British Cavalry approaching nearer to Damascus the Germans intended burning the city, a threat they were determined to carry out. Not only had we approached, but we had actually entered the city which was thus saved from destruction. No doubt our rapid advance had frustrated the plans of the Germans, much to the delight of the inhabitants.

Passing through the narrow alleyways of the Bazaar the head of the column reached the French quarter, where it received a great reception. The inhabitants turned out in force, almost blocking the narrow streets, and evidence of their great joy was apparent on all sides. Gifts were showered on the troops as they passed, whilst many of the women and girls shouted greetings and blew kisses from the windows along the route.

The Brigade moved along the Aleppo road to Jobar, at which place a halt was called. After a short spell the advance was continued, the advance Regiment coming in contact with the enemy rear guard in the vicinity of Narista el Basal. The Regiment moved up in support, and the opposition was speedily overcome. At 1 p.m. information was received to the effect that a large enemy force, protected by a strong rearguard, was retreating north-east along the main Aleppo road.

"B" and "C" Squadrons were therefore pushed forward to strengthen the flanks of the 10th Regiment, and later "A" Squadron was moved up to the left flank. At 2 p.m. Major T. J. Daly, D.S.O., with the balance of the Regiment also moved up to the left flank and pushed rapidly forward to within one mile of Khan Ayasn. At this point touch was gained with "B" Squadron, who were holding a position approximately one mile west of the village, the 10th being astride the main road one and a half miles south-west, and with advanced troops in the village.

The enemy were now moving up the pass leading into the hills north of Kubbel Asafur, thus securing their retreat. At 6 p.m. the Regiment concentrated on the main road two miles south-west of Khan Ayasn, and moved to Khan Kussier where it bivouacked for the night. Lieut. Hogan and 10 other ranks were moved out as a night outpost, being posted on the edge of the olive grove in which the Regiment was bivouacked, with orders to watch the main road.

The following members of the Regiment, who had been taken prisoners at Sasa on the 29th September, were reported to be in the German hospital at Damascus: No. 553 Sgt. A. E. King, 262 Cpl. A. L. Betteridge, 921 Cpl. A. C. Down, 1528 L.-Cpl. C. B. Clark,

2116 L.-Cpl. E. P. Hanrahan, 2140 Tpr. D. V. O'Donnell, and 702 Cpl. H. G. Adams.

At 6.15 a.m. on the 2nd October Lieut. Hogan, O.C. outpost, reported that a large force of enemy infantry were moving north, one mile east of his post. Doubt existed as to whether the advancing troops were actually enemy or Sheriffian troops, and a mounted patrol of "B" Squadron was rushed out to investigate and report. A message was despatched to Brigade Headquarters reporting the presence of approximately 2,000 infantry, and asking for information.

The Regiment was at breakfast when the report from Lieut. Hogan was received, but within 10 minutes horses had been saddled and the Regiment paraded ready to move. At 6.30 a.m. a few shots were heard from the direction of the column, and shortly afterwards a galloper from the outpost reported that the column was composed of Turkish infantry.

Orders were at once issued, and the Regiment moved out to the attack, and as the head of the Regiment cleared the olive grove the following message was received from B.H.Q.: "Party believed to be Germans; move and investigate at once; 8th Light Horse Regiment with four machine guns will be ready to support, if required."

With "B" Squadron in advance and Lieut. Sharp's troop of "A" Squadron as right flank guard, the Regiment moved at a rapid pace north-east along the main road for about half a mile, then swung to the left among the vineyards. The rear of the enemy column was now observed about one mile along the road.

By increasing the pace and moving towards the foothills the Regiment rapidly gained on the enemy, who had now mounted several machine guns, and pushed out several small parties to their left flank, in an endeavour to hold up our advance. In spite of the heavy machine gun fire the Regiment pushed forward and reached a favourable position about one mile to the left, and opposite the centre of the enemy column.

Orders were given to "A" Squadron to move rapidly and seize Khan Ayasn, and to "C" Squadron to seize the main road in the vicinity of Kubbet-I-Asafur. "C" Squadron immediately galloped forward, followed by "A" Squadron, under heavy fire, whilst "B" Squadron dismounted and opened a heavy fire on the centre of the enemy column. Regimental Headquarters established themselves near the water channel and gained touch with Brigade Headquarters by heliograph.

The two squadrons who had been sent forward were now seen to be well ahead of the enemy advance guard, and to be swinging in towards the main road to seize the villages, thus cutting off all chances of escape for the enemy. The head of the main body of the enemy seemed to hesitate as if doubtful of its next move, and their leaders appeared to be holding a conference.

"C" SQUADRON, 9th LIGHT HORSE, TRIPOLI
C.O., Major T. A. Brinkworth. *Australian Official Photograph*

OFFICERS 9th LIGHT HORSE, TRIPOLI

(Back row, from left) Lieuts. Cattle, Hahn, Barker, Aikman, Sharp ; Captains McDonal, Luxmore ;
Lieuts. Stephens, Bridger-Lane, and Wagg

THE FALL OF DAMASCUS

As the two squadrons swung round the remainder of the Regiment under orders from Major T. J. Daly, mounted, and with drawn swords, charged the main enemy column, detaching a small party of "B" Squadron to move round the flank. This move had the desired effect; the main body of the enemy promptly hoisting the white flag before the charging troops reached them.

In conjunction with this move, "A" and "C" Squadrons drew swords and charged the enemy cavalry advance guard. This was the first time the Light Horse, armed as cavalry, had the chance to try conclusions with the Turkish cavalry who were armed with sword and lance, and it was expected that they would put up a fight. The determined front shown by our men must have taken all the heart out of the enemy cavalry, as they surrendered without the slightest show of resistance.

"A" Squadron, moving forward, rushed a machine gun just as it was mounted and ready to open fire, whilst "C" seized the pass into the hills, and captured two 75 cm. guns near Kubbet-I-Asafur.

The Regiment collected together the various portions of the enemy force and proceeded to take stock of the bag, which gave the following totals: 91 officers, 318 cavalry, 1,064 infantry, eight German machine gunners, 26 machine guns, one mountain gun (No. F 7524), two 75 cm. (M 15, G.K.N.) guns, 12 automatic rifles, 264 rifles, and 285 animals. This force was captured within one hour of leaving the bivouac at Khan Kussier, seven miles distant.

Amongst the officers captured was the General who commanded the Turkish Division defending Shunet Nimrin in the Jordan Valley, against our attack in May, 1918. The standard of the 46th Regiment was also captured, and is believed to be the only enemy standard captured during the war. That such a force could be taken in open country in such a short time and with so few casualties, appears astounding, but the fact must not be lost sight of that they had been driven from pillar to post for the past three weeks, with no rest and little food, facts which had, no doubt, taken the heart out of them.

The rapidity of our movements contributed largely to the success of the operations, but great credit is due to both Major Charley and Major Bleechmore for the manner in which they manoeuvred their squadrons, in seizing the pass and main road ahead of the enemy columns. Major T. J. Daly, who conducted the operations, deserves special mention for his quick decisions and plan of operations, in which he was ably seconded by Lieut. O. J. Shaw, the Adjutant.

In spite of the hard work of the past three weeks, the horses responded bravely to this additional call, and covered the ground in fine style. The ground passed over was devoid of cover and fairly rough, being covered with stones and broken by numerous small wadis.

When the main column surrendered Signallers J. M. Smyth and N. C. Halliday, who were moving to the Regimental signalling station, in galloping over a rise were suddenly confronted by a party of the enemy composed of three Germans and 85 Turks, who were taking up a position within a few hundred yards of the signal station. A German officer was mounting a machine gun when Smyth and Halliday, with great gallantry, and under a shower of bombs, rushed at the officer and snatched his revolver, which he had hastily drawn, from his hand. With this revolver they fired into the enemy and seized the machine gun, the prompt action so surprising the enemy that they surrendered.

Signallers Smyth and Halliday were both awarded the Distinguished Conduct Medal for this gallant act, which prevented the enemy establishing a post from which a destructive fire could have been turned on the rear of the Regiment.

Lieut. Freebairn, with one troop, escorted the prisoners to Brigade Headquarters, where they were handed over. After collecting the captured war material into one dump, which was placed under a guard, the Regiment returned to bivouac to finish its breakfast, which had been so rudely interrupted. At 2 p.m. "A" Squadron was sent out to reconnoitre the country six miles east of the bivouac for stragglers, returning at 5 p.m. and reporting "all clear."

At 2 p.m. on the 3rd October Lieut. Freebairn, with a troop of "B" Squadron, moved out and mounted an outpost in the Wadi Maraba to guard the approaches to Damascus from the north. The inhabitants of these parts were very friendly disposed towards our men, bringing baskets of grapes, eggs, etc., into our lines. The country surrounding the bivouac was covered with flourishing vineyards and orchards which were abundantly watered. The grapes were ripe and of exceptionally good quality and flavour, being grown chiefly for drying into raisins.

On the following day "C" Squadron moved out at 9 a.m. to relieve "A" Squadron of the 8th Regiment who were holding the pass at Kubbet-I-Asafur. Lieut. Hahn with a working party, and with "A" echelon of the transport, collected the captured war material, which filled five wagons. The captured guns were also brought in and sent to Damascus. At 11 a.m. orders were received for the Brigade to move to a point south-west of Damascus, leaving "C" Squadron of the Regiment at Dumar to hold the main Aleppo road, and the Wadi Maraba.

At 3 p.m. the Regiment, less "C" Squadron, moved *via* the main Aleppo road, through Damascus to a point two and a half miles south-west of El Mezze, where it bivouacked for the night. Four of the men who had been taken prisoner at Sasa on the 29th September and who had been recaptured on the fall of Damascus, rejoined the Regiment at this bivouac.

CHAPTER XXXII

KAUKAB

After a good night's rest at El Mezze, the first since Kunneitra, the Regiment moved out at 8.30 a.m. and marched to a bivouac site two miles south of El Muadhamiye, where lines were laid out, and all ranks quickly settled down for a well-earned spell. The hard work of the past three weeks had caused many casualties amongst the horses, chiefly sore backs, and these received immediate attention. About 60 horses were placed on the sick list and received daily treatment, and owing to the splendid work of F.Q.M.S. Turner, most of them were fit and ready for work within a few days.

On October 6th a combined church parade and thanksgiving service for the recent victory was held, being attended by the whole Brigade.

Many thousands of prisoners, taken during the recent operations, had been collected at a point close to the village of El Muadhamiye, and on the banks of the stream which flowed through that place. This stream, which provided our drinking water supply, quickly became polluted to a degree which rendered it beyond the possibility of human consumption. Thousands of these prisoners were in urgent need of medical attendance, and there was the gravest suspicion of cholera, as they were dying like flies.

None of these men appeared to have the slightest idea of sanitation and their camping area was soon a place to be avoided. This state of affairs needed drastic action, and as their own officers appeared to take no notice of the deplorable condition of their men, Colonel Todd, 10th Light Horse, was appointed Commandant of the Prisoner of War Compound, Kaukab.

On the 9th a suspicious case of sickness occurred in the Regiment, and a few hours later Pte. E. K. Smith died of cholera. The Regiment was therefore hastily moved to a point half a mile above the prisoners' camp. Reports were received that Cpl. A. C. Down and L.-Cpl. Hanrahan had died of wounds in the German hospital at Damascus. Capt. A. H. Nelson proceeded to Damascus to assist in the administration of the hospital which had been formed in the captured barracks.

On the 11th Pte. A. A. Johns was suddenly taken ill, and died a short time later, evidently from the effects of cholera.

Attention was now directed to the enemy prisoners. It was no question of how they had treated our men who had been so unfortunate as to fall into their hands, but of how best to relieve them of the awful conditions under which they were at present existing. As we had no cover of any description for ourselves it was impossible to provide any for them, except for a few of the more serious cases, who were taken into the shelter of the field ambulance.

This small field ambulance with its two medical officers and a few orderlies was daily surrounded by hundreds of Turkish prisoners, many of whom were suffering from the effects of recent wounds, whilst the remainder were seriously ill. The lack of medical comforts was deplorable, but this state of affairs was speedily remedied by supplies being rushed up country in motor cars.

The handful of troops of the 4th Light Horse Brigade, who had been guarding the prisoners, had done all they possibly could, but met with little success. The unfortunate Turks, enduring their great hardships without a murmur, were dying in hundreds, their death rate being from 150 to 170 per day.

It could not be said that the British were responsible for this awful state of affairs. The desperate effort of the 4th Turkish Army to escape, their long retreat from the Jordan Valley, coupled with the breakdown or capture of their transport and supply columns, had contributed largely to the pitiable plight they were now in. Other influences were now at work, far more sinister and sordid than the sudden overwhelming of an honourable foe in battle, which had to be faced and fought for fear that this camp would remain a blot on the British conquest of Syria.

Damascus, apart from being the capital and by far the most important city in Syria, had also been, from the beginning of the war the main depot of supply for the whole Yilderim Army, which had been driven back, step by step, from the banks of the Suez Canal. It contained huge stores of everything necessary to equip and maintain an army in the field. For over two years the troops of the British Empire had fought and struggled through the burning sands of the Sinai Peninsula, through Palestine, Judea, and Syria, until the enemy were beaten to the ground, and their dreams of conquest shattered.

Twelve thousand British and Indian Cavalry, breaking through the gap prepared for them by the British and Indian Infantry and Artillery, had fought and ridden until the capture of the Syrian capital marked the culmination of their great effort. Now that the armies of Turkey and their allies in this theatre of war were broken the British role in the drama appeared to be one of self-effacement. To Amir Feisal, the son of the King of Hedjaz, who with his Arab rabble had followed in the wake of the conquering army, as jackals follow a wounded animal, the government of Syria was immediately handed, with Damascus as headquarters.

The city was soon a blaze of colour, the Hedjaz flag being flown from every building of importance, the flag of Arab independence. Feisal and his motley crew, ever a standing joke to any British soldier with the slightest sense of humour, installed themselves in the public offices and palatial residences of the city, and proceeded to administer the affairs of state, assisted by a handful of British officers, called liaison officers.

The few hundred Arab irregulars who comprised the "Army of the Hedjaz" at this stage, spent their time in galloping madly up and down the main streets on their little ponies, brandishing their rifles and calling for recruits. As long as they confined themselves to these antics they simply caused amusement to our troops, and a scarcely concealed feeling of disgust amongst the more decent residents, but the deeper mischief underlying all this was soon seen when the Arab officials began to assume control of the various departments.

These people had long since persuaded themselves that it was owing to their own efforts that the city, with its huge booty of stores and supplies, was now a prize in their hands. Seized with the Arab lust for gold and backsheesh, their chiefs soon indicated that they meant to turn these supplies to good account. Whether they were required for friend or foe, they were determined that they would have to be paid for at top price.

The records of the heartbreaking efforts of our medical personnel to obtain drugs and stores for the sick and dying during those early days of Arab administration would make surprising reading, if it did not stir one's blood to indignation. In the huge stores there was a plentiful supply of food, drugs, tents, and clothes, but these they would not part with except for cash, and at most exorbitant prices.

Such then was the condition of affairs when that splendid officer, Lieut.-Colonel Todd, was faced with the problem of organizing the prisoner of war camp at Kaukab, but no better officer could have been selected. A man of untiring energy, and of great administrative and organizing ability, he threw himself heart and soul into the task. Not only did he work himself, but he instilled the same spirit into the whole of his Regiment, with the result that the unfortunate prisoners were soon enjoying a certain amount of comfort, regular meals, and proper medical treatment.

A cemetery was formed in which the dead were decently interred, their graves being marked with the crescent, the symbol of their faith, and their names and unit carefully listed. In the adjacent villages he established two hospitals, which were soon crowded with patients, and organized the remainder into companies, each under the command of one of his squadron leaders.

Each day the prisoners who were fit to work were divided into groups of various sizes and sent to the units of the Brigade, where they were employed in clearing the camp area of stones and various light tasks. This work not only kept them healthy, but kept their thoughts occupied, and certainly put them into a much better state of mind. It can safely be said that the unfortunate prisoners received the kindliest treatment at the hands of our troops wherever they went.

After a few weeks the death rate dropped to practically nil under the splendid management of their camp. With the regular meals and good cooking, things they had not enjoyed since the war started, they soon grew strong and well, and when things had settled down orders were received for their transfer to the compound at Ludd. Each day a party of 1,000 were paraded, and after being rationed for the journey, were despatched under escort, *via* Nazareth to railhead. It is certain that many of these men were sorry to part with the members of the 3rd Light Horse Brigade, who had done so much to make their hard lot as easy and bright as possible.

Lieut.-Colonel Todd was warmly thanked for his splendid services by Lieut.-General Sir H. G. Chauvel, who commanded the Desert Mounted Corps.

After many pleasant days spent in the vicinity of Kaukab the Brigade was notified that it would march northward to rejoin the remainder of the Division, who were pushing on to the support of the 5th Cavalry Division in the vicinity of Aleppo.

CHAPTER XXXIII

HOMS AND TRIPOLI. THE ARMISTICE

At 9.45 a.m. on the 27th October, 1918, the Brigade, less 10th Light Horse Regiment, moved out on its long march to Homs. Passing through Damascus for the last time, it was cheerfully greeted by the inhabitants, especially those in the French quarter. A party of 21 other ranks with 70 spare horses, under the command of Major Charley, was left at Damascus to collect reinforcements, which were coming up country by train, whilst the Regiment proceeded to Jobar, where it bivouacked for the night.

By easy stages the Regiment moved to Kuteife, which place was reached at 10.45 a.m. on the 29th. At 7 a.m. on the following day the column moved to Nebk, which was reached at 4.45 p.m., after a long and trying march. Orders were issued to the effect that the last two stages of the march to Homs would have to be completed in one stretch, owing to the total absence of water in that area, and that a short halt would be made at Hasie.

At daybreak on the 31st the column moved off on this march, passing through Kara at 8.30 a.m. At 3.50 p.m. the Regiment arrived at Hasie, where the horses were off-saddled and fed. At 5 p.m. the march was resumed, but after covering roughly six miles the column again halted. About 10.30 p.m. orders were issued to saddle up and get ready to move, and as this order was being carried out a message was received from Headquarters to the effect that the Turkish Government had asked for and been granted an armistice, and that hostilities had ceased from 12 noon on the 31st October, 1918.

This news, which may safely be said was not unexpected, in view of their recent crushing defeats, caused great excitement amongst the troops, and sustained them during the long, weary hours of the night march to Homs.

At 11.30 p.m. the column moved off and arrived on the outskirts of the town just as day was breaking. Passing through the main street of the town, the Brigade proceeded to a point two miles to the north, and bivouacked near the banks of the famous Orontes River. The distance traversed from Kaukab was 109 English miles, over rough and hilly country, the last stage being over 50 miles.

Details of the Armistice terms were received, and pointed to an almost unconditional surrender. This precipitated the fall of Austria, and the war seemed to be practically over. The projected move of the Division to Aleppo was cancelled, and the Brigade received orders to move to Tripoli, on the Mediterranean coast.

At 5.30 a.m. on the 6th the Regiment moved from Homs and proceeded to Tel Kale, watering *en route* at the Nahr Kebir. On the following days the Regiment moved by easy stages *via* Jisr Ayash, Nahr Aarka, Nahr Berid, to Sheikh Bedawi, where it halted at 10 a.m. At noon the march was resumed through the northern edge of Tripoli to Mejdelaya, where we camped in the olive groves.

On the following day a standing camp was formed, roads being constructed through the groves to the various Regimental lines. A good supply of much-needed clothing and boots was soon procured by the Quartermaster, and issued to all ranks. A splendid canteen had been established by the 7th Indian Division, under Major-General Sir V. B. Fane, who were occupying Tripoli, from which a large supply of goods was purchased.

On the evening of the 11th November, 1918, the news arrived that Germany had asked for and been granted an armistice. This unexpected news was received by the majority of the Brigade very calmly, but the remainder proceeded to celebrate it with due honours. Red, white, and green flares were soon flying in all directions, the artillery fired a few blank rounds, and the bells of the quaint old monastery were rung, until the noise was deafening.

Away in the harbour a number of ships were lying at anchor, and these soon received the information, immediately setting up a screeching with their sirens, until they apparently ran out of steam, when the noise died down. A few of the more sober souls gathered together round a bottle of Johnny Walker, to drink the health of His Majesty, and the downfall of his enemies.

The eternal question was now, "When will we embark for home?" and no doubt many thought we would be off within a week or two, but these were to be sadly disappointed, as the black cloud of rebellion in Egypt was growing blacker each day, quite unknown to our men in Syria.

The troops settled down to their work cheerfully, and leave parties were allowed to visit Tripoli daily. General Sir H. G. Chauvel inspected the Brigade, and expressed entire satisfaction at the appearance of the Regiment.

A few miles to the east of this beautifully situated camp was the high range of the Lebanon Mountains with its snow-capped peaks. Half-way to the summit was a clump of ancient trees, surrounded by a high stone wall, the remains of the famous "Cedars of Lebanon," whilst across the mountain itself and the fertile plain was the ancient town of Baalbek with its wonderful ruins of the magnificent temples of Jupiter and Bacchus.

Leave was granted to visit these places, and parties, each under the supervision of an officer, set out. The party proceeding to Baalbek were allowed six days for the journey, whilst the Besherri party were allowed three. The route travelled was of remarkable beauty, pretty villages being dotted here and there amongst the hills. As the inhabitants of these villages invariably spoke English, they were soon on the best of terms with our men. Several people were met who had an intimate knowledge of Australia, and in the beautiful village of Besherri was found a Mr. J. Arida, a merchant from Queensland, who had the misfortune to be paying a visit to his native land when the war broke out in 1914, and was thus prevented from returning.

Lieut.-Colonel McLaurin, of the 8th Light Horse, had recently been admitted to hospital and died, the 8th Regiment thus losing a popular officer within a few days of the armistice. Major T. J. Daly, D.S.O., was therefore transferred to the 8th Regiment, promoted Lieut.-Colonel, and took command. This popular officer was a great loss to the Regiment, but the 9th's loss was the 8th's gain, and the appointment was very popular.

The remainder of the Regiment was kept busy, but in view of a possible early return to Australia, classes of instruction in various subjects of an educational nature were organized. Captains Ragless and Shelley and Major Charley were selected as the Regimental representatives of the scheme, and it was decided to make the best possible use of the facilities available.

As the winter was setting in, and the Lebanon Mountains and road to Besherri were covered with snow, the leave parties to Baalbek and Besherri were suspended. The heavy rains which were now frequent were turning the camp site into a quagmire, making it necessary to find fresh quarters, and a party was sent out for that purpose.

Major Darley, in charge of a party of officers and men from each unit of the Brigade, was sent to Cairo to obtain stores to augment the supply of rations for Christmas. This party proceeded to Beirut by motor lorries, a distance of roughly 76 miles, thence by the French railway across the Lebanon Mountains to Damascus, a journey of remarkable interest. The grades climbed, at a fairly fast rate, on this line is astounding, but is accounted for by the fact that in the centre of the track is a rack, and under the engine an arrangement of cog wheels, which, when the lever is pulled, drop and connect with the rack, the power being transferred to this system.

After a day in Damascus the party proceeded by train, via Semakh, El Afuleh, Jenin, Tul Keram, and Ludd, to Kantara, where it transferred to the Port Said-Cairo express and arrived in Cairo after a four days' journey. On completion of its business, the party assembled and proceeded by train to Kantara, and after a delay of some days embarked and returned to Tripoli by sea.

In the meantime a new camp site had been obtained, and the Brigade had shifted to its new quarters a few miles south-west of the town and close to the sea. As a good stretch of sand ran for a distance of roughly 1,000 yards inland, this camp was greatly appreciated by all.

Christmas, 1918, was ushered in, a bright and sunny day, which, combined with the pleasant surroundings, soon put everyone in the best possible mood. It was a decided contrast to the previous Christmas, which had been spent in the rain and mud at Suffa in the Judean Hills. With good camping arrangements, good cook houses and cooks, not to speak of the good things which had been brought from Cairo, all hands set to work to keep the day in the good old style. After dinner, the health of the dear ones in far-off Australia was drunk, not once, but many times, the evening being brought to a close by a fine concert which had been arranged some days in advance.

On the 12th January, 1919, the commander-in-chief, General Sir E. H. Allenby, G.C.B., G.C.M.G., inspected the Brigade. After inspecting each Regiment in turn, he delivered a short address, thanking the members for the splendid work they had done throughout the campaign. Turning to the Brigadier, he concluded his remarks by saying in loud, clear tones, "General Wilson, I congratulate you on your magnificent Brigade."

As there appeared to be no prospect of an early move, sports of all descriptions were organized. A splendid meeting was held by the Brigade on the sea front, the natives from the surrounding country attending in large numbers. A football tournament was also held, to find the champion team of the Egyptian Expeditionary Force, and after many exciting games the Regiment proved to be the champions, the final match being played in Cairo.

It was also decided to hold a race meeting, and a committee was formed for the purpose. As the first thing to be arranged was the construction of the ground, a sub-committee was appointed and commenced operations, assisted by large working parties. The spot selected was between the lines of the 10th Regiment and the hills, but required an immense amount of work before it would be suitable. Huge masses of rock were blasted out, the holes filled with sand, and after some weeks of work a beautiful circular course was laid out. The foot of the high cliff facing the sea was terraced and formed a splendid grandstand, roughly 150 feet high, and the top side of the course was railed in.

During the time these preparations were in hand, orders were received that the horses were to be disposed of. It had been found impossible to take them to Australia, and arrangements had been made to hand selected horses to the 5th Cavalry Division. As a large number were considered to be unfit for further Cavalry service, other arrangements had to be made as to their disposal.

The Syrians and Arabs were extremely anxious to purchase these animals, and had money in plenty for the purpose, but long experience of these people, and their cruel treatment of all animals, decided our humane government that it would be far more merciful to shoot

HOMS AND TRIPOLI. THE ARMISTICE

them, and this course was decided on. The veterinary officers, therefore, made a careful inspection and weeded out those condemned to die. The manes and tails of these horses were cut off as a means of identification, and at a later date they were taken over the hill and shot.

On the 21st orders were received for the 8th and 9th Regiments to proceed to Egypt, and by the irony of fate they had to move on the very day appointed for the race meeting. The tents were struck at daybreak, and all heavy baggage transported to El Mina, the port of Tripoli. At 8.30 a.m. on the 22nd the Regiments paraded dismounted, marched to the point of embarkation, and at 10 a.m. were all on board H.M.T. "Ellinga," which sailed at noon for Kantara.

The great race meeting was now the chief topic of conversation, and the final preparations were pushed forward. It appeared to be the first time such an event had been held in this country, and every effort had been made to get some of the better class natives to enter their thoroughbred Arab ponies for a special race. Some appeared anxious to do this, until someone sent out the rumour that we were only trying to find out which were the best ponies, so that we could commandeer them, which frightened them out of the race.

Six events were set down on the programme, and all were well contested. The riders had gone to a great deal of trouble and expense, and turned out in full racing kit, with silk jackets and caps of all colours, whilst the committee had provided numbered saddle cloths.

Marquees had been erected for afternoon tea, and were well stocked. Enormous crowds gathered, and all the troops for miles around flocked to the races, while thousands of natives attended to see the show. A large totalizator had been erected and placed under the charge of Major Darley. This was a large wooden structure with an enclosure at either end, one being for 100 piastre (£1), and the other for 20 piastre bets. A very large sum of money passed through these totes during the day, and the manner in which they were worked proved entirely satisfactory.

The racing was of a very high order and would have done credit to any racecourse. The natives grew tremendously excited as they saw the desperate finish of race after race, and some of those who had ridden to the meeting, expressed a wish to try their ponies against our horses. As this would have been a one-sided affair, the President of the Committee, Lieut.-Colonel Olden, 10th Light Horse, induced them to take part in a race, for natives only. A good number of entries were secured, and after a little delay they were got away to a fair start; but stopping them was a totally different matter.

Round and round the course they flew, flogging their ponies along with their light canes, and taking not the slightest notice of the attempts to stop them. Dropping out one by one as their ponies were winded, it appeared that the race would soon end, but the last man did two laps alone before he was finally stopped by the crowd on the course. He appeared to be a bit surprised and offended at being stopped, but became all smiles when he was informed that he had won by about three-quarters of a mile.

It was a great day for all, and the committee deserved special credit for the splendid show. From information gained from civilian friends in Tripoli, it proved to be the topic of conversation amongst the natives for weeks afterwards.

A few days later, after a general clean up of the camp site, and disposal of the remaining horses and equipment, the balance of the Regiment, under the command of Major Darley, embarked at El Mina and proceeded to Port Said, where they disembarked and proceeded to Moascar by train.

The Regiment, on leaving Tripoli, had proceeded to Port Said, and disembarked there at 4.30 p.m. on the 23rd, proceeding by train to Kantara. A good hot meal was secured at the Soldiers' Club, after which they crossed the Canal and bivouacked at Kantara East. On the following day they proceeded, by the desert railway, to Rafa, where camp was formed one mile west of the station.

It was surmised by all that we were to wait at this camp for a few days, and then embark for Australia. Rumours of all descriptions flew round the lines all day, and every day, but these received a sudden shock when the news of the Egyptian rising came to hand, and that the Regiment would proceed to Egypt immediately.

At 2 p.m. on the 2nd March, 1919, the baggage was transported to the station by camels, and at 6 p.m. the Regiment paraded and marched to Rafa Station, where it entrained and proceeded to Moascar, arriving at that place at 4.20 p.m. on the following day.

CHAPTER XXXIV

THE EGYPTIAN RISING

Although it was intended to deal solely with the doings of the Regiment in this book, it is necessary to make a few remarks on the astonishing upheaval which took place in Egypt at this period, and became known as the Egyptian Rebellion.

That the Egyptian of the Effendi class, fat, rich, and prosperous, should breed sedition and foster animosity towards British rule caused little surprise, as any rule which protected the poorer classes from their clutches, would prove obnoxious to them. The Fellaheen, tillers of the soil, who for centuries had been crushed by taxation, and who had, under British rule, become owners of their land, appeared to be contented and prosperous.

That they should suddenly turn on the Government which had raised them from the status of slaves, and made them what they were at this time, could hardly be expected, and proved that some very subtle influence was at work.

During the course of the Great War, Egypt was one of the few countries which had every reason to be happy and contented. She had seen nothing of the war beyond a few bombs dropped on Cairo one day by an insane German airman, and had gained great wealth by the sale of her products at advanced prices. In addition to this she had lacked nothing in the way of the necessaries of life, and her frontiers were protected by a Great British Army, yet at a moment's notice the whole country was aflame from end to end.

The cry of "Egypt for the Egyptians" was screamed in every town and village throughout the land by frenzied mobs, whose sole ambition appeared to be to murder and destroy all that came in their way. Railways were torn up, the rails and sleepers being thrown into the canals, telegraph and telephone wires cut, and the railway stations burnt to the ground. Other mobs, specially interested in this particular kind of work, proceeded to raid the properties of the British and other European residents.

Parties of British officers and men, who had become isolated owing to the destruction of railways, were set upon, although unarmed, and beaten to death. Eight officers travelling by the Luxor express were murdered, and property of immense value, mostly belonging to their own government, was totally destroyed. All over the country acts of violence were perpetrated, until it seemed that the whole Moslem population had gone stark staring mad.

The outlying districts suffered most owing to their isolated nature, the larger cities, owing to the presence of regular garrisons, being safeguarded against any great damage. Huge demonstrations, however, were held by the frenzied natives, who missed no opportunity to smash the windows of shops and tramcars. The situation was rapidly becoming more serious, and General Headquarters took action accordingly.

All available troops were collected and rushed out in all directions to guard the railways, stations, and bridges, and for the protection of Europeans. As the English troops available for this task fell far below requirements, the embarkation of the Light Horse Regiments was suspended, and they were called upon to play a part in this newly-staged drama, or shall we say, tragedy.

Within a few hours the Regiment was being re-fitted, armed, and equipped for service. The rifles, machine guns, and ammunition, which had been returned to ordnance after the armistice, were reissued. Supplies for a protracted period were arranged for, and the Regiment was ready to move. One squadron, made up of 76 officers and men of "A" Squadron, and 74 from "C," were fitted out for mounted duty, and placed under the command of Major Bleechmore.

On the morning of the 15th March, 1919, exactly four years to the day since the Regiment had landed from Australia, news arrived that a train had been attacked on its journey from Cairo to Kantara. At 9.45 a.m. a party consisting of three officers and 50 other ranks from the 8th and 10th Regiments, proceeded by train to Zag-a-Zig.

At 11 a.m. on the 16th, the Regiment, less the mounted squadron, paraded and proceeded by a construction train to Zag-a-Zig. The line was found to have been torn up at various points, and the culvert near the town had been damaged. Repair gangs were immediately set to work to repair the line and culvert, also the telegraph lines, which had been cut. On arrival at the town, "B" Squadron, under Major B. B. Ragless, was sent back to Abu Hammad, reports having been received that the Christians at that place were in great danger.

The appearance of this squadron, which marched through the village, soon put an end to the trouble, and the squadron bivouacked.

On arrival at Zag-a-Zig the Regiment camped for the night near the supply depot, and early on the following morning the Brigade paraded and marched through the principal streets of the town. The town is an important distributing centre on the main Cairo-Port Suez-Port Said line, and was a hotbed of sedition. It was the seat of the Arabi Pasha Rebellion in 1882, and it was near this place that the battle of Tel el Kebir was fought.

The appearance of the Brigade made a great impression on the natives, who appeared quiet and orderly, but sullen, and all thoughts of serious participation in the rebellion disappeared when it was found that the Brigade was here to stay.

THE EGYPTIAN RISING

On arrival of the baggage train, a comfortable camp was soon pitched a few yards from the sweet water canal, and opposite the Turkish officers' compound. The mounted squadron arrived on the following day, and were immediately employed in patrolling the country districts and bringing in the European residents.

The Regiment took over the protection of the railway from Zag-a-Zig to Bilbeis, and to Abu Hammad, being split up into small groups for the purpose, important points being strengthened by the addition of machine guns. A strong guard was posted at the big railway station, and troops were also sent to guard the aerodromes at El Rimal and Abu Sueir.

For the next few weeks the Regiment was employed on these duties, the mounted squadron making daily excursions to outlying villages. In some cases trouble was encountered, but a few shots and a determined front soon put all ideas of resistance out of their minds.

On the 26th March, at about 9 p.m., the sky was suddenly illuminated by a great blaze from the direction of the railway station, and the troops turned out to investigate. It was immediately surmised that the natives had deliberately set fire to it, but it was found that the cook in the station refreshment room had upset a lamp, the place becoming a mass of flames in a few seconds. The troops set to work with a will, and in a very short time the fire had been got under, and the main portion of the station saved.

Many natives had been arrested on charges of murder and pillage, and a Military Tribunal was established for their trial. Major H. M. Parsons, D.S.O., was appointed President of the Military Court, Zag-a-Zig section, and was assisted by Major B. B. Ragless and some English officers. At a later date Major Brinkworth relieved Major Parsons, and later still was appointed President of No. 2 Court.

As affairs became more settled, the number of detached posts was reduced, and parties left for early repatriation to Australia. On the 10th May, 34 other ranks moved to Moascar for embarkation and passage to the United Kingdom, under the 10 per cent. leave scheme. This scheme provided for three weeks' leave in the United Kingdom for men of long war service and of exemplary character, and was much appreciated.

On the 16th the Regiment entrained and proceeded to Tel el Kebir, where a camp was formed opposite the railway station. The duty of guarding the line and the aerodromes was continued, whilst the mounted squadron furnished the daily patrols. Every opportunity was taken of continuing the instructional and educational classes, which were well attended. Lieut. V. K. McNamara did splendid work for the men who were anxious to improve their education during this period and during the voyage home.

Sports of various kinds were taken up, and a first-rate cricket team was organized. This team visited Cairo to play the A.I.F. Headquarters team, and gained an easy victory. It also played the team of the English Regiment at Bilbeis on two occasions, the first match ending in a draw and the second in an easy victory for our team.

Thousands of Turkish prisoners were interned at Tel el Kebir, and from time to time parties consisting of one officer and 50 other ranks were detailed to escort batches of these prisoners to Alexandria, *en route* to Turkey. Each party of prisoners numbered roughly 1,500, and, strange to say, there were many amongst them who were far from anxious to return to their native land. I asked one, whom I considered to be far from pleased at the prospect, as to his reasons, and he told me that many of them would be shot when they returned.

There was also a large and well laid out camp a few hundred yards from ours, occupied by 1,100 Russians, who had been prisoners with the Turks for about four years, and who had been released on the signing of the armistice. They were an exceptionally fine body of men, mostly of the peasant class, and showed traces of the terrible treatment they had received at the hands of their inhuman captors.

They were formed into companies of roughly 200, being well fed and clothed by the British Government. Each company had formed a choir of magnificent singers, and their headquarters also had its choir, conducted by the man who, prior to the war, had been the principal bass in the Czar's opera. When the unit was out on its early morning route march, the beautiful singing of their marching songs could be heard for miles across the desert. The choir would sing a portion, after which the whole column would join in, making a volume of sound hard to realize.

On several occasions the headquarters choir, augmented by picked men from the company choirs, gave a concert in our lines, and those who had the pleasure of hearing their magnificent voices will never forget it.

On the 5th June permission was granted for leave parties to proceed to Jerusalem, each party having leave for six days. Many men took advantage of this privilege, and a little later leave was granted to Cairo, which place was yet very unsettled, and arms had to be carried by the officers.

On the 27th the horses were handed over to the remount depot at Bilbeis, and the saddlery returned to ordnance.

Lieut.-Colonel W. H. Scott, who had been in indifferent health for some time, and who had recently returned from hospital, was again evacuated to hospital, Major H. M. Parons, who had been relieved of his duties in connection with the Military Court, assuming command of the Regiment.

On the 30th June the Regiment handed over its duties in the Tel el Kebir area, and proceeded by rail to Moascar, collecting the troops at El Rimal and Abu Sueir *en route*.

EMBARKING AT TRIPOLI FOR EGYPT
H.M.T. "ELLENGA"

OUR CAMP AT ZAG-A-ZIG, EGYPT

CHAPTER XXXV

THE RETURN TO AUSTRALIA

The Regiment arrived at Moascar at 1 a.m. on the 1st July, and took over the camping area opposite the railway siding. Orders were received to the effect that the Regiment would embark for Australia on the 10th July, the information being received with great rejoicing. After breakfast the whole Regiment paraded and marched to Lake Timsah, where all ranks enjoyed a good swim, after which they marched back to camp.

On the following day, all equipment, except cooking and sanitary gear, was checked and returned to ordnance. All available new clothing was issued, and surplus and worn-out clothing disposed of.

Heavy baggage was packed ready for the voyage, and transported to the rail siding. The whole camping area was subjected to a thorough clean-up, and everything prepared for the final departure.

On the 9th July Major Parsons and Major Darley, with an advance party from each unit of the Brigade, proceeded to Port Said to take over the ship. Immediately on arrival the party proceeded on board H.M. Transport "Oxfordshire," Major Parsons being appointed ship's commanding officer, and Major Darley ship's quartermaster.

At 2 p.m. the ship left its moorings and proceeded to Kantara, where it tied up to the eastern bank of the Canal for the embarkation of the remainder of the Brigade. By 3 p.m. on the following day all troops and stores had been taken in, and the men were settling down to their new quarters. Friends from all quarters had come along to bid us good-bye, and at 4.30 p.m. the good ship "Oxfordshire" started on its long voyage to Australia.

Besides 16 officers and 360 other ranks belonging to the Regiment, there were on board the 10th Light Horse, 3rd Machine Gun Squadron, 3rd Field Troop, Engineers, 3rd Field Ambulance, and Brigade Headquarters. There were also 50 details from France, and a number of British officers and their wives who were proceeding to Colombo, making a grand total of about 1,200 troops on board.

Passing through the Canal the troops on board were heartily cheered by the various camps in the Canal zone. On reaching Lake Timsah the engines were stopped, and the huge vessel slowed down to allow Brigadier-General Wilson, commanding the Brigade, to come on board.

During the hours of daylight of this first day on board, all was bustle and excitement, but as darkness set in the troops, who had been on the move from a very early hour, began to settle down, and long before Port Suez was reached were fast asleep in their hammocks.

The following day all troops were paraded and allotted their decks and boat stations. Life belts were issued and the method of adjustment explained. Ship's and fire orders were read and explained to all ranks, and after inspection the men were dismissed to their quarters.

The voyage through the Red Sea was dull and uninteresting, everyone feeling the intense heat, which seemed to scorch the life out of one, but on nearing Colombo a welcome change took place, good fresh winds clearing the atmosphere.

Large stocks of clothing and boots had been taken on board at Kantara, and the Quartermaster's staff had a busy time, fitting out the troops and packing the unserviceable clothing for return to store on arrival in Australia. Thanks to the Australian Comforts Fund Commissioner, a good supply of comforts had been sent to the ship, and issues were made daily to all on board by the Padre, the Rev. R. C. Turner. Several gramophones had also been sent down, together with a good supply of records, but, strange to say, most of these machines disappeared during the stay at Colombo.

Large supplies of material had also been put on board for the use of the educational classes, which were to be carried on during the voyage. An old motor cycle had also been put on board, and a class of instruction in motor mechanics was conducted by Pte. Walker, 12th Light Horse, attached to the Brigade. Concerts were held from time to time, some splendid talent coming to light. Several of the English officers and their wives contributed items, which were greatly appreciated.

Arrangements were made by wireless so that on arrival at Colombo all who wished to do so could proceed to Kandy. Arriving in harbour early on the morning of the 22nd July, 17 officers and 163 other ranks took advantage of this trip and proceeded by the special train, provided by the courtesy of the Ceylon Government. Leave to visit Colombo was granted to the remainder, with the result that by 10 a.m. the ship was practically deserted, all being anxious to stretch their legs on mother earth.

This beautiful town, with its fine avenues and wonderful gardens, was well worth a visit, but those who took advantage of the trip to Kandy were well repaid by the magnificent scenery of the hills.

On the following day leave was again granted ashore for all ranks, very few remaining on board, but as the ship was due to sail on the 24th, all leave was stopped on that date. The troops, although confined to the ship, were able to spend a very pleasant time by indulging in a diving and swimming display. Hundreds of the

THE RETURN TO AUSTRALIA

men passed the time away in this manner, and some of the more expert ones gave a fine display of high diving from the upper decks of the ship.

At 5 p.m. the good ship moved out on its voyage to Fremantle, and all were well satisfied to be once more on the move, especially as the next land to be sighted would be the home-land. Rough weather was experienced for the next few days, which kept most of the men below, where they passed the time with various card games or read books borrowed from the library.

On the weather clearing a sports meeting was organized, but owing to the confined space the events were not well contested. The Regiment's team, captained by Sgt.-Trumpeter Watts, after a prolonged struggle, won the heavy-weight tug-of-war.

At daybreak on the 4th August, exactly five years from the date of the declaration of war, the land of Australia was seen in the distance, and all ranks were early astir and on deck to see the welcome sight. The 10th Light Horse, who were to be landed at Fremantle, handed over their ship's stores and got everything ready to disembark.

The "Oxfordshire" entered the harbour at 8 a.m., being welcomed by vast crowds ashore, and by everything in the harbour which could possibly make a sound of any sort, with the result that the noise was deafening. At 9.30 a.m. the 10th Light Horse paraded on the hurricane deck, and after a few preliminaries marched ashore. They were immediately dealt with by the embarkation staff, and in a few minutes were allowed to depart with their friends. As soon as they had departed, leave was granted to those men who were to be disembarked in other States, orders being issued that they were to be back on board by 10 p.m., and most of the troops availed themselves of the privilege.

At noon on the 5th the moorings were cast off, and the good ship turned her nose towards the Bight. As soon as the harbour entrance was cleared heavy seas were encountered, and for the next two days the troops had a rough time, many of them being only too glad to hide themselves in any old corner.

On the 9th August a meeting of the members of the Regiment was held in the first saloon to discuss a proposal to form an Old Comrades' Association. A large number of all ranks attended and listened to the scheme as outlined by Major Darley. On being put to the meeting the proposition was carried unanimously, and the following members were elected as a temporary committee to get the scheme in working order:

President, Major T. A. Brinkworth.
Secretary, Major T. H. Darley.
Members, Lieut. H. Lawrence, S.S.M. Virgo, S.S.M. Steinwedel, Sgt. C. Allen, and Pte. Curtin.

On the 10th August, 1919, the "Oxfordshire" steamed into the roads opposite Largs Bay, and was tugged to the wharf at the Outer Harbour. In spite of the fact that no trains were running, owing to the seamen's strike in New South Wales, thousands of friends and relatives had by some means managed to get to the wharf to greet the returning troops, and gave them the heartiest of welcomes. The famous Sammy Lunn was, as usual, well to the front in tendering a welcome to the boys of South Australia, and was ably seconded by those present.

The disembarkation was quickly carried out, and the troops dispersed after receiving orders to parade at the Cheer Up Hut at 9 a.m. on the following day.

At 9 a.m. on the 11th August, 1919, the Regiment paraded at the Anzac Arch, and was inspected by Brig.-General J. M. Antill, C.B., C.M.G., who complimented them on their smart appearance and steadiness. After the inspection the Regiment marched through the city, *via* King William, Grenfell, Pulteney, and Rundle Streets, to the railway station, where it entrained for Keswick.

Each man was then paraded before a board of medical officers and given his leave pass, after which they paraded by squadrons in front of the barracks for final dismissal.

A short address, which included much good advice, was then made by the acting Commanding Officer.

After being associated for nearly five years, during which time many hardships and dangers had been cheerfully shared, the time had come for the Regiment to be disbanded, and its members scattered to all quarters of the Commonwealth.

Many life-long friendships had been formed amongst its members, and the final dismissal was akin to the breaking up of a great family.

With a hearty, but in many cases a silent, grip of the hand, these members of the **gallant** 9th dispersed to face their new and more peaceful life.

CHAPTER XXXVI

CONCLUSION

After an absence of four years and six months overseas, the Regiment was once more back in the home land, and its members scattered to all parts of the State.

Leaving Australia in February, 1915, with a total of roughly 500, nearly 4,000 men had passed through its ranks during its service abroad, and helped to uphold its traditions. The magnificent spirit with which the Regiment was founded carried its members through the periods of trial and danger, and never once did that spirit waver.

Through the dark days of Gallipoli, the trials of the desert, and the torments of the Jordan Valley, the Regiment was at all times a credit to the country of its origin, and its members ever eager to play their part in the greatest drama of all time.

I cannot close without paying a tribute to its members, those splendid men who were ever ready to cheerfully undergo the greatest hardships and danger. The greater the danger of the operations, the more cheerfully were they undertaken, and Australia may well be proud of its sons who served with the 9th Light Horse.

"For Glory and Honour" was the Regimental motto, and in Glory and Honour their names should ever be remembered, for duty nobly done.

FINIS

APPENDICES

APPENDIX I

THE WORK OF THE TRANSPORT

The question of transport for an Army in the field is one of the biggest problems a commander has to face, as on the performance of its difficult and arduous duties the success of the whole operations may depend.

As the Army advances, the work of the transport becomes more difficult, and only perfect organization can lead to success. During operations it becomes a matter of unceasing movement, for after a long and trying march wagons must be unloaded, and after the shortest possible halt start on the return journey to refill.

On the Regiment proceeding to Anzac the horses and wheeled vehicles were left at Heliopolis, as it was found impossible to land them on the Peninsula. The only transport available at Anzac was the Indian Mule Corps, which was chiefly used for the carrying of ammunition and shells to the front line.

All rations and water had to be carried from the beach to the trenches by the men, and it was by no means a light task to carry a case of biscuits or bully beef to a height of about 400 feet in a distance of about three-quarters of a mile. For carrying drinking water, round cans with swing handles, each holding two gallons, were provided, each man carrying two cans.

After the Suvla landing in August, the Regiment moved to Hill 60, and from that time to the evacuation pack mules were used.

On the return of the Regiment to Egypt, we reverted to the old organization of wheel transport, viz.:

- 1 general service wagon for cooks' gear.
- 1 limbered wagon for signalling gear and tools.
- 1 limbered wagon per squadron for ammunition.
- 1 limbered wagon per squadron for tools.
- 4 limbered wagons for the machine gun section.
- 1 water cart and 1 Maltese cart for the medical officer.

With this establishment the Regiment moved out to the Canal zone on the 27th February, 1916, and went into camp at Serapeum.

About May, 1916, the four general service wagons per Regiment allowed for the cartage of baggage, which up to that time had formed part of the Brigade Train, were added to the Regimental establishment, bringing it up to a total of 18 vehicles.

On the Regiment moving to Bally Bunion, the transport soon got into difficulties on leaving the metalled road, which had been constructed into the desert by the Engineers, the wheels of the heavily laden vehicles sinking into the soft sand. This clearly showed that for operations in the desert, wheeled transport in its present form would be practically useless. The idea of fitting broad iron tyres on the wheels was therefore introduced, and in many cases the whole wheel was encased with tin.

After a few days spent at Bally Bunion, the Regiment was ordered out for operations. Wheels were left behind and camel transport taken into use for the cartage of rations and water. During the attack on the redoubt at Abd, rations and water had to be brought out each night from the refilling point, a distance of about eight miles. This night work with long strings of camels was very trying and difficult owing to the huge sandhills and the pitch darkness of the desert.

On the first night the orders were to take the convoy to Hassanieh, a small hod about six miles away. After loading, a start was made at 1.30 a.m., and for a couple of miles, owing to the sand formations, the column had to move in exactly the opposite direction. After much difficulty in crossing high sand formations, the convoy arrived in the vicinity of the hod, but as it was hidden away amongst high sand dunes it could not be located until daybreak.

The following night the orders were to take the convoy to the old Artillery position in front of the redoubt, the Regiment being on outpost. The convoy moved off at 1 a.m., and at 3.30 a.m. reached the Field Ambulance, at which place the Ambulance and Artillery portions were detached. On reaching the old Artillery position no signs of troops could be seen, and the convoy was halted. After much riding round in the dark, the Regimental Headquarters were located in a small gully, the remainder of the Regiment being scattered in its outpost positions.

Before leaving each night for the refilling point, I had asked that the Signaller on duty be made to flash a light in the direction of the convoy at intervals after 2 a.m. to guide the convoy in, but this had not been done, and much valuable time was wasted.

After the Romani operations the Regiment went into camp at Nabit and started to accumulate baggage, with the result that an establishment of camels for all units had to be arranged. Seventy-three camels were allowed per Regiment, and were employed for the following purposes: 16 for ammunition, 3 sanitary gear, 3 water troughs and pumps, 1 medical panniers, 1 office gear, 18 drinking water, 4 cooks' gear, and 27 for general baggage.

With this establishment we operated in the desert, the camels being brought daily from the camel transport unit as required. As the men accumulated stores, the loads generally grew in size until in some cases the camel would almost be hidden. It was no uncommon sight to see a camel trekking with two or three long tables tied on, and in some cases with a five-seated latrine across the saddle. The load was not supposed to exceed 300 lbs., but often reached nearer 500. In addition to the bulky loads, many camels would have strings of pots and pans tied to every odd corner, and as a camel never misses an opportunity to scratch himself against anything solid, the pots and pans came in for much ill treatment.

Camel supply convoys would consist of hundreds of camels in strings, one driver to each three camels, and moving four strings abreast to shorten the column. Each camel would carry three sacks of grain or two bundles of Dries or Tibben. The bales of Dries or Tibben were compressed and bound with iron bands. The camel in rear of one of these loads was no trouble to lead, as he would keep close up quietly munching the stuff, thereby lightening the load, whilst the camel in his rear rendered him the same service, with the result that the bales reached their destination very much the worse for the journey.

On entering Palestine, the wheel transport, which up to that time had been located at Kantara on the Suez Canal, was brought forward. For the operations against Gaza a fresh scheme was adopted. The idea was to make the troops self-supporting for a period of five days by carrying their rations on saddle horses, in improvised packs.

These packs were made out of sacks in the form of large saddle bags, each side being large enough to hold two tins of biscuits. The scheme had many faults, the worst being that it took too many men from the firing line to lead them, and that the loads, which were in all cases awkward, could not be made to ride easy, with the result that the corners of the tins rubbed the horses' sides and galled them.

On the morning of the 26th March the troops moved out for the attack, the improvised packs following in rear of the Brigade, and carrying three days' rations, whilst the men carried two days', and an iron ration. The animals were, as far as possible, to live on the country, which at that time

APPENDICES

was covered with good crops of barley. The pack horses did not take too kindly to their loads, and two broke loose, galloping off across country, with the result that tins of bully beef, jam, and milk were soon flying in all directions.

A big camel convoy carrying ammunition and water, and wheeled transport carrying grain, left shortly afterwards to rendezvous at Sheikh Abbas Ridge, arriving there at 1 p.m. On the Brigade moving forward, 44 camels, carrying 176,000 rounds of ammunition, were collected and taken in rear of the Brigade as a reserve. On the return of the Brigade it was found that the horses carrying the improvised packs had not had their loads taken off, owing probably to their awkward adjustment, and had thus carried the load for 29 hours.

The wheeled transport now joined up with their own units, and came under fire for the first time at the battle of Attawineh on the 19th April, 1917.

The next operations found us in the Shellal area and a fresh scheme was adopted. The scheme was to divide the transport into three echelons as follows: "A" echelon to carry water, ammunition, and tools; "B" 1, supplies; and "B" 2, baggage. "A" echelon consisted of the water cart, the Maltese (medical officer's) cart, 1 limbered wagon for ammunition, 1 limbered wagon for technical gear and tools, and 1 for officers' mess gear. "B" 1 echelon consisted of 1 general service and 4 limbered wagons, to carry supplies on the following scale: Biscuits, 13 ounces; bully, 9 ounces; sugar, 3 ounces; and tea, $\frac{5}{8}$ ounce, per man, per diem; and $9\frac{1}{2}$ lbs. of crushed barley or oats per horse for each day.

"B" 2 echelon consisted of 4 G.S. wagons to carry general baggage, such as men's kits, cooking and sanitary gear, etc. Each echelon was placed under the command of an officer detailed by the Division, and on all moves formed up as a Divisional unit. "A" echelon was to follow and keep touch with the fighting line, "B" 1 to follow the rear of the Division, and "B" 2 to bring up the rear.

During the Beersheba-Jerusalem operations this scheme proved entirely satisfactory. On arrival at Ludd the rains broke, and the work of the transport became extremely hard owing to the scarcity of good roads.

On the Brigade taking up dismounted duty in the hills, the transport was sent to camp at Surafend, near Ludd, and was moved later to Katra, where it did good work in assisting the Divisional Train in bringing supplies from Esdud, the only track from which, owing to the continual rain storms, soon became almost impassable, the wheels sinking to their axles.

At the end of December the Division was sent into reserve at Belah, four days' march south-west, the transport of the Brigade being moved as one unit for the journey, and placed under the orders of Major Darley. The second day's march was exceptional, as for the first three miles the country was under water and in many places boggy, making the task of getting through 112 heavily-laden wagons a matter of great difficulty. On reaching the higher ground about mid-day, one of the worst rainstorms one could ever expect to see started, and continued for the rest of the journey.

About one mile from Mejdel a large stretch of bog was met, and although most of the wagons got through, the last three became bogged for three hours, owing to their drivers not taking the track ordered.

After a month's stay at Belah, during which time the transport was thoroughly overhauled, the Division moved out and proceeded by easy stages to Sarona, near Jaffa. On the expected operations being abandoned, orders were received for the Division to proceed to the Jordan Valley. The first day's march on this journey was a severe test for the draught animals, owing to the sandy nature of the country traversed, the teams beginning to show signs of distress by the time they reached camp. The second day brought us to Latron at the foot of the hills.

We were now faced with the problem of crossing the Judean Hills, and with this in view the brakes had been put in a good and serviceable condition. The roads were in fairly good order, but long stretches of new metal were met, the inhabitants—men, women, and children—being kept busy repairing the roads by laying new metal.

This move through the hills with a string of over 100 five-horse teams was very difficult, as they had to be kept closed up to prevent the column stretching for miles. The drivers also had an inclination to straggle all over the road, instead of keeping to their own side, as was absolutely necessary, owing to the winding nature of the roads and the amount of motor traffic met with.

After a few days' halt at Talaat ed Dumm, the Brigade was ordered to the Valley and proceeded *via* the old road. It is hard to understand why the transport was ordered to proceed by such a road, when a splendid new road had been constructed and was available, but this was kept solely for motor traffic.

On arriving at the top of the hill the transport was halted, the hind wheels, in addition to having the brakes put full on, being lashed with rope. When all was ready, the first wagon was dispatched, and had nearly reached the bottom when the ropes broke, with the result that the wagon became out of control and overturned. After being righted it was ordered to proceed for about 600 yards on the flat and then halt until the remainder were down. As each wagon reached the foot of the hill, the ropes were removed, and the wagon moved along the flat, halting as they came in rear of those already down. When all except the Maltese cart were down, I moved down the hill to send the column forward, and in my absence someone gave the driver the order to descend. After the worst part of the road had been safely passed and the cart was within 50 yards of the level, both wheels struck a deep rut, and both shafts broke off close to the cart.

The driver was thrown forward and fell between the cart and the mules, which immediately galloped off dragging the cart after them by the traces. Although stopped by several men before they had gone 30 yards, the driver was so badly injured that he died a few minutes later in the Field Ambulance, which was alongside the road at the spot where the accident happened.

In spite of the thousands of miles of difficult country traversed by the transport during the war, this was the only serious accident met with. (One driver was killed at Sarona whilst out with his wagon, but this was not a case of an organized party of transport.) The authorities, when the fatal accident to Pte. Learmouth referred to above was reported, wisely gave an order to the effect that all wheel transport would use the new road.

The work of the transport in the Jordan Valley was exceptionally trying, as in addition to the intense heat, clouds of choking dust would rise at every movement, it often being impossible to see the wagon immediately in front. It was with great relief, therefore, that orders were received for the march to Ludd, and in this move the Judean Hills were crossed without the slightest difficulty.

For the operations of September-October, 1918, as it was possible that the wheels might have to be abandoned, each off-side horse was fitted with pack saddlery, and carried this in addition to his harness. The articles which must be carried in any case were arranged in loads and tied with the loading ropes before being placed in the wagon, so that in the event of emergency the change could be effected in the shortest possible time.

The number of additional pack saddles and their loads were as follows: Signalling gear, 2; water equipment, 3; ammunition, 3; drinking water, 3; medical stores, 2; and supplies, 8; bringing the number of pack horses up to 57.

On the 18th September, 1918, the Division moved to and bivouacked at Sarona. At dawn on the 19th the attack started, and the fighting troops moved off, followed by the transport in the following order: "A" echelon following and keeping close up to the fighting force, "B" 1 (supplies), and "B" 2 (baggage).

"B" 1 echelon consisted of the supply wagons of the 3rd, 4th, and 5th Brigades, Corps Troops, and French Troops, and was under the command of Major T. H. Darley, whilst the baggage echelon of the same units was commanded by Capt. B. B. Ragless.

At Yellow House bridge the transport was parked by echelons and the animals watered, on completion of which the column moved off, making for Sheik Muhammed. This proved to be one of the hardest marches the transport was ever subjected to, as in addition to the distance being roughly 33 miles, the country for the greater part was of a loose sandy nature, and without roads. On reaching the Turkish lines wire entanglements had to be removed and trenches filled in before the wagons could proceed, causing the loss of valuable time. At 6 p.m. the column halted to water and feed, and the men had tea. At 7 p.m. the advance was continued, and at about 10.30 p.m. the convoy struck large sand beds, and found hundreds of wagons trying to get through. The state of affairs at this place defies description, and the frantic shouts of hundreds of drivers must have been heard miles away. In many cases teams of 12 horses failed to shift a single wagon, many of which were sunk to their axles in the loose sand, and great care had to be taken to prevent our own column of over 100 wagons from getting mixed up with the many teams floundering in the sand.

Halting the convoy, I rode forward and searched for more solid ground, and on my return took the convoy along the foot of the hills, where the ground was fairly good, although it meant adding a mile or two to the journey, but it paid handsomely, as we got through without a single wagon stuck, and reached our position at 3.30 a.m. after a journey of 17¼ hours.

After watering at Yellow House bridge, "B" 2 echelon was left well behind, and it was found later that they had had to abandon most of their loads on striking the sand beds. They were not seen again until the echelon caught us up at El Afuleh five days later.

At 5 a.m. the transport was once more on the road and started to cross the Nahr Iskanderun by means of a very flimsy bridge, which had one side completely open, the approaches to which were very steep and on the turn. The wagons of the Regiment crossed in safety, but the first wagon of the 4th Brigade landed in the stream, a fall of about 10 feet, much valuable time being lost in rescuing the mules and stores.

After a long march, the latter part of which was fortunately done on a good hard road, the column arrived at Lejjun at 5 p.m., where it unloaded its supplies and bivouacked for the night. At daybreak fresh supplies were loaded, and the column moved to Jenin, which was reached at 10.30 a.m.

At 5 p.m. on the 25th, the column moved off on the march to Tiberias. After a few miles of fairly level road, the long and trying climb to Nazareth began. The roads were strewn with smashed enemy motor transport, and twisted and turned every few yards. Passing through the town the transport was halted for a spell, after which the journey was resumed under better conditions. The Brigade reached Tiberius at 5.30 a.m. and passed through the town to Mejdel, where the column formed up and halted near the Sea of Galilee.

As soon as the horses were watered and fed and the men had a meal, the transport delivered its supplies and returned to Tiberius to await the motor supply column. This column arrived about 3.30 a.m. on the following morning and the transports were loaded, leaving immediately for Mejdel.

At about 10 a.m. the column moved off on the march to Benat Yakub. The first eight or ten miles was along a winding road, which rose about 800 feet, and the wagons soon began to straggle, so that frequent halts had to be made to allow the slower teams to close up. Some of the teams were showing signs of exhaustion as the high ground was reached, as in addition to the difficult road, the wagons were well laden.

On arrival at Rosh Pinar it was found that the enemy were opposing the crossing of the river, and the transport was taken off the road and parked for the night. At 7 a.m. on the following day the transport moved off and proceeded to Jisr Benat Yakub, where it halted to await the completion of repairs to the bridge, which had been partly blown up by the enemy. At 3 p.m. a move was made, and the bridge safely crossed. On reaching the eastern bank the road was found to be very narrow and steep, so that it took some time before the column was on the high ground.

At this point the column was halted in accordance with orders from Headquarters to allow the fighting troops of the 5th Cavalry Division to pass, followed by their "A" echelon. About an hour later the fighting troops had passed, and we anxiously awaited their echelon, but there appeared to be no signs of it. As it was beginning to get dark, I walked down the hill to investigate, and came across the echelon, halted with nosebags on and poles down. I had been assured by a Staff Officer of the 5th Cavalry Division that they had been given orders to push on past our transport, so that we could move.

Seeing a Staff Officer near at hand, I asked him why the echelon was halted when we had been waiting for over three hours for them to pass, and was told that they were waiting for my column to get out of the way. I therefore got them to move forward, and eventually got my own column on the move towards Kuneitra, a distance of 18 miles away. The night was very dark and cold, and both men and horses were beginning to feel the strain by the time that place was reached about 3.30 a.m.

At 5.30 a.m. the horses were fed and the men had breakfast, after which the transport moved off for the Brigade bivouac and rationed the units, returning to the bivouac about 10 a.m. Orders were received from Division to load fresh supplies on arrival of the motor transport, and be ready to continue the march at 10 p.m.

The column moved off at the appointed hour, and after about two hours' march came to a halt behind the 5th Cavalry Division. Firing could be heard in front for some time, and after a two hours' halt I walked along the road to see if there was any chance of a move, but after going about two miles along the closely-packed road I gave up the job as hopeless and decided to await events. All through the night the column, miles in length, stood in the roadway, and it was not till 7 a.m. that the column was once more on the move. At 11 a.m. the column was halted to water and feed, and moved off at mid-day to Sasa. After passing this place the whole of the echelons were moved off the road and parked, and placed under the escort of an Indian Cavalry Regiment, as there was a probability of enemy forces crossing the rear of our fighting force.

At 5.30 p.m. the advance was resumed, and shortly afterwards the 5th Cavalry Division transport pulled off the road and bivouacked for the night, but as the Australian Mounted Division had pushed forward to Damascus, I decided to follow, and marched until 3 a.m., at which hour we halted for the remainder of the night. At 5.30 a.m. we were once more on the move, and reached Divisional Headquarters about 7.30 a.m.

On arrival at Division it was found that although the Brigade had passed through the city, it still contained a number of enemy troops, and was not considered safe for a big convoy to pass through. After repeated requests to be allowed to proceed, consent was finally given at 3 p.m., and the column moved off. It was found that the enemy had blown up the bridges and torn up the roads in all directions, so that it was not till after dark that the column reached the native quarter on the other side of the town.

This part of the town consisted of very narrow streets, the first part of which was completely covered in, and had a right angle turn about 100 yards from the entrance. The task of getting the big general service wagons round this turn was a difficult one, as the tunnel was pitch dark. By lighting bunches of about a dozen candles, and holding them in the corner, the task was at last accomplished, and the transport reached the open streets, which were so narrow that the wheels in some places touched the kerb on either hand. On reaching the French quarter the drivers were given a great reception, also many gifts of flowers and fruit.

Moving along the Aleppo road, which had been damaged in many places by the retreating enemy, the transport reached Brigade Headquarters at 11.45 p.m. Several unpleasant experiences were met with during this run, the chief being that in crossing the bridge over the river one of the off-side horses fell through a hole which had been blown in the bridge. After much hard work and harder swearing, the poor beast was got back onto the road not much worse for its experience.

At 5 a.m. supplies were issued to the various camps, and the column moved off on the return journey, reaching Mejdel at 1 p.m. Orders were then received to reload and return to the Brigade with further supplies, and at 3 p.m., the transport, having reloaded, started on the return march and reached the Brigade at 11 p.m. A very welcome rest was now given to the transport, which had only bivouacked for eight hours out of the last 75.

Two days later the Brigade moved back to El Mezze, and on the following day moved to Kaukab, where it stayed until the 27th October. It then marched out on its trek to Homs.

For most of the journey the roads were in a very bad state, the final stage being exceptionally trying owing to the long track of waterless country which had to be passed. For this particular journey the transport moved off at 7 a.m. and watered in the vicinity of Nebk. It then started on the 50 miles stretch of waterless country.

The roads were very dusty, and in some places stretched so far into the distance as to appear almost endless. By 7 p.m. the column had made good progress and was halted for one hour to feed. On arrival at Hasie the welcome news was received that an armistice had been agreed upon, and that hostilities had ceased.

At 11.30 p.m. the march was resumed, and after marching all night the outskirts of Homs was reached at daybreak. Passing through the town a camp was formed about two miles along the Aleppo road. The few days spent in this camp formed a welcome rest, although the transport was by no means idle, and on the 6th November the Brigade once more struck camp and started on the journey to Tripoli.

The march proved a hard one, as in addition to stretches of the road which were in a deplorable condition, the Lebanon Mountains had to be crossed. This journey was, however, of great interest, some fine villages being passed through, the beautiful scenery being admired by all.

After a lengthy stay at Tripoli, during which the transport had a fairly easy time, we handed over the wagons and horses with deep regret, and embarked on the "Ellenga" for Egypt.

During the whole of the operations mentioned, except Beersheba, I was in command of the Brigade transport or "B" 1 echelon of the Division, and I cannot conclude without mentioning the splendid work done by all ranks. No matter what the conditions, or how hard the task, they never failed, and this is the more praiseworthy as, although they played such an important part in the general scheme, their only reward was the satisfaction of having done their duty, as in no single instance did any member of the transport receive special commendation.

During the Es Salt operations two drivers of the Regiment, Drivers Rattley and Rolland, were, with their limber, part of a force attached to the Field Squadron on special duty. This force got into difficulties with the large enemy reinforcements which attacked the 4th Light Horse Brigade. The teams of all the wagons and guns had been unhooked and taken to the wadi for shelter. The rapid advance of the enemy upset all calculations, and orders were given to retire and abandon the vehicles.

In spite of the fact that the whole of the remainder retired, and the closeness of the enemy, Drivers Rattley and Rolland took their horses from the wadi, hooked them in, and started out to save their wagon. To effect a crossing of the wadi, it was necessary to gallop towards the oncoming enemy for some distance, and in spite of the heavy fire they succeeded in reaching their lines in safety, this being the only vehicle of that force to be brought out. For their bravery and devotion to duty, these two men deserved some recognition, but none was awarded.

The fighting force undoubtedly did great work, but their part is always interesting and full of excitement. Not so the work of the drivers, monotonously plodding along, hour after hour and night after night, just an endless column of wagons enveloped in clouds of dust, and I have nothing but admiration for the men who did this work faithfully and well for the long period of the war.

APPENDIX II

SPECIAL ORDER OF THE DAY, BY GENERAL SIR E. H. H. ALLENBY, COMMANDER-IN-CHIEF, EGYPTIAN EXPEDITIONARY FORCE

Now that the Australian Mounted Division and Anzac Mounted Division are leaving my command, I wish to express to all ranks my admiration of and gratitude for the work they have done.

The units composing these Divisions, landing in Egypt after gallant service in Gallipoli, have been constantly engaged with the enemy since the formation of the Egyptian Expeditionary Force, and have taken a leading part in all the victories won.

In the advance through the Sinai Desert, the capture of Beersheba, the pursuit of the enemy which ended in the taking of Jerusalem, the operations in the Jordan Valley, in the mountains east of the Jordan, and in the final defeat and pursuit of the Turkish Army in September and October, 1918, Australian and New Zealand troops have been always in the forefront. They have borne with cheerful endurance the thirst and glare of the desert, the heat and dust of the Jordan Valley, and the fatigue of long and exhausting marches. They have responded to every call, and have fully earned the welcome which will reward them on their long-deferred return to their homes.

I send them my congratulations, my thanks, and my best wishes.

(Signed) EDMUND H. H. ALLENBY,
General.

General Headquarters,
    Egyptian Expeditionary Force,
        June 28th, 1919.

The following is an appreciation of the Australian Light Horse in Palestine:

"I knew the New South Wales Lancers and the Australian Light Horse well in the Boer War, and I was glad to meet some of my old friends of those days when the Light Horse came under my command just two years ago.

"When I took over command of the Egyptian Expeditionary Force in July,

THE QUAY AT KANTARA, SUEZ CANAL.
9th Light Horse proceeding to embark. Captured Turkish guns awaiting transport to Australia

"THE ORIGINALS."

The only members who left Australia and returned with the Regiment

APPENDICES 193

1917, the Light Horse were already veterans, tried and proved in many a fight. Since then they have shared in the campaign which achieved the destruction of the Turkish Army and the conquest of Palestine and Syria, and throughout they have been in the thick of the fighting. I have found them eager in advance and staunch in defence. At Beersheba a mounted charge by a Light Horse Regiment, armed only with rifles, swept across the Turkish trenches and decided the day. Later some of the Regiments were armed with swords, which they used with great effect in the pursuit of last autumn.

On foot, too, they have equally distinguished themselves as stubborn fighters. They have shown in the dismounted action the dash and enterprise of the best type of Light Infantry.

The Australian Light Horseman combines with a splendid physique a restless activity of mind. This mental quality renders him somewhat impatient of rigid and formal discipline, but it confers upon him the gift of adaptability, and this is the secret of much of his success, mounted or on foot. In this dual role, on every variety of ground—mountain, plain, desert, swamp, or jungle—the Australian Light Horseman has proved himself equal to the best. He has earned the gratitude of the Empire and the admiration of the world.

(Signed) EDMUND H. H. ALLENBY,
General.

APPENDIX III

NARRATIVE OF SGT. WATTS—THE EGYPTIAN RISING

The Regimental Football Team, which had proceeded to Cairo to play in the final for the Championship of the Egyptian Expeditionary Force, which they won, were, on the outbreak of the Egyptian rising, detailed for special duty with a composite force, organized by Army Headquarters, at Kasr el Nil Barracks.

At noon on the 19th March this force boarded a barge and proceeded to the barrage, a distance of about 20 miles down the Nile. After a three hours' journey the troops disembarked and proceeded to the village, round which a cordon was placed. Parties were then sent to search the village and to arrest some 50 natives, whose names had been supplied by the secret police.

The Mudir (Governor) of the District was given a list of the men required, and was ordered to produce them. Within two days these orders were carried out and the party returned to Cairo. On arrival the party proceeded to Ghezireh, where they were addressed by Colonel Fulton as to their next task.

Two hours later the party proceeded to the embarkation pier at Giza and boarded the river steamers "Puritan" and "Vic," owned by the American Nile Company. Reinforcements, consisting of 110 Australians and a party of the 10th (Irish) Division, with two machine guns, also embarked. As soon as the rations and stores had been taken aboard the steamers proceeded up the river to Maadi, at which place they anchored for the night.

As a large supply of good bedding had been put on board for the use of the refugees whom we were to bring from the interior, the troops soon made themselves comfortable for the night. At daybreak the journey was continued to Wasta, which was reached at noon. At this place stores were loaded for Assiut, and whilst this was being done a number of the troops went ashore and inspected the damage done by the frenzied natives during the riots a few days earlier. The railway station had been completely wrecked, and the unfortunate station-master butchered before the eyes of his family.

A boat containing 15 natives attempted to pass down stream, but was ordered to pull in for examination. This order was promptly disregarded, with the result that they were fired on by the sentry. As they still made no effort to comply, a machine gun was turned on them and soon had the desired effect, as they pulled in to the ship after having one man killed and one wounded.

At 3 p.m. the steamers cast off and proceeded up stream, but after travelling a short distance were stopped owing to the channel being blocked, and the journey was not resumed till daybreak. At 10 a.m. a seaplane signalled the captain to stop, and landed alongside, the pilot reporting that he was out of petrol. After filling his tank he rose from the water, and the steamer proceeded on its journey.

During the day many villages and ancient ruins were passed, and were of great interest. On nearing Minia our boat ran aground, causing a delay of about an hour, Minia being reached at 2 p.m. A party of Egyptian Cavalry were drawn up at the landing stage as the steamer drew in, and owing to the local conditions the troops were not allowed to land. The drinking water of both steamers was replenished and we moved off immediately. A few miles up the river the second steamer was fired on, the fire being promptly returned with good effect and causing several casualties to the party of rebels.

The steamers anchored for the night in mid-stream and resumed the journey at daybreak, Assiut being reached at mid-day. A party was immediately organized and sent across the barrage, and it was here that we witnessed one of the most impressive sights that had come our way. An American lady had in her charge some 50 odd native children, whom she had been educating for their battle through life, entirely at her own expense, which work she had been carrying out for the past seven years.

She had been warned on several occasions that if she remained she would be murdered, and for the past three days had hidden away, together with the children, in a disused brick kiln, to escape the fury of the mob. She had done untold good for the people, who were now, without reason, anxious to take her life, but our timely arrival frustrated their plans and she was taken on board and conveyed to safety.

Aeroplanes had on the previous day bombed the mobs of rioters, whom they dispersed after inflicting numerous casualties, thus gaining time for the arrival of the troops. An examination of the town revealed the fact that great damage had been done to the residences of the Europeans, many beautiful homes being completely destroyed. On the following day the European residents were collected and taken on board the two steamers, about 100 being placed on each.

On our boat the refugees were mostly Americans, but they had been subjected to the same treatment as all Europeans. At mid-day the boats moved off on their return journey, and all hands went to work to make our guests comfortable. Anchoring in mid-stream for the night, we moved away at daybreak, and reached Minia at 10 a.m.

At this point we were met by a patrol boat, the commander of which informed us as to local conditions, and as a consequence all ranks were ordered to the top deck under arms, ready for any emergency. On arrival at the town the commandant asked that the boats be stopped and an armed force landed, as the situation was far from satisfactory, five Egyptian soldiers having been killed on the previous night. Thirty men from each boat were therefore landed, and the boats continued their journey.

By this time the Americans and ourselves were "hitting it great," and it was decided that when we anchored for the night a concert would be held. Therefore, as soon as the boats dropped anchor, all on board, with the ex-

APPENDICES

ception of the sentries, assembled on the deck for the concert, which went off in great style. The night passed without incident, and the steamers moved off at daybreak. All went well until about 11 a.m., when our boat ran aground on a sand bank, and all efforts to shift her proved useless. Church service was held in the evening, all on board attending.

At daybreak further effort was made to get afloat, but proved of no avail, until the "Vic," who had herself been aground, came up and towed us off. Two hours later we passed Wasta, at which place a great change had occurred, troops appearing to be everywhere, and the town to be quite under control.

The two steamers continued their journey, passing many boats loaded with troops, guns, and stores. A second concert was held during the evening, at which the troops were cordially thanked by the refugees for the services rendered to them.

On arrival of the steamers at Giza, the refugees with their baggage were landed and conveyed to Cairo, where they were given suitable accommodation. The troops were employed for the remainder of the day in handing over stores, after which they disembarked and proceeded to the Australian Kit Store at Ghezireh.

In summarizing the trips we came to the conclusion that it was the most enjoyable time we had spent during the whole course of the war. It had been an enjoyable experience to be once more amongst poeple speaking our own language and with the same ideals, and for once our work was appreciated because we were understood.

After two days spent at the Kit Depot, the party proceeded to Zag-a-Zig and rejoined the Regiment.

APPENDIX IV

DESCRIPTION OF GUNS CAPTURED BY THE REGIMENT.

4 FIELD GUNS, 75 MM. Captured at Rafa on the 9th January, 1917.

When the New Zealanders came over the ridge west of the enemy position, the Regiment, with the Imperial Camel Corps, and followed shortly after by the 10th Light Horse, pushed forward to the assault on the south-west.

"C" Squadron of the Regiment, having crossed the first line of trenches, where the enemy surrendered, sent a party forward under Capt. J. C. Chanter. This party pushed on to the gun pits, capturing the four guns, together with some members of their crews.

1 HOWITZER, 15 CM. Captured at Huj on the 8th November, 1917.

After the capture of Huj, the Regiment pushed on through the enemy depot to a position overlooking the flat country in the vicinity of Simsin and Burber. Lieut. L. M. S. Hargrave, with a troop from "A" Squadron, was sent forward to reconnoitre a position. On arrival he found a party of the enemy in the act of removing a gun which a short time previously had been firing into our advancing troops. He led the troop to a favourable position and brought a heavy fire to bear, killing part of the escort and team. He then led the troop forward and captured the gun.

2, 4-IN. FIELD GUNS. Captured at Huj on the 8th November, 1917.

Lieut. Mueller was sent forward with a patrol of "B" Squadron, after the capture of Huj, to reconnoitre the country on the right of the 5th Mounted Brigade, who had just made a successful charge. During this move he found

196 WITH THE NINTH LIGHT HORSE

a party of the enemy in the act of withdrawing a field gun. The patrol immediately shot down the bullock team and forced the escort to withdraw, capturing the gun. A few minutes later the patrol captured a second gun with team complete.

2 HOWITZERS, 15 CM. Captured at Neby Huj on the 8th November, 1917.

On the 8th November, 1917, the Regiment was detailed as advance guard to the Brigade, for the attack on Huj. "A" Squadron on the right, and "B" on the left, supplied the advance patrols.

Strong opposition was encountered, but the enemy were eventually driven from their positions. The right flank patrol, under the command of No. 705, Lance-Cpl. K. C. Bennett, pushed forward to Neby Huj, at which place, after shooting one of the escort and taking three prisoners, they captured two modern 15 cm. Krupp Howitzers.

Great credit is due to the members of this patrol for the splendid initiative and dash displayed in effecting this capture. Unfortunately, Lance-Cpl. Bennett was killed in action at Berkusie, four days later.

NAVAL GUN, 10 CM. (manufactured by William Armstrong, England). Captured at the wadi north of Huj on the 8th November, 1917.

As the Regiment pushed forward after the capture of Huj, a patrol of "A" Squadron, with a section of the 3rd Machine Gun Squadron, came towards the wadi where the enemy were attempting to withdraw this gun. After shooting down the team and escort, the gun was captured.

2 FIELD GUNS, 7.5. Captured at Khan Ayash on the 2nd October, 1918.

At 6.15 a.m. on the 2nd October, 1918, an enemy column 1,500 strong was observed retreating near the main Aleppo road, north-east of Damascus. The Regiment quickly turned out to attack, and galloping towards the hills to cut the retreat of the force, the Squadrons formed line and charged with the sword.

"C" Squadron, under the command of Major Charley, charged and captured these guns near Khan Ayash.

1 MOUNTAIN GUN AND 26 MACHINE GUNS. Captured at Khan Ayash on the 2nd October, 1918.

These were captured by various units of the Regiment in the operation briefly described above, together with a number of automatic rifles.

APPENDIX V

TRANSLATION OF CAPTURED DOCUMENTS

Correspondence between Field Marshall Limon Von Sanders, Major Von Papen, Chief of Staff, IVth Turkish Army, and Djemal Pasha, Commander IVth Army.

4th May, 1918.

His Honour,
    Major Von Papen,

I regret to have to inform your Honour that I am not in any way in agreement with the various measures recently adopted by the Chief Command of the 4th Army.

The VIII Army Corps fought well and bravely under Ali Fuad Bey, and but for this, results would have been very different.

I give my criticism below:

1. It would have been advisable for the Headquarters of the 4th Army to keep in close touch with the VIII Army Corps when a serious attack was to be delivered. I cannot in any way approve of its move northwards.

2. The whole of the enemy operations were directed against Es Salt.
    The enemy wishes to create a strategical bridgehead, whence he can advance later against Amman, Daraa, or Beisan; consequently it is necessary to retake Es Salt at all costs.
    This would be difficult by day as the enemy has so many machine guns with his Cavalry, but at night it would always be possible from the north, with Infantry, as the enemy has there only two Cavalry Brigades (1) and, later on, indeed, a fifth Regiment, besides some Artillery.
    Only on the north is co-operation possible with the 3rd Cavalry Division, which has fought splendidly.
    I recommend pushing forward a light screen of Infantry on to the former battle ground at the first sign of the light failing; with this, at dusk, Artillery and machine guns should come into action.
    The remainder of the Infantry should be collected on the right wing, and should take Es Salt with the bayonet from the north.
    Intead of that, in this morning's report there appears a statement that the right wing of the Infantry is advancing on Es Salt, and that the 8th Cavalry Regiment is already there.

3. I would suggest that in such a position there should not be so much talk of losses and shortage of water. In severe fighting of this kind, losses are inevitable. Water could be brought from Suweileh.
    Other troops have had far greater losses. It is we, as Prussian officers, who are charged with the duty of pushing forward with the greatest energy, satisfying complaints as far as possible, but otherwise insisting with an iron-like resolution on our wishes.

4. Had the VIII Army Corps taken up the flanking position which I have advised since the beginning of April, such a break through by Cavalry would never have occurred. Water can be no excuse, for there is sufficient in the Jordan, and the men's supplies could have been boiled.

5. I recommend, in the VIII Army Corps' position, to give each Cavalry post that has been pushed out a group of Infantry with a machine gun; these can later be protected by barbed wire. Perhaps this cannot take place everywhere, but it must be done on the most important roads.

6. I have repeatedly drawn attention to the fact that it is necessary to close the important roads at suitable places, or at least prepare them for closing. But on the 30th of April, at 7.30 a.m., the English were at Jisr ed Damie with Artillery and motors, and shortly before 11 a.m. a few squadrons had arrived opposite Es Salt. I am going to send Major Effuert to Es Salt to arrange a few supporting points on decisive heights, the early completion of which I request, if possible, with the help of the inhabitants.
    I beg that the above named work may be taken in hand as soon as possible on the roads leading to Es Salt, as well as on the roads to Tell Hamman (2). The barricades can be watched during the day by patrols in order not to employ too many groups. At night they must be manned, also as soon as strong enemy forces are being concentrated west of the Jordan, or at the bridgehead.

7. I recommend alternative positions being prepared for the Artillery, and more use made of Dummy positions.
    This will lessen our losses.

(Signed) LIMAN VON SANDERS.

4th May, 1918.

To Major Von Papen,

During the night 3rd Cavalry Divisions took the heights north of Es Salt, and it is now in immediate possession.

The enemy has retired in a S.W. direction, and is being pursued by a Battalion and some Cavalry, moving on a parallel course.

I hold you personally responsible if, through any delay on the part of Shukri Bey's column, a set back should occur.

I request an immediate report from the scene of the fighting.

(Signed) LIMAN VON SANDERS.

N.B.—(1) Liman Von Sanders evidently estimated each Cavalry Brigade at two Regiments.

(2) Close to Ain Hammam, three miles S.W. of Amman.

The draft letter below is undated, but from contemporary correspondence is undoubtedly of about the 5th May, 1918.

Marshall Liman,
   Nablus,

Now that the normal situation is restored, I respectfully notify your Excellency of the following:

1. The Army most emphatically protests against the untrue announcement of the 7th Army, that the 3rd Cavalry Division took the heights north of Es Salt.

    These heights are covered with the dead of the 66th Infantry Regiment, only one patrol of the 8th Cavalry Regiment was there.

    Just as strange is the assertion of the 3rd Cavalry Division, that for two days past they have been in possession of the western heights, as yesterday evening the English Cavalry, entirely unhindered, withdrew beyond Es Salt in the direction of El Mandesi.

    The 66th Infantry Regiment fought very gallantly. Its high losses prove this. If they did not succeed in beating the enemy at the exact moment desired by your Excellency, this was due to circumstances into which I cannot enter in a "Clear" telegram.

    However, your Excellency will doubtless agree that when an attack repeatedly ordered does not develop, I should as in duty bound report with regard to the situation as it actually is, and should not make triumphant announcements.

    Your Excellency will be satisfied with the bearing of the VIIIth Army Corps, which during the foregoing weeks has been so equipped and furnished with directions from the Army, that no doubt could prevail as to its task.

2. Your Excellency has complained of deficient reports. In reply to this I respectfully report that the Army Headquarters only had one telephone operator at its disposal. The rest of the personnel took part in the defence of Es Salt, and are dead, wounded, or prisoners—besides this, Headquarters had only one line, generally out of order, which served at the time as operation line. Your Excellency will agree that this line, when in working order, should be used first of all for the transmission of operation orders. I may add that I had only one orderly officer. All other officers, despite urgent requests, were unable to keep up with the Headquarters as they were not mounted.

    The Army Headquarters working under such conditions has been for five days continuously in closest touch with its units. It left Es Salt one minute before the English forced their way in.

    It is evident that the limited communications of the Army Headquarters might give the impression that it was not informed as to the situation during this period in the same way as a Headquarters established in Nablus, with a great number of good lines. As a matter of fact, the Headquarters were always well informed as to the situation.

3. It must be an error if your Excellency assumes that the Army rushed an unplanned attack against the bridgehead—the Army Headquarters had no such incomprehensible arrangement, but only ordered that the Infantry of the 48th Division should press forward resolutely into the old positions, and that the Artillery should keep the Jordan bridge under continuous fire.

4. In yesterday's telegram your Excellency referred pointedly to my personal responsibility. From this I must assume that your Excellency believes that I am not aware of my responsibility as Chief of Staff, and did not fulfil my duty during these days. This is the first time in my military career that this reproach has been addressed to me.

Therefore I respectfully beg your Excellency to grant my immediate relief from my present position, and to employ me as a Battalion Commander on a battle front.

(Signed) VON PAPEN.

These documents were found in the Yilderin Headquarters, Nazareth.

CAPTURED DOCUMENT.

Letter to Kiazim Pasha, C.G.S., Yilderin, from apparently (the letter is unsigned) Djemal Pasha, G.O.C., 4th Army.

I humbly thank your Excellency for the kind words which you have been so kind as to address to me. In the 5th year of the War we are all accustomed to misunderstanding. In the meanwhile the point in question is that the Commander of Army must possess the entire confidence of the Army Group Commander, if he is to work successfully.

I learn from the discourse which his Excellency the Marshall has directed to me in writing that the decisions of the Army had not met with the approval of his Excellency.

Your Excellency, I beg to be allowed to take the following stand with regard to these criticisms:

1. The Marshall is of the opinion that Es Salt should have been taken during the night from the north with the Infantry of the 8th Army Corps, while simply a light Infantry screen should have been left on the front of the 8th Army Corps. This solution, which perhaps appears possible according to the map, is, as a matter of fact, a tactical impossibility.

At the first attack on the morning of the 30th April the foremost positions of the 48th Infantry Division, that is, the right wing of the 8th Army Corps, had already been lost.

If the 8th Army Corps was to hold on, which was an absolute necessity, then no man could be withdrawn out of its front.

This alone would have been wrong on account of the moral reaction on the troops who were fighting. Till 4 p.m. the Army command had positive hopes of holding Salt. If the Army command had withdrawn from here earlier the defence would have probably been smashed by mid-day. The position of the Army command was therefore close to Salt.

If the Army command had joined up with the 8th Army Corps after the fall of Es Salt, it would have been able to effect this by about 9 p.m.

An order given at this hour for the concentration of the Infantry of the 8th Army Corps on its right flank could have been carried out somewhere between 1 and 2 a.m. next morning. An attack on Es Salt could not have been made with less than three Battalions. They would have had to be taken from Lufty Bey's Division, which itself is only three Battalions strong. In that case the Infantry would have had to carry out a six hours' night march from Jebel Hot to Salt from a south-westerly direction. Hence follows the technical impossibility of the operation required by his Excellency. If it were determined on, the danger was imminent that the front of the 8th Army Corps would be crushed in, and the attack on Es Salt, which could not be managed with this Infantry from the north, would likewise miscarry.

There is not the slightest doubt that Salt must be captured from the enemy again as soon as possible. This could, however, according to views taken here, only come to pass through a co-operation of forces from the direction of Ed Damie and Amman.

The task of the 8th Army Corps was clear. It had to hold on. In consequence of this, the only thing the Army command could do was to exercise as much influence as possible on the battle front which was developing round Es Salt. Hence the decision to take to the heights to the north of Es Salt, which had already been discussed before, when your Excellency was present.

Had the Army command joined up with the 8th Corps Commander, then it would have been cut off from every communication, and not even in the position to provide for the reinforcements of the 8th Army Corps.

2. The Marshall reproaches the Army for not taking the flank position recommended by him since the beginning of April. If the 48th Division had been situated on a flank position on the Jordan, the rapid break through of the enemy Cavalry towards the north would of course have been prevented. I, however, venture to leave it at the judgment of your Excellency whether the Lufty Division, with three Battalions (not yet 1,000 strong) would have been in the position to hold the front attack of the 60th Infantry Division; on the other hand, I venture to remind your Excellency that the Army has four times requested that the 2nd Caucasus Brigade be placed under it for tactical purposes. This request was rejected. The result was that the 9th Cavalry Regiment immediately withdrew before the enemy Cavalry to Mafid Jozele, whilst the 11th Cavalry Regiment obstructed the right flank of the 48th Division; if the 2nd Caucasus Brigade had been attached, it would have been withdrawn into the mountain passes leading to Es Salt, and would have delayed the enemy until the weak local defences of Salt could have been strengthened.

3. The Marshall considers that not too much be said in such a position of losses and scarcity of water. The attack on the 66th Infantry Regiment had come to a complete standstill at noon on the 3rd May, and encountered energetic resistance. The Infantry lay, on the whole, 100 to 200 meters in front of the enemy. Then the telegram from the Marshall arrived that Salt must be taken on that very afternoon. I reported, as in duty bound, how things stood, and said that it was not possible to continue the attack before night set in—at the same time, however, as the action of the enemy seemed with regard to the whole position to be threatening, I requested that the pressure on Salt be continued by the 3rd Cavalry Division.

It of course goes without saying that all the difficulties mentioned in this report, such as ammunition supply, the provision of water, have been surmounted, and that we continue the attack with the utmost energy. The Marshall must not therefore construe a faithful report as lack of energy on the part of those beneath him. I have certainly been in a more difficult situation in war than this, but never has this reproach been made to me.

Your Excellency will understand that with such differences of opinion, confidential and profitable work is not possible.

An Army command can demand that tactical decisions which can only be formed on the basis of a judgment made on the spot should not be characterized without further ceremony as entirely unreasonable.

I therefore think it best for all parties if his Excellency the Marshall responds to the wish I directed to him. I further report briefly to your Excellency on the position here.

It is not improbable that the enemy will shortly make a renewed attempt to capture the east Jordan region.

Considering the importance of an English success in the east Jordan region to the general position of the Army group, the Army feels bound in duty to make the following proposals:

A fresh attack may be attempted, with the numerous British Cavalry, by encircling both flanks of the 8th Army Corps (especially the left) with a simultaneous holding down of the front of the Army Corps and the break-through of a Cavalry Division east of the Jordan towards the north.

The communications in rear of the 8th Army Corps must in all circumstances be kept open.

In addition, the following seem necessary to the Army up to the time when it is itself ready to attack:

1. A mixed group of all arms for blocking the roads leading to Es Salt, with its necessary mountain Artillery.
2. Grouping of the 3rd Cavalry Division on the east bank of the Jordan as "action" troops against enemy Cavalry thrusting through towards the north.
3. Formation of a reinforced Cavalry Brigade (out of the Caucasus Cavalry Brigade and 7th Cavalry Regiment) on the left flank of the 8th Army Corps.
4. Reinforcement of 8th Army Corps in mountain Artillery.
5. Better equipment of the Army in motor lorry columns and mule transport columns, in order to regulate securely the provisioning and munition supply.
6. Improvement of the battle leadership and assignment of the necessary materials thereto.

All these preparations are considered at the same time as preparations for an offensive against the English Jordan flank.

We are proceeding with the further restoration of those barriers which were already established on the heights of Es Salt on the occasion of the last attack. Similar barriers are necessary on the heights east of Es Salt against an enveloping movement from the south.

The Army would be grateful if Major Effnert could direct this work for some time, as the Army Pioneer Inspector has been sick for eight days.

I beg your Excellency, as far as it seems expedient to you, to give an exposition of my statements, as set forth in the foregoing, to his Excellency.

This document was found in the Yilderin Headquarters, Nazareth.

APPENDIX VI

LIST OF MEMBERS OF THE REGIMENT WHO GAINED DECORATIONS FOR SERVICES RENDERED DURING THE WAR

Regt. No.	Rank	Name	Decoration Awarded
	Col.	Arnott, J. M.	C.M.G.
	Lieut.-Col.	Scott, W. H.	C.M.G., D.S.O., and Bar
	Major	Daly, T. J.	D.S.O.
	,,	Weick, G. F. C.	D.S.O.
	,,	McKenzie, K. A.	D.S.O.
	,,	Parsons, H. M.	D.S.O.
	,,	Darley, T. H.	O.B.E.
	Capt.	Luxmoore, E. M.	M.C.
	,,	McDonald, J. M.	M.C.
	Lieut.	Sharp, R. C.	M.C.
	,,	Hargrave, L. M. S.	M.C.
	,,	Wastel, N.	M.C.
	,,	Smith, P. T.	D.C.M.
	,,	Cattle, H. J.	D.C.M.
	,,	Cruddas, G. F.	D.C.M.
	,,	Rickaby, T. N.	M.M.
255	Sgt.	Foreman, J. L.	D.C.M.
956	,,	Runn, H. E.	D.C.M.
769	Cpl.	Todd, A. H.	D.C.M.
902	Siglr.	Smyth, J. N.	D.C.M.
1458	,,	Halliday, N. C.	D.C.M.
645	Pte.	Currie, A.	D.C.M.
2451	,,	Footner, A. O. H.	D.C.M.
958	Cpl.	Beard, A. W.	D.C.M.
405	R.S.M.	Wuchatsch, B. G.	M.M.
150	Sgt.	Myren, R. J. G.	M.M.
1442	,,	Rodger, C.	M.M.
1212	Pte.	Smith, E. K.	M.M.
821	Cpl.	Hillgrove, J. D.	M.M.
580	Sgt.	Maxwell, H. C.	M.M.
605A	Pte.	Morgan, F. R.	M.M.
213	,,	Partington, N. L.	M.M.
1004	,,	Watson, W. H.	M.M.
6046	,,	Carroll, J.	M.M.
2809	Lance-Cpl.	Dennison, R. L. W.	M.M.
2830	Pte.	Whittlesea, W. P.	M.M.
271	,,	Harvey, T. W.	M.M.
	Capt.	Wilkinson, R.	Order of the Nile, 4th Class
	,,	Pascoe, W. E.	Order of the Nile, 4th Class

The above abbreviations stand for the following: C.M.G., Commander of St. Michael and St. George; D.S.O., Distinguished Service Order; O.B.E., Officer of the Order of the British Empire; D.C.M., Distinguished Conduct Medal; M.C., Military Cross; M.M., Military Medal.

APPENDICES

APPENDIX VII

ROLL OF HONOUR

OFFICERS:

Date of Casualty.		Rank.	Name.	Nature of Casualty.
3rd June	1915	Lieut.	McWilliam, S. A.	Died of wounds
4th July	,,	Major	Cook, A. E.	,, ,,
7th Aug.	,,	Lt.-Col.	Mieli, A.	Killed in action
13th ,,	,,	2/Lieut.	Maude, W.	,, ,,
28th ,,	,,	Lt.-Col.	Reynell, C.	,, ,,
29th ,,	,,	Capt.	Jaffrey, A. J.	,, ,,
,, ,,	,,	,,	Callary, P. I.	,, ,,
4th Sept.	,,	2/Lieut.	Cameron, W.	,, ,,
6th Aug.	1916	Lieut.	Palmer, A. D.	,, ,,
13th ,,	,,	,,	Robertson, G. O.	,, ,,
14th Jan.	1917	Capt.	Gibson, B. D.	Drowned
19th Apr.	,,	Lieut.	Mitchell, C. L.	Died of wounds
30th ,,	1918	,,	Farmer, M. O.	Killed in action

NON-COMMISSIONED OFFICERS AND MEN:

Date of Casualty.		Regt. No.	Rank.	Name.	Nature of Casualty.
5th May	1915	440	Pte.	Locke, J. L.	Died of wounds
29th ,,	,,	535	,,	Blackwell, H. A.	,, ,,
,, ,,	,,	589	,,	Clough, E. C.	Killed in action
30th ,,	,,	96	,,	Axtens, A. L.	,, ,,
,, ,,	,,	415	,,	Griffiths, T.	,, ,,
,, ,,	,,	844	,,	Binyon, H.	,, ,,
4th June	,,	55	,,	Mercer, O. T.	Died of wounds
7th ,,	,,	496	,,	Tudgey, R. G.	,, ,,
12th ,,	,,	273	,,	Hawson, A. L.	,, ,,
15th ,,	,,	204	,,	Weathers, T. F.	,, ,,
,, ,,	,,	12	,,	Riley, W. T.	,, ,,
17th ,,	,,	338	Sgt.	Smiley, P. V.	,, ,,
20th ,,	,,	469	Pte.	Petrusch, A. E. J.	,, ,,
22nd ,,	,,	575	,,	Blanch, H.	Killed in action
,, ,,	,,	548	,,	Gribble, W. J.	,, ,,
,, ,,	,,	357	,,	Wilson, L. S.	,, ,,
,, ,,	,,	302	,,	Makin, T.	,, ,,
28th ,,	,,	278	,,	Hildebrand, J. H.	,, ,,
,, ,,	,,	240	,,	Clark, E. G.	,, ,,
29th ,,	,,	477	,,	Radburn, E.	Died of wounds
,, ,,	,,	294	,,	Lane, C. H.	,, ,,
30th ,,	,,	789	,,	Flower, H. V.	,, ,,
,, ,,	,,	134	,,	Hopping, J. L.	Killed in action

Date of Casualty.			Regt. No.	Rank.	Name.	Nature of Casualty.	
10th July	,,	,,	292	L/Cpl.	Kent, F. B. ..	Died of	wounds
22nd	,,	,,	564	Pte.	Trebilcock, L. A. L. .	,,	illness
,,	,,	,,	274	Cpl.	Dickinson, A. B. ..	,,	wounds
23rd	,,	,,	277	Sgt.	Hennessy, J. ..	,,	illness
24th	,,	,,	280	Cpl.	Hockridge, R. C. ..	,,	,,
2nd Aug.	,,		631	Farr.	Johnson, D. T. ..	,,	,,
6th	,,	,,	143	L/Cpl.	King, A. ..	Killed in action	
7th	,,	,,	746	Pte.	Smith, F. J. ..	,,	,,
,,	,,	,,	361	S.S.M.	Harvey, W. E., D.C.M.	,,	,,
,,	,,	,,	62	L/Cpl.	Seager, G. B. . ..	,,	,,
8th	,,	,,	625	Pte.	Cooper, C. ..	Died of illness	
,,	,,	,,	542	,,	Drew, F. N. ..	,,	wounds
9th	,,	,,	772	,,	Wyman, L. J. ..	Killed in action	
,,	,,	,,	213	S.Q.M.S.	Judell, E. ..	,,	,,
,,	,,	,,	605	Cpl.	Smedley, A. C. ..	Died of wounds	
10th	,,	,,	675	Pte.	Morphett, W. . ..	Killed in action	
,,	,,	,,	600	,,	Day, A. T. ..	Died of wounds	
13th	,,	,,	60	,,	Schocroft, S. L. ..	,,	,,
14th	,,	,,	898	,,	Culph, T. W. ..	,,	,,
25th	,,	,,	360	S.Q.M.S.	Gott, A. H. ..	,,	illness
28th	,,	,,	945	Pte.	Spencer, H. ..	,,	wounds
,,	,,	,,	568	Sgt.	Willoughby, F. ..	Killed in action	
,,	,,	,,	69	,,	Gooch, H. L. ..	,,	,,
,,	,,	,,	322	Pte.	McGillivray, J. A. ..	,,	,,
,,	,,	,,	489	,,	Spinks, L. C. . ..	,,	,,
,,	,,	,,	897	,,	Levien, C. B. . ..	,,	,,
,,	,,	,,	530	,,	Mobbs, W. G. D. ..	,,	,,
,,	,,	,,	111	L/Cpl.	Capper, W. R. ..	,,	,,
,,	,,	,,	750	Pte.	Fitcher, J. M. ..	,,	,,
,,	,,	,,	591	,,	Capern, P. ..	,,	,,
,,	,,	,,	403	L/Cpl.	Dickenson, T. ..	,,	,,
,,	,,	,,	401	Pte.	Dawson, W.	,,	,,
,,	,,	,,	723	,,	McDougall, D. ..	,,	,,
,,	,,	,,	559	,,	Napper, L. T. ..	,,	,,
,,	,,	,,	772	,,	Weaver, F. H. ..	,,	,,
,,	,,	,,	324	,,	Pulleine, J. B. ..	,,	,,
,,	,,	,,	113	,,	Doris, A. D. . ..	,,	,,
,,	,,	,,	198	,,	Sampson, C. E. G. ..	,,	,,
29th	,,	,,	976	,,	Megan, J. H. ..	Died of wounds	
,,	,,	,,	135	L/Cpl.	Harrington, M. D. ..	Killed in action	
,,	,,	,,	254	Pte.	Fitzgerald, W. G. ..	,,	,,
,,	,,	,,	339	,,	Smith, H. E. . ..	,,	,,
,,	,,	,,	551	Cpl.	Humphries, C. ..	,,	,,
,,	,,	,,	214	Sgt.	Gill, J. W.	,,	,,
,,	,,	,,	719	Pte.	Knibbs, W. J. ..	,,	,,
,,	,,	,,	327	,,	Regan, L.	,,	,,
,,	,,	,,	347	Dvr.	Taylor, O. F. L. ..	,,	,,
,,	,,	,,	928	Pte.	Lear, W. E.	,,	,,
,,	,,	,,	756	,,	Kent, J. S.	,,	,,
,,	,,	,,	893	,,	Coverdale, R. ..	,,	,,
,,	,,	,,	374	Sgt.	Bugbird, A. M. ..	,,	,,
,,	,,	,,	711	Pte.	Craven, W. H. ..	,,	,,
,,	,,	,,	603	,,	Cairns, R.	,,	,,
,,	,,	,,	224	,,	Bates, W. G. ..	,,	,,
30th	,,	,,	211	,,	Yeates, A. P. . ..	Died of wounds	
,,	,,	,,	604A	,,	Cane, G. A.	,,	,,
,,	,,	,,	831	,,	Byrne, M.	,,	,,

APPENDICES

Date of Casualty.	Regt. No.	Rank.	Name.	Nature of Casualty.
3rd Sept. ,,	533	,,	Ball, W.	Killed in action
,, ,, ,,	263	L/Cpl.	Green, W. H.	Died of wounds
5th ,, ,,	476	Pte.	Rickard, H. C.	Killed in action
9th ,, ,,	158	Cpl.	McDonald, A. E.	Died of wounds
16th ,, ,,	769	Pte.	Jarrett, H. N.	,, ,,
,, ,, ,,	598	L/Cpl.	White, W. H.	,, ,,
,, ,, ,,	8	Sgt.	Richards, F. J. A.	Killed in action
,, , ,,	729	Pte.	Richards, R. H.	Died of wounds
16th Oct. ,,	378	,,	Brennan, J.	,, ,,
18th ,, ,,	529	,,	Keough, W. T.	,, illness
26th ,, ,,	843	,,	Betro, J.	,, wounds
28th ,, ,,	581	,,	Sabine, R. T.	Killed in action
28th Nov. ,,	835	,,	Baker, W. A.	,, ,,
29th ,, ,,	1100	,,	Collins, C. W.	,, ,,
4th Dec. ,,	560	,,	Norton, C. E.	,, ,,
9th ,, ,,	784	,,	Burrough, J. A.	Died of illness
29th Jan. 1916	1380	,,	Freeman, H. S.	,, injuries
22nd Feb. ,,	1978	,,	Johnston, H. M.	,, illness
26th Mar. ,,	1028	,,	Brown, A. R.	,, ,,
29th May ,,	1520	,,	Renton, G. D.	,, ,,
5th Aug. ,,	957	,,	Sharp, A. M.	Killed in action
,, ,, ,,	592	,,	Bruce, C. J.	,, ,,
,, ,, ,,	1115	,,	Litster, T.	,, ,,
9th ,, ,,	1385	,,	Gavin, J. W.	,, ,,
,, ,, ,,	153	L/Cpl.	Mounsey, G. C.	,, ,,
,, ,, ,,	830	Pte.	Powell, C. B.	,, ,,
,, ,, ,,	1046	,,	Shuttleworth, G.	,, ,,
,, ,, ,,	367	Cpl.	Travers, G.	Died of wounds
7th Dec. ,,	3013	Pte.	Dooley, L.	,, illness
23rd ,, ,,	179	L/Cpl.	Pix, R. H. A.	Killed in action
28th ,, ,,	1601	,,	Scroop, P. G.	Died of wounds
27th Jan. 1917	1130	Cpl.	Taylor, M. G.	,, illness
6th Mar. ,,	12	Sgt.	Sullivan, H.	,, ,,
19th Apr. ,,	2760	Pte.	Truman, P. O.	Killed in action
,, ,, ,,	1444	Tptr.	Samuels, H.	,, ,,
,, ,, ,,	1029	Pte.	Nettleton, W.	,, ,,
,, ,, ,,	804	Cpl.	McKenna, B.	,, ,,
,, ,, ,,	146	Pte.	Keane, F. T.	,, ,,
,, ,, ,,	1106	Pte.	Haines (Heinze), W.	,, ,,
,, ,, ,,	1214	,,	Cronin, M. P.	,, ,,
,, ,, ,,	118	L/Cpl.	Elsdon, C.	,, ,,
,, ,, ,,	1318	Pte.	Cork, A.	,, ,,
,, ,, ,,	1441	,,	Robinson, R. G.	Died of wounds
,, ,, ,,	495	,,	Tompkins, S. J.	,, ,,
20th ,, ,,	1497	,,	Linehan, T. M.	,, ,,
,, ,, ,,	181	,,	Roach, K.	,, ,,
22nd ,, ,,	1358	,,	Lawton, A.	,, ,,
23rd ,, ,,	648	Cpl.	Wheaton, R. A.	,, ,,
1st May ,,	1098	Pte.	Carey, L. H.	Drowned
15th June ,,	3131	,,	Smith, W. G.	
27th ,, ,,	139	,,	Johnson, R. J. J.	Killed in action
1st July ,,	1438	,,	Ridgway, E. B.	Died of wounds
26th Sept. ,,	933	,,	May, H. G.	,, illness
31st Oct. ,,	2815	,,	Leahy, C. M.	Killed in action
,, ,, ,,	2939	,,	Morrison, D. J.	,, ,,
1st Nov. ,,	3255	,,	Bodkin, J. L.	Died of wounds

Date of Casualty.			Regt. No.	Rank.	Name.	Nature of Casualty.
12th	,,	,,	705	L/Cpl.	Bennett, K. C. ..	Killed in action
,,	,,	,,	1021	Pte.	Thurlow, A.	,, ,,
,,	,,	,,	1602	Cpl.	Shadforth, W. H. ..	,, ,,
20th Jan.		1918	3371	Pte.	Wallace, G. B. ..	Died of illness
31st	,,	,,	1419	,,	Lowrie, A.	,, ,,
11th Apr.		,,	1050	,,	Williamson, G. ..	Accidentally killed
21st	,,	,,	1131	Sgt.	McDonald, J. F. W. .	Died of illness
22nd	,,	,,	2816	Pte.	Learmouth, W. J. ..	Accidentally killed
30th	,,	,,	1216	,,	Fleming, N. M. ..	Killed in action
3rd May		,,	373	L/Cpl.	Baker, W.	,, ,,
,,	,,	,,	1159	Pte.	McGinty, S. P. ..	,, ,,
,,	,,	,,	101	,,	Bockleberg, F. B. ..	,, ,,
,,	,,	,,	1577	,,	Medhurst, P. W. ..	,, ,,
7th	,,	,,	270	Sgt.	Harris, S.	Died of illness
13th June		,,	2115	Pte.	Hank, R. H.	,, ,,
24th	,,	,,	140	Sgt.	Jones, A. E.	Accidentally killed
20th July		,,	3012	Cpl.	Fletcher, G. E. P. ..	Died of wounds
12th Sept.		,,	3139	Pte.	Tuhera, R.	,, illness
29th	,,	,,	899	Cpl.	Mann, G. N.	,, wounds
3rd Oct.		,,	3542	Pte.	Harvey, A. H.	,, ,,
5th	,,	,,	3592	,,	Bone, E.	,, illness
8th	,,	,,	1618	Dvr.	Woods, A.	,, ,,
9th	,,	,,	921	Cpl.	Down, A. C. . ..	,, wounds
,,	,,	,,	2116	L/Cpl.	Hanrahan, E. P. ..	,, ,,
,,	,,	,	1212	Pte.	Smith, E. K.	,, illness
11th	,,	,,	142	,,	Johns, A. A. . ..	,, ,,
12th	,,	,,	255	Sgt.	Foreman, J. L. ..	,, ,,
13th	,,	,,	605A	Pte.	Morgan, F. R. ..	,, wounds
,,	,,	,,	3227	,,	Gallacher, W. ..	,, illness
16th	,,	,,	3413	,,	Dillon, J. B.	,, ,,
17th	,,	,,	1203	,,	Stevens, W.	,, ,,
,,	,,	,,	1535	L/Cpl.	Delanty, G.	,, ,,
20th	,,	,,	1729	Dvr.	Bavin, J. P.	,, ,,
21st	,,	,,	3672	Pte.	Uphill, F. R. . ..	,, ,,
25th	,,	,,	902	,,	Smyth, J. N. . ..	,, ,,
,,	,,	,,	3647	,,	Murray, M. G. D. ..	,, ,,
26th	,,	,,	3496	,,	Wallace, W. N. ..	,, ,,
29th	,,	,,	1532	,,	Dawson, C. M. E. ..	,, ,,
6th Nov.		,,	3439	,,	Allen, H.	,, ,,
11th	,,	,,	R2826	,,	Smith, L. J.	,, ,,
12th	,,	,,	1029A	Dvr.	Kither, J. F.	,, ,,
3rd Dec.		,,	1554	Pte.	Holloway, H. C. ..	,, ,,